Biofictions

Explorations in Science and Literature

Series Editors: John Holmes, Anton Kirchhofer and Janine Rogers

Explorations in Science and Literature considers the significance of literature from within a scientific worldview and brings the insights of literary study to bear on current science. Ranging across scientific disciplines, literary concepts, and different times and cultures, volumes in this series will show how literature and science, including medicine and technology, are intricately connected, and how they are indispensable to one another in building up our understanding of ourselves and of the world around us.

Forthcoming titles

Imagining Solar Energy, Gregory Lynall
The Diseased Brain and the Failing Mind, Martina Zimmermann
Narrative in the Age of the Genome, Lara Choksey
Fictions of Prevention, Benedetta Liorsi
The Social Dinosaur, Will Tattersdill

Explorations in Science and Literature

Series Preface

In spite of the myth of the 'Two Cultures', science and literature have always been shaped by one another. Many of our most powerful scientific concepts, from natural selection to artificial intelligence, from germ theory to chaos theory, have been formed through the careful – and sometimes careless – use of written language. Poets, novelists, playwrights and journalists have taken up scientific ideas, medical research and new technologies, exploring them, reworking them, at times distorting or misjudging them, but always shaping profoundly the wider culture's understanding of what they mean. This intimate and productive relationship between literature and science generated a steady stream of insightful scholarship and commentary throughout the twentieth century and has grown into a substantial field of study in its own right since the turn of the millennium. Where the idea of 'Two Cultures' does still have a hold, however, is in academic disciplines themselves. In schools and universities, we study science and arts subjects in different classrooms, taught by different people with different expectations. Literature and science studies has, so far, been largely a sub-discipline of literature, with only rare contributions from or addressed to scientific experts. In a world of ever-increasing specialization, failure to communicate across these disciplinary divides risks failing to appreciate the contribution that the study of literature can make to our understanding of science, medicine and technology, the uses that science makes of images, narratives and fictions, and the insights that scientists can bring to bear on literature and on culture at large.

Explorations in Science and Literature aims to speak across this divide. It has a particular mandate to bring the insights of literary study to bear on science itself; to consider the significance of literature from a scientific point of view; and to explore the role of literature within the history of science. The books therefore examine the complex interrelations between science and literature in cross-disciplinary ways. They are written equally for scholars and students of literature and for scientists and science students, but also for historians and sociologists of science, as well as general readers interested in science and its place in culture and society. By showing how each field can be enhanced by a knowledge of the others, we hope to enrich scientific as well as literary research, and to cultivate a new cross-disciplinary approach to fundamental questions in both fields.

The series will encompass topics from across the physical, biological and social sciences, medicine and technology, wherever literature can inform our understanding of the science, its origins and its implications. It will also include books on literary forms and techniques that are informed by science, as well as studies that consider how science itself has been articulated. Along with literature in the broad sense of written texts, books in the series will also consider other cultural forms including drama, film, television, and other arts and media.

John Holmes, Anton Kirchhofer and Janine Rogers

Biofictions

Race, Genetics and the Contemporary Novel

Josie Gill

BLOOMSBURY ACADEMIC
LONDON • NEW YORK • OXFORD • NEW DELHI • SYDNEY

BLOOMSBURY ACADEMIC
Bloomsbury Publishing Plc
50 Bedford Square, London, WC1B 3DP, UK
1385 Broadway, New York, NY 10018, USA
29 Earlsfort Terrace, Dublin 2, Ireland

BLOOMSBURY, BLOOMSBURY ACADEMIC and the Diana logo are trademarks of Bloomsbury Publishing Plc

First published in Great Britain 2020
This paperback edition published in 2021

Copyright © Josie Gill, 2020

Josie Gill has asserted her right under the Copyright, Designs and Patents Act, 1988, to be identified as Author of this work.

For legal purposes the Acknowledgements on p. ix constitute an extension of this copyright page.

Cover design: Toby Way
Cover image © Getty Images

This work is published subject to a Creative Commons Attribution Non-commercial No Derivatives Licence. You may share this work for non-commercial purposes only, provided you give attribution to the copyright holder and the publisher.

Bloomsbury Publishing Plc does not have any control over, or responsibility for, any third-party websites referred to or in this book. All internet addresses given in this book were correct at the time of going to press. The author and publisher regret any inconvenience caused if addresses have changed or sites have ceased to exist, but can accept no responsibility for any such changes.

A catalogue record for this book is available from the British Library.

A catalog record for this book is available from the Library of Congress.

ISBN:	HB:	978-1-3500-9983-8
	PB:	978-1-3502-3745-2
	ePDF:	978-1-3500-9984-5
	eBook:	978-1-3500-9985-2

Series: Explorations in Science and Literature

Typeset by Integra Software Services Pvt. Ltd.

To find out more about our authors and books visit www.bloomsbury.com and sign up for our newsletters.

Contents

List of Figures ... viii
Acknowledgements ... ix

Introduction ... 1
1 The Roots of African Eve: Science Writing on Human Origins and Alex Haley's *Roots* ... 31
2 Race, Genetic Ancestry Tracing and Facial Expression: 'Focusing on the Faces' in Kazuo Ishiguro's *Never Let Me Go* ... 57
3 'One Part Truth and Three Parts Fiction': Race, Science and Narrative in Zadie Smith's *White Teeth* ... 79
4 'The Sick Swollen Heart of This Land': Pharmacogenomics, Racial Medicine and Colson Whitehead's *Apex Hides the Hurt* ... 101
5 Mutilation and Mutation: Epigenetics and Racist Environments in Octavia Butler's *Kindred* and Salman Rushdie's *The Satanic Verses* ... 121
Conclusion ... 145

Notes ... 154
Bibliography ... 191
Index ... 209

List of Figures

1. Front cover of *Out of Eden: The Peopling of the World* by Stephen Oppenheimer. London: Constable and Robinson, 2003. Reproduced with the permission of Little, Brown Book Group. 51
2. Rachel Dolezal Meme. Anonymous, http://www.quickmeme.com/p/3w42zi. 102

Every effort has been made to trace copyright holders and to obtain their permission for the use of copyright material. The publisher apologizes for any errors or omissions in the above list and would be grateful if notified of any corrections that should be incorporated in future reprints or editions of this book.

Acknowledgements

This book is the product of many years' research and thinking that have taken place both inside and outside the academy. It has been shaped as much by my academic teachers, mentors and peers, as it has by my family, friends and work colleagues, all of whom have supported and influenced this book in different ways. I am thankful for the support, generosity and kindness of David Clifford, whose steady guidance was invaluable during my time as a postgraduate at the University of Cambridge. I am indebted to Patricia Waugh and Steve Watts for their incisive comments and advice during the earlier stages of this project, as well as to Megan Jones, Alice Hall and Ben Etherington for their helpful suggestions and friendship. This book has been informed by many conversations with scholars in literature and science studies, often at meetings and conferences of the British Society for Literature and Science. I would in particular like to thank John Holmes, Alice Jenkins, Anton Kirchhofer, Greg Lynall, Peter Middleton, Janine Rogers, Martin Willis and Michael Whitworth for their engagements with my work. Thank you to Sharon Ruston for organizing the Arts and Humanities Research Council Literature, Science and Medicine network, which provided me with important training in the field and a community of like-minded peers. Thank you to Peter Middleton and Clare Hanson for inviting me to participate in the Beyond the Gene project at the University of Southampton, which was crucial to my thinking on the racial implications of epigenetics. Thanks also to Priscilla Wald for her help, encouragement and scholarship.

I am very lucky to have had the support of many colleagues at Bristol who have offered advice and wisdom at various stages of this project, and I'd like to thank Helen Fulton, Ulrika Maude, Josie McLellan and Sumita Mukherjee for their thoughtful suggestions and comments. Special thanks go to my writing retreat companions Michael Malay and Andrew Blades for their generosity and care in reading and commenting upon drafts of this work. Thanks to my colleagues in the Centre for Black Humanities for their solidarity and for creating a community of scholars in which I could feel at home. I also thank my anonymous reviewers for their helpful feedback, and David Avital and Lucy Brown at Bloomsbury for their patience and support. Thank you to the librarians and archivists at the

Schomburg Center for Research in Black Culture in New York and the Wellcome Library in London for their assistance.

The funding I have received at various stages of this project has been essential to its completion and I gratefully acknowledge the support of the Leverhulme Trust, the Arts and Humanities Research Council and St John's College, Cambridge. At the University of Bristol I have received a number of research grants from the Faculty of Arts, for which I am grateful, and I would also like to thank the Institute for Advanced Studies at Bristol which granted me a fellowship in order to complete this book.

Parts of this book were developed and written during times of unemployment and precarity, other parts written during intense periods working within the academy. Throughout I have had the love and support of friends and family, many of whom have put me up and put up with me talking about this book for years. Thank you to Katharine Sprigge for your friendship, and for being so hospitable, with Ralph McLelland, in London and Cornwall. Thank you to Rebecca Ryan for listening and for offering space in Wales, to Roisin Hood for London accommodation and fun, to George and Helen Lovesmith, Sarah Hollingworth, Megan Blomfield, Tara Puri, Victoria Bates and many other friends in Bristol for your support. Thanks to my friends Pantelis Avaliotis, Lauren Couch, Andre Faure, John Rothwell, Charmaine Jelbert, Cristina Patriarca and DM Withers. I'd like to thank Jessica Gill for the reality checks and Angharad Ameline, Eleanor Woodward and Jennie Wood, whose friendship has helped me to 'stay cool and keep smiling'. This book is dedicated to my parents, Eric and Christine, who have been unwavering in their support of me and my work. They gave me the confidence to go my own way and to take the opportunities that they did not have, and for that I thank them.

Some of the material in this book has been adapted from published articles and I gratefully acknowledge the permission granted to reproduce the copyright material in this book. Chapter 3 is adapted from 'Science and Fiction in Zadie Smith's *White Teeth*', *Journal of Literature and Science* 6, no. 2 (2013): 17–28; Chapter 2 is a revised version of 'Written on the Face: Race and Expression in Kazuo Ishiguro's *Never Let Me Go*', *MFS: Modern Fiction Studies* 60, no. 4, (2014): 844–862, ©2014 The Johns Hopkins University Press; and Chapter 5 contains some material from '"Under Extreme Environmental Pressure, Characteristics Were Acquired": Epigenetics, Race and Salman Rushdie's *The Satanic Verses*', *Textual Practice* 29, no. 3 (2015): 479–498.

Introduction

Race: Beyond Fact or Fiction

Is race a biological fact or a fiction? At the beginning of 2018, scientists working with ancient DNA in the UK and the United States offered two very different public responses to this long-asked question. In the UK in February 2018, Channel 4 aired the documentary *The First Brit: Secrets of the 10,000 Year Old Man*, in which geneticists at the Natural History Museum and University College London sequenced the DNA of Cheddar Man, a 10,000-year-old skeleton that is the oldest to have been found in Britain. Focusing on the question of what Cheddar Man looked like and where he came from, model-makers reconstructed the head of the man using information derived from his DNA to reveal that the person the programme dubbed 'the first modern Brit' had dark skin and ancestors who came from the Middle East.[1] Overturning the previously held scientific assumption that Cheddar Man was white, the scientists then compared Cheddar Man's DNA to that of modern-day Britons in order to answer the other question posed by the programme, 'How Cheddar Man are we?'[2] The answer, the programme's narrator playfully informed the audience, is that according to the DNA 'we're all a little bit Cheddar Man'.[3] It was a finding which, combined with the man's dark skin, led one of the scientists interviewed to conclude that 'these imaginary racial categories that we have are really very modern constructions... that are not applicable to the past at all'.[4] With its suggestion that some ancestors of modern white Britons were black, the programme and its participants positioned race as a modern social construct, a genetic fiction, and situated their findings as a means of fighting against racism. *The First Brit* opens with a montage of images of people with varying skin colours against the London skyline while the generic sounds of parliamentary debate play as the narrator claims 'there's been a lot of talk lately about Britain; about who belongs and who doesn't'.[5] The programme's scientific findings are then offered as an intervention into the contemporary debates about immigration which are evoked by these scenes, science becoming the justification for a national reassessment of 'our notions of what it is to be British'.[6]

Yet only a month later the idea put forward by *The First Brit* – that contemporary racial categories are 'imaginary' – was challenged by Harvard professor of genetics and ancient DNA expert David Reich. Reich published an article in *The New York Times* in which he claimed that 'it is simply no longer possible to ignore the average genetic differences among "races"'.[7] While Reich acknowledged that 'it is true that race is a social construct', he argued that this widespread assumption had become a scientific 'orthodoxy', to the degree that it was no longer being questioned for fear of reviving scientific racisms of the past.[8] Geneticists now need to recognize, he contended, that 'differences in genetic ancestry that happen to correlate to many of today's racial constructs are real', a fact that could be used to 'improve health and save lives'.[9] Future research in genetics and on ancient genomes would likely make it indisputable, he claimed, that not only physical but behavioural traits differ across 'human populations' and 'it will be impossible – indeed, anti-scientific ... to deny those differences'.[10] What Reich's statements amount to is an affirmation of the genetic basis for race: his claim that racial groupings and widely recognized patterns of genetic variation can be correlated with each other reinforces the idea that race is biologically real (even if it is somehow also, as he paradoxically claims, a social construct). While coming to the opposite conclusion of the scientists involved in *The First Brit*, Reich similarly framed his claims in anti-racist terms, stating that he had 'deep sympathy for the concern that genetic discoveries could be misused to justify racism', but that scientists articulating a genetic understanding of race are in fact needed to counter those who might misuse this understanding 'as "scientific proof" that racist prejudices and agendas have been correct all along'.[11] Reich was no doubt writing with the knowledge that 'those who might misuse' have become increasingly vocal in the United States which, as in the UK, has seen a resurgence of the far-right and a rise in attempts to use science to assert the biological reality of race and, consequently, to justify racial inequality and racist violence.[12]

These contrasting conclusions about the genetic status of race drawn from studies of ancient DNA offer a snapshot of the opposing scientific positions which have characterized debates about race in the biosciences across the late twentieth and early twenty-first centuries. The rise of DNA sequencing techniques in the 1970s and subsequent research on human genetic diversity overturned the post-war scientific convention that race was 'an illusory object constructed by bad science',[13] and thus an inappropriate object of scientific investigation. Instead, major genetic research projects in fields including biological anthropology, population genetics, genomics, pharmacogenetics and epigenetics have made highly publicized discoveries about the nature of race. These include the African Eve hypothesis (1987), which traced the origin of all humans to a population in Africa approximately 200,000 years ago; the Human Genome Diversity Project (HGDP), begun in 1991, which sought to map human genetic diversity through a focus on isolated populations believed to be vanishing; the Human Genome Project (HGP), the draft of which was completed in 2000 and which famously affirmed that human 'races' are genetically more similar than they are different; the development of BiDil, a drug approved in 2005 to treat heart failure exclusively in the African American population; and the study of the intergenerational effects of slavery in epigenetic science in the first decades of the twenty-first century. Race is explained variously across these developments as constituted in the genes, or as not constituted in the genes, as a socio-political construct, as determined by self-identification and as a biological effect of environmental circumstances, to name only some of the genetic reasoning which has characterized recent interventions into the race debate. Yet, while differing significantly in their conclusions about the nature of race, what has united these diverse positions and studies (and is demonstrated by the examples from the field of ancient DNA) is scientists' insistence that their research and its conclusions are anti-racist, and is research carried out for the benefit of people once dehumanized by racist science.

There is no scientific consensus as to whether race is biologically real, and the array of genetic standpoints about what race means and how it functions is such that it might seem that science has lost any ability to answer the question of whether race is fact or fiction. And yet, the opposite is true: regardless of whether geneticists argue for the non-existence of race, biologically, or for its genetic reality, genetic science has become the ultimate authority on race, the final arbitrator of race's meaning, as politicians, doctors, public officials, academics and journalists turn to science as a means of getting to the 'truth' of race. Those uncomfortable with the findings of the Cheddar Man documentary sought to counter them with recourse to a scientist who emphasized that Cheddar Man's dark skin colour was only 'probable',[14] while in an open letter to David Reich protesting against the unacknowledged politics of his genetic racial realism, a group of scholars from the natural sciences, medical and population health sciences, social sciences, law, and humanities asserted that Reich was wrong because a 'robust body of scholarship' has shown that 'geographically based genetic variation' is 'not consistent with biological definitions of race'.[15] The fictional or factual status of race has become something to be determined by genetic science, the question of whether race is real one to be answered at the molecular level, by the genes. As Chris Stringer, a palaeoanthropologist interviewed in the Cheddar Man documentary, asserted in his discussion of the findings, 'we're not just conjuring this up out of nowhere, we really do have scientific data'.[16] Science is presented as an objective, neutral authority through which the public can be reassured they are getting the facts about race. What matters in these debates is not only whether race is a biological fact or fiction, but that the facts of science can be upheld over the 'made up' ideas about race that exist more widely in culture.

This book is about the role of the conjured up, the imaginary and the fictional in the formation of racial ideas in contemporary genetic science. It contends that, contrary to the common assumption espoused by Stringer that the concrete findings of science are the opposite of the imaginary, fiction is integral to contemporary scientific conceptions of race. The fictional, understood inclusively as narratives and stories about race in literature as well as narratives formed in the political, social and cultural spheres, is intimately and inextricably bound up in the formation of scientific fact, shaping and impacting upon the development, expression, transmission and ultimately the public understanding of the new science of race. This relationship between fiction and science encompasses more than the way popular science writing has long employed literature, literary language and metaphor as a means of communicating scientific ideas to a wider public, something which Reich does in his discussion of race. Writing about the significance of the 'genome revolution' for creating 'a new understanding of human difference and identity', Reich cites Alex Haley's 1976 historical novel *Roots* as the inspiration for modern-day root seekers who have 'realized the potential of the genome' by using genetic ancestry testing to create narratives of African ancestry, much as Haley did in *Roots*.[17] This is true enough, but far from simply inspiring black Americans to use 'the new science of the human past' (as Reich subtitles his book), I contend that Haley's novel played a significant role in shaping the development of that science: the narrative structure and tone of Haley's tale of his African ancestry informed emerging ideas in biological anthropology about the relationship between ancient African ancestors and modern-day humans that were crystallized in the African Eve hypothesis. As I will discuss in detail in Chapter 1, Haley's novel and its television adaptation did more than assist scientists to communicate their findings about ancient human ancestry; it provided a formally conservative account of African origins, which was itself influenced by earlier anthropological writing on Africa, that operated as a narrative model for the racialized conceptions of genetic ancestry promoted by scientists such as Reich today.

This is but one instance of the way in which race in genetic science is what I name biofiction: an idea constituted through the complex entanglement of scientific and fictive forms, the dynamics between which produce the dominant racial imaginaries of Britain and the United States in the contemporary era. This book is about how contemporary fiction explores, actively participates in, and might inform, the biofictional formation of racial ideas in genetic science. It examines novels by Alex Haley, Kazuo Ishiguro, Zadie Smith, Colson Whitehead, Salman Rushdie and Octavia Butler which illuminate how race, racism and racial identity have come to be increasingly understood through the lens of genetic science and medicine. Rather than simply contesting or challenging scientific visions of race, the novels both intervene in and respond to the language, images, theoretical frameworks, methodologies and narrative structures deployed by genetic science. I argue that these novels develop their own biofictional narrative forms that incorporate scientific stories, discourses and methods, as a means of highlighting the imbrication of the factual and the fictional in genetic racial formations. In so doing, the novels enable us to apprehend how genetic science functions narratively, rather than neutrally or objectively, within the racialized contexts in which it is embedded. They also help us to comprehend how the avowed anti-racism of contemporary genetics is narratively constructed, and thus not impermeable to the older racial scientific ideas and contemporary socio-political racisms which press in upon it. These contemporary fictions demonstrate that the question is less about whether race is real or imaginary, than about how it could ever be conceived as either, given that genetic facts and cultural fictions of race are mutually informing; together they create the stories about history, ancestry and kinship, as well as racism, illness and the environments in which these arise, which characterize our understanding of race today.

It is a commonplace that the idea of race, as it developed across the eighteenth and nineteenth centuries, was constructed and defined across disciplinary lines from a combination of scientific, philosophical, historical and literary discourses.[18] As Robert J.C. Young notes, racial theory emerged in the era of British and European colonial expansion when racism knew 'no division between the sciences and the arts'.[19] Racial ideas flowed, 'from the natural sciences to the humanities and vice versa',[20] the formation of race across academic fields contributing to what W.E.B. Du Bois identified as the 'continuous change in the proofs and arguments advanced' for its existence.[21] These changing arguments included (but are by no means limited to) Immanuel Kant's claim in 'Of the Different Human Races' (1775) that 'we only need to assume four races in order to be able to derive all of the enduring distinctions immediately recognizable within the human genus. They are (1) the white race; (2) the Negro race; (3) the Hun race (Mongol or Kalamuk); and (4) the Hindu or Hindustani race';[22] Johann Blumenbach's naming of 'five principal varieties of mankind' in 1795 as Caucasian, Mongolian, Ethiopian, American and Malay, of which the Caucasian was the most handsome, beautiful and becoming;[23] and Arthur de Gobineau's division of races into white, black and yellow (1853).[24] Such theories contributed to an emerging science of race which was 'inextricable from the need of colonialist powers to establish dominance over subject peoples and hence justify the imperial enterprise'.[25] The science of race was integral to the politics of Empire, and its emergence coincided with what Michel Foucault identifies as 'an explosion of numerous and diverse techniques for achieving the subjugation of bodies and the control of populations, marking the beginning of an era of "biopower"'.[26] The emergence of biopolitics – when the state began to exercise power over life itself, bringing birth and mortality rates, health, longevity and the whole biological existence of populations into its purview – required, according to Foucault, racism, as a means of fragmenting the field of the biological that power controls.[27] Racism provided the state with justification for killing when functioning in this biopolitical mode, and 'biological theory' became 'not simply a way of dressing up a political discourse in scientific clothing, but a real way of thinking about the relations between colonization, the necessity for wars, criminality, the phenomena of madness and mental illness, the history of societies with their different classes, and so on'.[28]

Given that the emergence of the concept of race is widely accepted to be the product of the intersection of the scientific, political, social and cultural spheres, it is somewhat curious that a comparable understanding of how contemporary scientific concepts of race have been formed and informed by political, but also cultural and literary discourses, has been largely absent from critical analyses of race in the humanities and literary studies. Prominent critical race scholars have instead often simply accepted the claims of geneticists – most often the idea promoted by the HGP that race has no biological meaning – and have approached genetic science as an objective, anti-racist authority on race because its findings support their own long-held views.[29] In 2016, philosopher Kwame Anthony Appiah claimed in his Reith lecture on 'Colour' that race meant nothing in 'scientific terms'.[30] In an interview preceding the lectures, he stated that 'if you try to say what the whiteness of a white person or the blackness of a black person actually means in scientific terms, there's almost nothing you can say that is true or even remotely plausible' and that 'if everybody grasped the facts about the relevant biology and the social facts, they'd have to treat race in a different way'.[31] Biology and science more generally become conduits for the 'truth' about race in this formation, scientific facts neutrally authoritative despite the fact that Appiah spends a greater part of the lecture discussing how in the eighteenth century ideas about race emerged across disciplinary lines. Examining a range of thinkers and figures, he states that 'ideology – enlisted by forms of domination from slavery to colonization – does help explain why... scientists... made extraordinary efforts to assert the continuing reality of race' and he acknowledges in his discussion of English literary critic Matthew Arnold that 'literary history was part of the scientific study of race'.[32] Yet he then almost immediately switches to consider 'the rise of modern genetics' which he argues represents a period when 'race and science became untethered from each other' because science has shown that 'the vast majority of our genetic material is shared with all human beings'.[33] The possible cultural and literary entanglements of this scientific racial idea are left unexplored.

Henry Louis Gates Jr. makes a similar move. Reflecting on his life's work in 2008, he noted that he had begun his academic career exploring 'pseudoscientific theories of race in creative and philosophical writings in the Enlightenment in Europe',[34] before explaining his more recent endorsement of genetic ancestry tracing technologies on his television shows including *African American Lives*, in which African Americans, often celebrities, use genetic information and historical records to recover their ancestral roots. For Gates, genetic science is 'deconstructing the typological categories of racial purity... through the results of the genetic admixture tests that we administer to the subjects in the series, even if these tests are in their infancy and even if their precision may only increase after more individual genomes are sequenced'.[35] Genetic testing, despite its imprecision, is where the real answer to race lies, revealing 'the fiction of race through scientific evidence'.[36] While Gates acknowledges that 'we also need to interrogate the limits of genetic constructions, or models, to account for their social valences',[37] this is work which he has yet to do. Instead, he positions science as the final arbiter of questions of racial ancestry; 'If the database reveals an exact match with a person of, let's say, Yoruba descent, then the subject – indisputably – shares a common ancestor with that person. This is not an opinion; it is a fact.'[38]

Paul Gilroy goes further in attempting to unpick the origins and basis of racial thinking in contemporary genetics. He is wary that we must keep 'the pathological problems represented by genomic racism' in view, as well as 'the contingencies of truth-seeking, the pressures of institutional location, the active power of language to shape inquiry, and the provisional status of all scientific enterprises'.[39] Yet, in *Against Race* (2000), the main evidence he marshals to support his suggestion that humanity might now be in a position to move beyond race is the 'DNA revolution', which he claims has caused a crisis in racial thinking and offers a way to 'free ourselves from the bonds of all raciology'.[40] In agreement with many geneticists working on questions of race, he asserts that contemporary genetics is far removed from older racial thinking in science: for Gilroy the new scientific focus on the molecular level, rather than on physical morphology – the 'bones, skulls, hair, lips, noses, eyes, feet, genitals' which preoccupied racial scientists – means that race is now signified at a different scale, skin colour being replaced by the cellular, so that if race has any meaning, it is now contained within the body as an internal, rather than external, marker of identity.[41] Published in the same year that the mapping of the human genome was announced to worldwide acclaim, it is unsurprising that Gilroy's highly influential book on race sought to harness the racial findings of that project. Yet Gilroy's position pays little attention to the ongoing role of physical appearance in many genetic studies of racial difference, examples of which I will discuss in this book. The stresses and frameworks of earlier racial science have not always been left behind.

These intellectual positions articulated by scholars working across the disciplines of philosophy, critical race studies and cultural studies (but who each have academic origins in literary studies), have been highly influential in literary scholarship. Invocations of contemporary genetics are now common in literary analyses of race, where scholars frequently maintain that race is a fiction, a sociocultural phenomenon that 'bad science' once made biological, but which contemporary genetics has shown to be biologically meaningless. Considering biological understandings of race to be redundant and disappearing, literary analyses of race focus on culture as the nexus of racial meaning and read race in contemporary fiction as resistant to scientific explanations. Recent examples of this stance in literary criticism include the following formulations: 'race is a social construct which assigns non-necessary meanings to common phenotypical features of humanity...There is no genetic basis for race';[42] 'In discussing "white" and "black" readers, texts, and authors, then, I refer to identities that are ideologically (rather than biologically) "real"';[43] 'The project of contemporary British fiction...is a two-fold exercise: first, to deny the primacy of biology...second, to use the "unreality" of race to explore the idea of communities and relationships in which race is not seen'.[44] Race is considered real only in the sense that 'the reality of race lies in the experience of the racial subject, the experience of racism'.[45]

To be clear, it is not that literary critics or critical race scholars are wrong about the genetic status of race. Rather, the problem is that the critical position which can be summarized as 'genetic science has proved that race is fiction' not only fails to recognize the existence of long-standing, contrary contemporary genetic standpoints on race,[46] but fails to interrogate the social and cultural environments which gave rise to the genetic view that race is not real. This is the point made by Jenny Reardon in her analyses of the work of critical race theorists who, she argues, turned in the 1980s 'to scientists and historians of science to legitimate their claims that race had no naturalistic meaning'.[47] Reardon contends that 'rather than continue to subject scientific ideas about human biological diversity to critical analysis, most critical scholars of race have embraced Gates's view that, biologically speaking, race is a fiction. Rather than interrogating how claims about the biological meaninglessness of race emerged and how they shape and are shaped by broader social, political, and technical contexts, most scholars of race merely enlist these claims to bolster their argument that race is mere ideology'.[48] Reardon's scholarship has been dedicated to exploring how, 'instead of viewing these claims through a frame that opposes science's truths to society's ideologies', we might 'reread them through an analytic frame that draws into view the mutual constitution of natural, social, and moral orders'.[49] This is an approach to race which I contend might be extended to literary studies, expanded to include literature as a central element of the cultural orders which shape and are shaped by the formation of racial ideas in genetic science.

Biofictions addresses the socio-political, cultural but most significantly literary contexts in which racial scientific ideas arise, reading contemporary fiction alongside, rather than in opposition to, genetic science, in order to apprehend the biofictional constitution of race. In the following sections of this introduction I explore how the idea of race as a social construct gained ground in the 1970s when anti-racist activists, alongside humanities scholars, social scientists and some scientists, began to argue that scientific ideas were deeply political and thus socially constructed, rather than separable from politics as many scientists believed. While this led to the widespread understanding that race was a political, rather than biological, concept, this stance resulted in a movement away from anti-racism and towards a fight against the concept of race itself. The ironic consequence of this was that the separation of science and politics returned. For with the erasure of race, the possibility of racism could also be erased, meaning that scientists were able to begin positioning themselves and their work as non-racial, and beyond the influence of social and political racisms (regardless of their view of the biology of race) – a stance seemingly endorsed by critical race theorists who positioned certain genetic ideas about race as truth beyond social or political influence.

I offer the concept of biofiction not only as a description of the constitution of race in science but as an approach which necessarily rejects the separation of the scientific from the socio-political and the fictional. Yet my approach does not represent a return to some of the constructionist approaches of the 1970s, which could be characterized, as Donna Haraway contends, by an 'appropriationist logic of domination', whereby criticism of science and its values set itself apart from the very social construction it identified in science.[50] That critical tendency simply reversed the traditional view that nature is the truth underlying culture, rather than accounting for the fact that 'evaluation is also implicated, bound, full of interests and stakes, part of the field of practices that make meanings'.[51] My biofictional approach instead understands that in order to comprehend the mutual constitution of the natural and the cultural, it is necessary to bring the disciplines which examine these entities – science and literary studies – together; to recognize, while also approaching critically, the value of both scientific and literary theorization. For, following Susan Merrill Squier, in order to 'discover the sources and significance of the new [biomedical] forms emerging in our era, we must engage in the same kind of boundary crossing that characterizes the new biotechnologies'.[52] *Biofictions* draws upon recent insights from the genomic sciences concerning the entanglement of biological and cultural factors in gene development and expression, as a means of thinking about race in contemporary fiction. At the same time, it builds upon the work of literature and science scholars and sociologists of science to argue for fiction, specifically the literary, to be included in the expanded understandings of genetics for which they advocate. That is, for literary conceptions of the biofictional formation of race to be recognized for their involvement in, and capacity to impact, the new genetics of race; for fictional narrative to be understood as a site where the imbrication of biological fact and fiction is ultimately laid bare.

The genetics of anti-racism and colourblindness

In the early 1970s Francis Crick, one of the discoverers of the double helix structure of DNA, became involved in a transatlantic argument about the use of race in scientific research. Arthur Jensen, an American educational psychologist, had published a paper in 1969 which argued that black people had a genetically lower IQ than white people, a finding which he used to criticize educational programmes designed to provide support for schoolchildren from deprived and low-income backgrounds.[53] Jensen's paper prompted another scientist, William Shockley, to call on the US National Academy of Sciences to make research into IQ differences a priority. Crick became involved in the affair when some members of the Academy wrote a letter to their President which was critical of Shockley's views on race and human genetics (Shockley was motivated by his belief that rates of reproduction among groups with lower IQs, which included black people, were too high). Crick decided to support Jensen and Shockley, threatening to resign as a Foreign Associate of the Academy, eventually signing a resolution on the right of scientists and academics to pursue research into the role of inheritance in human abilities and behaviours. In February 1971 Crick wrote a strongly worded letter to Dr John Edsall, a biochemist at Harvard, saying that he was 'very distressed' at discovering that Edsall had signed the letter to the President of the National Academy against Shockley's proposal. Crick wrote:

> Unlike you and your colleagues I have formed the opinion that there is much substance to Jensen's arguments. In brief I think it likely that more than half the difference between the average I.Q. of American whites and Negroes is due to genetic reasons, and will not be eliminated by any foreseeable change in the environment. Moreover I think the social consequences of this are likely to be rather serious unless steps are taken to recognize the situation ... Would you and your colleagues please state in detail why they think the arguments put forward by Jensen are either incorrect or misleading ... the most distressing feature of your letter is that it neither gives nor refers to any scientific arguments, but makes unsupported statements of opinion. This, I need hardly remind you, is politics, not science. The voice of established authority, unsupported by evidence or argument, should have no place in science.[54]

Crick's letter and his involvement in the affair provide a snapshot of the political culture of the early 1970s in the United States and in Britain, which saw both the questioning of the objectivity of science and increasing activism around the issue of racial prejudice. Despite arguing for the separation of science and politics, Crick's concern with the 'serious social consequences' that might ensue if genetic racial differences were not recognized is demonstrative of the very 'non-scientific' thinking against which he is reacting, a point that Edsall made in his reply to Crick.[55] Social scientists, humanities scholars, as well as some scientists themselves, were increasingly arguing that science could not be separated from the social and political conditions under which it was produced, and the use of race in science seemed to epitomize this. As part of their campaign for racial equality, anti-racist organizations began to criticize scientists directly for using race in ways which were considered far from neutral.[56] The work of scientists was increasingly understood to be socially constructed and race was similarly conceived as a social construct, while sources of racism were located in political, social and indeed scientific institutions.[57] The argument for inherited racial differences in IQ which situates whites above blacks, what Stephen Jay Gould called an 'argument as old as the study of race',[58] was made new in the Jensen case. However, Jensen and his supporters were in the minority as other scientists, most famously Richard Lewontin, used the latest genetic information available to refute Jensen's arguments and to reassert the idea at the heart of the 1951 UNESCO Statement on Race, that race had no real genetic significance.[59]

Lewontin's ideas initially bolstered the growing anti-racist movements of the 1970s and 1980s, as well as academic sociological and cultural theories on the social construction of race. In Britain, anti-racist practice began to be institutionalized following the Race Relations Act of 1976, which made racial discrimination in employment, education and public services illegal. Although race was not considered by many activists to be a biological fact, its power as a social reality which produced racism justified the need for its continuing usage as a way of analysing inequality. However, it was the idea that race is a social construct, rather than genetically real, which would eventually contribute to the decline of the anti-racist movements of this period. For, as David Theo Goldberg has shown, 'In the wake of whatever nominal successes, anti-racist struggle gave way... to anti-racial commitments at the expense of antiracist effects and ongoing struggle.'[60] The fight against racism gradually became a fight against the idea of race itself, as anti-racist campaigns were deemed to have largely achieved their goals and science had proved that race, as biological difference, did not exist.

In the UK, attention began to shift from popular and structural forms of racism to more subtle aspects of cultural stereotyping and discrimination which constituted 'the new racism'.[61] The 1980s and 1990s witnessed a turn away from political blackness as a form of synchronized action among the victims of racism, and a turn towards more complex ways of fixing and instrumentalizing culture and difference, a development which made anti-racism less politically focused and thus more difficult to organize.[62] In its place, multiculturalism became the predominant way of conceptualizing the state of race relations in Britain, questions of ethnicity, identity and culture coming to dominate the agenda, rather than inequality and racism.[63] While in the wake of the racist murder of Stephen Lawrence in 1993 the Race Relations Act was amended in 2000 to include a duty on public authorities to promote race equality, attitudes towards race were beginning to shift. The Labour government's response to the Northern riots in 2001 was to emphasize 'community cohesion' as a new framework for race relations, a framework which, as Claire Worley has shown, involved the negation of racialized language in favour of the more ambiguous language of 'community'.[64] This political movement away from race was publicly confirmed with the disbanding of the Commission for Racial Equality in 2007, an institution which was subsumed into the newly created Equality and Human Rights Commission. Under the Equality Act of 2010, race became one of several 'protected characteristics' within a broader framework of human rights, a movement overseen and endorsed by Labour politicians and policymakers who believed racism was no longer a significant issue and that government policy should reflect a British society that had apparently transcended racial discrimination and inequality.[65]

In the United States, the public and political consensus on race was also beginning to shift at the end of the twentieth century, premised on the belief that racism had been defeated, that the civil rights movement had successfully ended racial inequality, and that there was thus little need or justification for affirmative action or other colour-conscious policies. The initially naïve concept of colourblindness, which had been put forward as an antidote to Jim Crow during the civil rights movement, had by the late 1980s developed into a conservative ideology characterized by the belief that 'if racial inequalities in income, employment, residence and political representation persist… it is not because of white racism. Rather, the problem is the behavior of people who fail to take responsibility for their own lives'.[66] Re-situating race as an issue for individuals, rather than for institutions, colourblind policies were increasingly adopted as US government policy into the 1990s and 2000s, as race became a banned consideration in public employment across several states, and courts dismantled affirmative action programmes designed to desegregate schools, erasing racism as a factor in the lives of the US citizens.[67] The election of Barack Obama in 2008 only seemed to reinforce the legitimacy of these moves, as commentators in the media, politics and academia rushed to claim that the United States was now a post-racial society.

This gradual disappearance of race from policy and political dialogues in the UK and United States initially gained traction from scientific ideas about the biological non-existence of race, which high-profile scientists and projects continued to promote.[68] However, it was the denial of the significance of racism at the heart of colourblind ideology that also, ironically, enabled the growth in research into the genetic basis of race at the same moment in time. Invocations of colourblindness enabled genomicists to position their research as beyond the influence of race and racism, as the 'color-blind metanarrative of human genetic sameness' operated to 'inhibit scientists' ability to critically assess the racialized cultural and ideological considerations contained within it'.[69] Geneticists' presupposed 'antiracist investigation into the biology of race'[70] was seen to make the use of race 'safe' in their hands, and liberal-minded scientists erected what Dorothy Roberts calls an 'imaginary wall... separating racial science from racial politics'.[71] This 'imaginary wall' meant that geneticists could begin to once again invoke genetic understandings of race, and, as evident in cases such as the development of the racially targeted drug BiDil, to invoke their own anti-racist beliefs as a defence against the charge levelled at them that their invocations of race risked a return to racial (racist) science.[72] Even if such geneticists were and are motivated by anti-racism, the idea that racial difference is genetic also began to be simultaneously invoked by political conservatives in the United States as alternative evidence that affirmative action schemes should be dismantled, on the basis that inequality could be explained by genetic difference.[73] Genetic definitions of race came to be increasingly used 'to explain why stark racial disparities persist despite the abolition of official discrimination on the basis of race'[74] even though it is more evident than ever that discrimination persists.

The reinvigoration of genetic investigations into race at a moment when genetic science was also denying the biological existence of race is a situation which is both the product and enabler of the denial of the persistence of racism in the UK and US public spheres. The current era is characterized by what Goldberg calls 'racism without race';[75] an erasure of the possibility of racist beliefs and practices on the basis that race itself does not exist and on the understanding that racism has been consigned to the past. Experiences of racism become unnameable, as it becomes increasingly unacceptable to even speak in racial terms. In the UK the former head of the Commission for Racial Equality, Trevor Philips, suggested that the term 'systemic bias' should be adopted to talk about racial discrimination,[76] while even the fascist English Defence League avoid speaking in racial terms about what are overtly racist beliefs.[77] In the United States, Donald Trump has claimed that he is not a racist and is 'the least racist person',[78] while instituting some of the most racist policies the United States has witnessed in recent times.[79] The language of genetics has been characterized by a similar reflex, for not only do geneticists consistently deny the possibility of racism, but the term 'race' itself is often avoided (as I will discuss further in Chapter 2), in favour of terms such as 'population', 'ethnicity' and 'ancestry' which nevertheless continue to signal and to correspond with older racial categorizations.

New developments in genetics have tended to fit comfortably into this emerging racial schema and have harnessed the commercial possibilities of the downplaying of racism in favour of the promotion and bolstering of identities which are racial in all but name. Racial minorities (or perhaps formerly racialized individuals as the commentators who deny the significance of racism might have it) are encouraged to focus not on racism as the central and defining experience of being raced, but on identity. For example, Black Britons and African Americans (nearly always the populations at the forefront of scientific investigations of race) have been encouraged to trace their ancestral roots using the genetic ancestry tracing technologies which have emerged from the Mitochondrial DNA and Y Chromosome analysis developed in the African Eve project and the HGDP, respectively. Such technologies focus on carefully selected, individualized lines of ancestry which have encouraged the idea that knowing 'who you are' is about 'genetic differences', genetics appearing, as Catherine Nash contends, 'neutralized, just a means to something else, to knowledge of ancestry, something positive, rewarding, meaningful but politically neutral'.[80] Where once such scientific racial interventions were considered to be politically charged, they now assume a political neutrality which has been largely accepted by the populations at which genetic technologies are aimed, as well as by some scholars of race in the humanities.

Indeed such developments – the denial of the possibility of racism, and the celebration of individual ancestry tracing which makes race an issue of personal identity, rather than collective experience – are racial arrangements that have been accepted and to a degree promoted in some scholarship on the new genetics of race. Such scholarship views these developments not as evidence of a renewed (false) separation of science and politics as I do, but as evidence of new kinds of interaction between the scientific and the socio-political which supersede older binaries between biological and social definitions of race. Alondra Nelson, for example, attempts to 'triangulate' the binary between biological and social understandings of race through an examination of genetic genealogy testing, the users of which, she contends, utilize genetic results in ways that are meaningful to them to construct their identities.[81] Genetic genealogy testing is not reducible to a form of genetic determinism or racial realism in Nelson's view, but operates complexly as it is also applied to a range of political and social efforts to bring issues of inequality into view – reconciliation projects which she argues shape race in new and innovative ways.[82] Nikolas Rose argues in a similar vein that the new genetics of race 'is intrinsically linked to the delineation and administration of biosocial communities, formed around beliefs in a shared disease heritage, demanding resources for the biomedical research that might reveal the genomic bases of these diseases, and mobilized by the hope of a cure'.[83] Black and minority ethnic communities' apparent embrace of race-based medicine and genetic ancestry tracing makes them 'active biological citizens', ushering in a new biopolitical era where race is located between biology and culture: 'race now signifies an unstable space of ambivalence between the molecular level of the genome and the cell, and the molar level of classifications in terms of population group, country of origin, cultural diversity and self-perception'.[84] Catherine Bliss comes to a similar conclusion through an investigation of how genetic scientists integrate their own political beliefs into research on race. She contends that geneticists approach race through an anti-racist lens, 'drawing on their own experiences, memories, and racial values', in effect 'biosocializing' in the way that minority communities had previously been understood to do.[85] For Bliss, this means that we need to 'rethink the character, aims, and implications of scientific knowledge' as scientists are 'expanding the definition of biology to include social factors'.[86] Genetics is infused with social meanings which in turn are being shaped by science in these accounts, in which social theorists seek to work with, rather than against, new genetic discoveries and practices. Rejecting critical approaches which link recent developments in genetics with older racial science as a form of outdated 'sociocritique',[87] these stances take the anti-racist outlook of contemporary science as a given, and understand genetics to be a non-deterministic science, far removed from the determinism of racial ideas in science past.

Such accounts usefully bring to the fore the ways in which the idea of race is being shaped in novel ways across social and scientific lines in the twenty-first century, going further than the aforementioned critical race theorists in recognizing how contemporary science is actively determined and informed by the social, and acknowledging that genetics has not left biological conceptions of race behind. Yet these approaches to race differ from that which I will propose in this book, as the conceptual frameworks they employ to understand the interconnections of science and society draw upon a model of hybridity which, when deployed in relation to questions of race, is potentially limiting. Nelson's triangulation of race between social construction and biological reality, Rose's vision of race as occupying an 'unstable space of ambivalence between' science and culture, and Bliss's understanding of race as a 'hybrid of molecular science, social epidemiology, public health and bioethics',[88] each has a tendency to conceive of race as the hybrid product of pre-existing entities (at their broadest, 'science' and 'society'). Science studies scholar Bruno Latour proposed the concept of hybridity as a means to overcome the modern distinction between nature and society, hybridity describing how 'all of culture and all of nature get churned up every day', and the 'imbroglios of science, politics, economy, law, religion, technology, fiction' that he argued characterize modern societies but which such societies attempt to separate out into 'pure disciplines'.[89] In a highly influential move, Latour viewed the work of the critic as being the work of hybridity; to re-tie the Gordian knot by crisscrossing the divide between nature and culture, to understand how these entities are networked.[90] Around the same time the concept of hybridity was being theorized and developed in postcolonial studies, where it came to describe the fusion of cultures that results from 'third world migration'; 'the hybrid strategy', Homi Bhabha writes, is 'a space of negotiation' which is 'neither assimilation nor collaboration' but in which hybrid agencies 'deploy the partial culture from which they emerge to construct visions of community ... that give narrative form to the minority positions they occupy; the outside of the inside: the part in the whole'.[91] Hybridity came to signify the unsettling of notions of essentialism and, as Pnina Werbner has noted, 'in the postmodern imaginary, hybridity invades whole areas of sociological discourse, subverting and conflating long-established classes and categories'.[92]

Yet hybridity can be a problematic concept, not only for its tendency to imply that the objects, entities and ideas of which a hybrid consists are somehow pure and separable from each other in the first place. The use of hybridity as a means to describe purportedly new formations of race in genetics is particularly problematic because ironically it recalls the very history of racial science that these theorists so consciously seek to avoid. The concept of hybridity was used extensively by nineteenth-century racial scientists to describe racial mixing and became central to debates about whether different races were different species, the test for different species being whether the progeny would be infertile, a charge often levelled at mixed-race populations in the colonies.[93] The lack of attention paid to this racialized history has resulted, as several scholars have shown, in the repetition of ideas and structures from past racialized discourses in contemporary theorizations of hybridity.[94] For Robert J. C. Young,

> The question is whether the old, essentializing categories of cultural identity, or of race, were really so essentialized, or have been retrospectively constructed as more fixed than they were. When we look at the texts of racial theory, we find

that they are in fact contradictory, disruptive and already deconstructed … in deconstructing such essentialist notions of race today we may rather be repeating the past than distancing ourselves from it or providing a critique of it.[95]

For Young, contemporary theoretical and conceptual invocations of hybridity cannot be separated from the roots of the idea in racial science. Yet when Bliss states firmly that 'genomics does not mark the reemergence of a prior science of race; rather, it is devoted to a new understanding of race',[96] or when Rose claims that whereas race in the nineteenth century was understood at the molar level – in terms of visible, physical characteristics – the molecular scale of the new genetics creates a complexity which is simply not deterministic in the way that racial science was,[97] Young's point is missed. While the mechanics of measuring race might have changed, these claims do not take account of the fact that race (in science) has never been wholly deterministic, essentialized or biologized. As recent studies have emphasized, the non-deterministic nature of much post-genomic biology has a precedent in the non-deterministic way that race emerged in the work of Darwin and the mid-to-late Victorians.[98] In a similar manner to the repetition of the 'already deconstructed' discourses of racial theory, contemporary theorizations of race as being ambivalently in between biology and culture reiterate the 'ambiguities, contradictions and discrepancies'[99] of racial theory in nineteenth-century science, ambiguities and ambivalences built into the concept of hybridity from its inception in racial science. Far from providing a new, radical framework for conceiving of race and its relationship to the biosciences, the hybrid model of an ambivalent in between race risks having the same impact as older discourses on race where the 'ambiguities … manifest within particular racial theories and racialised medicine are more likely to strengthen than weaken racial discourses'.[100] The critical privileging of questions of identity over an engagement with the social and political struggles of the people whose experience hybridity is supposed to describe, simply repeats, rather than challenges, the tired focus on the politics of identity, at the expense of an engagement with history, which characterized postcolonial formations of hybridity.

A biofictional approach

How can we conceive of the contemporary biofictional nature of race in a way which recognizes the complex imbrication of biology and culture, scientific fact and fiction, but resists re-inscribing the artificial separation of these entities? How can we move beyond these dichotomies while accounting for and acknowledging the history of the race concept, which has never been either wholly biological or cultural? How can we keep the realities of racism and racial inequality in view, recognizing that, as Dorothy Roberts puts it, 'just as we cannot apply the same old sociocritiques or paste the same label of eugenics on contemporary biopolitics, nor can we uncritically assume that the new biocitizenship necessarily fosters individual life and choice and necessarily intervenes on the consequences of inequality, rather than legitimizing inequality'?[101] This book proposes a biofictional approach which situates contemporary fiction as key to comprehending how the current racial formations dominant in the UK and United States (namely the movement from anti-racism to an anti-racialism which obscures racism while making race an issue of personal identity rather than collective experience) are the product of entanglements of scientific fact and fiction, neither of which can be conceived without the other. For, as Donna Haraway has long maintained, 'both science and popular culture are intricately woven of fact and fiction'.[102] As Amade M'Charek has argued, facts and fictions are not pre-given entities; a previous fact might become fiction and vice versa, fictions being partial truths in the sense that they are both made and made up.[103] Facts cannot be privileged over fiction (as they have often been) in this relational understanding because fiction is part of truth-making, and facts are fluid and unfixed as they materialize in different ways over time.[104] I contend that an examination of contemporary novels enables an apprehension of the overlapping, mutually constituting facts and fictions of race which circulate across the boundaries of genetics and literature, illuminating, in Caroline Levine's terms, how 'forms migrate across contexts', how 'aesthetic and political forms may be nestled inside one another' and how 'each is capable of disturbing the other's organizing power'.[105] Rather than simply contesting socio-scientific racial formations, or reinforcing a social constructionist paradigm, contemporary literary engagements with race underscore that 'science is not a single origin, with literature, or sociology, or economics, or philosophy as its interpretative followers',[106] but that racial forms emerge from the entanglement of literature and science in ways which highlight both historical precedents for contemporary racial formations and continuing racist realities.

While the interwoven relations of facts and fictions (literary, cultural and social) have preoccupied postmodernist literary criticism for some time, my approach draws upon emerging insights in post-genomic biology, in which the relations between biology and culture are being reconfigured in ways that, I contend, might act as a model for thinking about the relations between genetic science and literature. Where once the gene was understood as a fixed, stable entity, and the discourse of classical genetics was dominated by the idea of 'gene action' which gave causal priority to genes in the development of characteristics, post-genomic science has revealed the genome to be 'an exquisitely sensitive reaction (or response) mechanism', in which genes are embedded in and acutely responsive to their environment.[107] This environment includes not only the immediate cellular environment, but the environment external to the organism (or human), the 'complex socio-cultural environments' that humans construct and engage in.[108] For Evelyn Fox Keller, any sense of a binary between genes and their wider environments therefore becomes obsolete; she writes:

> Not only is it a mistake to think of development in terms of separable causes, but it is also a mistake to think of the development of traits as a product of causal elements interacting with one another. Indeed, the notion of interaction presupposes the existence of entities that are at least ideally separable – i.e., it presupposes an a priori space between component entities – and this is precisely what the character of developmental dynamics precludes. Everything we know about the processes of inheritance and development teaches us that the entanglement of developmental processes is not only immensely intricate, but it is there from the start.[109]

We must abandon, Keller contends, the 'mirage of a space between nature and nurture' (terms which she has demonstrated correspond, although not un-problematically, with biology/culture distinctions), in favour of a relational understanding of genes and their environments which acknowledges that neither can be understood in the absence of its apparent opposite.[110] This new conception of the gene, together with other theorizations of complexity and entanglement in science, has been highly influential within the humanities and social sciences, prompting calls for a renewed understanding of how remapping the borderlands between nature and culture requires a concomitant rethinking of the borders between the corresponding disciplines which study these objects.[111] Recent theorizations of the 'bio-humanities',[112] the 'bio-social'[113] and the 'biocultural'[114] seek to do just this, to articulate not only how the humanities can 'add to our understanding of biology itself'[115] (in the case of the first) but how moving towards what Keller terms a 'biocultural synthesis' would mean admitting the biological into social (and in this case literary) theory.[116] The challenge is to develop an approach which in Gillian Beer's words can 'find ways out of the circle of current presumptions ... to create knowledge or fresh insight', for 'all description draws, often unknowingly, upon shared cultural assumptions which underwrite its neutral and authoritative status and conceal the embedded designs upon which describing depends'.[117] In the case of some sociological work on race in contemporary genetics, such presumptions include the long-embedded impulse to triangulate and hybridize binaries which never existed in the first place, an impulse which Levine contends can distract attention from the way that power operates.[118]

The biofictional approach to race proposed here brings contemporary genetic narratives of race, biology and culture into dialogue with a broad range of fiction published in the UK and the United States from the 1970s onwards, responding to Squier's call to craft new ways of making sense of the configurations and assemblages of relations produced by new biomedical developments.[119] Following Squier I understand (fictional) narratives as offering 'an alternative to the impossible attempt to distinguish nature from culture, science from society' and instead as 'a site where we can productively consider their mutual imbrication and cogeneration'.[120] Each chapter considers a different genetic intervention into the race question in relation to a work or works of fiction originating in the UK or the United States where these scientific developments took place. Chapter 1 explores the African Eve hypothesis (1987) and Alex Haley's *Roots* (1976); Chapter 2 the Human Genome Diversity Project (1991) and Kazuo Ishiguro's *Never Let Me Go* (2005); Chapter 3 the Human Genome Project (2001) and Zadie Smith's *White Teeth* (2000); Chapter 4 the development of BiDil (2005) and Colson Whitehead's *Apex Hides the Hurt* (2006); Chapter 5 the rise of epigenetics (*c.* 2008) and Octavia Butler's *Kindred* (1979) and Salman Rushdie's *The Satanic Verses* (1988). The novels range widely in style and genre, differ in their approaches to race and their authors' level of engagement with genetics. Where Smith, Ishiguro and Whitehead make reference to recent racial developments in genetic science through novels which adopt realist, science fictional and satirical modes, the novels of Haley, Rushdie and Butler – ranging in genre from family saga to magic realism and fantasy – contain no overt references to contemporary genetics. These latter novels were published before the developments in genetics alongside which they are considered took place, and thus cannot be considered to respond to or interact directly with a particular scientific idea. Instead, each of the six novels evinces different kinds of relationships to science: for example, where Chapter 1 explores how the narration of African ancestry in *Roots* came to shape the structure and tone of popular science books on human origins in Africa, Chapter 3 examines how the comic form of *White Teeth* operates as a rebuttal to attempts by scientists to delimit the meaning of race and the significance of literature in discourses surrounding the Human Genome Project, while Chapter 5 more speculatively explores how fantastic representations of racism in *Kindred* and *The Satanic*

Verses might aid understanding of the epigenetic effects of racism on the body. The inclusion of two novels in the final chapter reflects this chapter's aim to consider how fiction might be actively and critically engaged as a means of thinking through the implications of an emerging strand of genetics: it offers more than one example as a gesture towards the multiple and specific possibilities that contemporary fiction affords for scholars across disciplines grappling with the import of race in (epigenetic) science. Together, the chapters evince a range of possible entanglements between concepts in genetics, scientific discourse, fictional narrative, literary criticism and sociological discourse, biofictional assemblages that move us away from understanding these relations through sociological triangulation models of race, and which go beyond Beer's 'two-way traffic'[121] model for the relations between literature and science.

My approach reflects the fact that racial forms know no generic boundaries; race is an idea which is portable across time, space and context, and while always historically inflected and determined, race confounds attempts to delimit its boundaries through types of literary categorization (by either style, temporality, or the racial or geographical origins of a writer) rooted in the institutional patterns of nineteenth and early-twentieth-century English departments.[122] The creation of race in the eighteenth and nineteenth centuries occurred not only through exchanges between scientific and literary texts but through literary scholarship, which has continued to attempt to distinguish aesthetic patterns of difference between writers on the basis of racial background. This study makes no such taxonomic attempt, but in reading different kinds of literary texts alongside one another it aims to demonstrate how the formation and transmission of racial ideas call into question not only the internal disciplinary organization of English studies but the boundaries between science and literary studies; for race unsettles the presumed stability of both scientific truth and literary hierarchies of knowledge. Following this, *Biofictions* reads scientific writing and narrative including research papers, popular science and journalism, as well as racial and genetic theories, alongside the novels as a means of illuminating how stories about race emerge across the generic boundaries of these different texts. I work with an expanded definition of science as 'an evolving set of technological, material, narrative, and affective practices' in which the boundaries between the lab and science journalism, scientific commerce and fiction, collide to produce genetic narratives, metaphors and language.[123] What Deborah Lynn Steinberg calls the 'spectacle of science' is not an artefact which can be tacked onto 'real science' but a core part of scientific cultures and scientific work.[124] Contemporary scientific culture is characterized by a range of practices and forms which influence how scientific ideas are received by both scientists themselves and the wider public; science, like fiction, functions narratively and operates agentially within the wider sociocultural context in which it is embedded.

I consider genetic science to be inextricable from what Stefan Timmermans and Sara Shostack call 'gene worlds', that is 'the social worlds in which genes flourish, which include the political, financial, and professional contexts that enable genetic knowledge'.[125] However my approach calls for literature to be considered and included as a key element of the 'gene worlds' from which scientific ideas emerge; for fiction to be acknowledged and interrogated alongside sociocultural considerations; for the definition of genetics to be expanded to include not only the social or cultural, but also the literary; perhaps, even, that fiction be considered a part of the wider environment without which, it is now understood, genes cannot be conceived. In this, I join a growing number of scholars who have sought to understand how cultural representations, including the fictional, are involved in the production of genetic knowledge and the creation of a biomedical imaginary.[126] My focus on fiction alone is designed not only to highlight the narrative origins and histories of the contemporary sociocultural – scientific entanglements that produce race concepts, but to centralize narrative form as key to comprehending how processes of racial formation occur. For while the novels range widely in style, context and their level of engagement with genetics, they each develop narrative forms which are informed by (often older, racial) scientific theories and methodologies, forms which highlight continuities between the interdisciplinary creation of race in the past and in the present. For example, in Chapter 2 I will explore how *Never Let Me Go* evokes a Darwinian theory of human (racial) unity through a narrative which emphasizes facial expression over physical characteristics as a means of thinking differently about contemporary understandings of race in genetic ancestry tracing; while in Chapter 4 I examine how *Apex Hides the Hurt* recalls the fictionality and overt racism of the mid-nineteenth-century racial medical theories of Samuel Cartwright through a signifying narrative mode which links this history to contemporary, purportedly anti-racist racial medicine.

Biofictions seeks not only to follow and to trace connections between literary and scientific texts and forms, to map entanglements which have already occurred, but to consider how knowledge of these relationships might offer new ways of understanding race in the age of the genome that might challenge the false anti-racism of colourblindness and restore a historically conscious approach to race in contemporary genetics. I read the novels not only as revealing the biofictional nature of new racial formations – that 'bodies are always both natural and cultural, both biologically and socially raced'[127] – but as offering ways to harness this imbrication for anti-racist ends, as a means of overcoming the creeping privatization of race that genetic science enables. In this, *Biofictions* departs from recent literary approaches to science which, much like the sociology of science I have discussed, have called for the abandonment of a critical mode characterized as 'critique'. For Rita Felski, critique encompasses 'a spirit of skeptical reflection or outright condemnation; an emphasis on its own precarious position vis-à-vis overbearing social forces; the claim to be engaged in some kind of radical intellectual and/or political work; and the assumption that whatever is *not* critical must therefore be *uncritical*'.[128] Critique, in this view, is a negative mode which literary scholars have used to defend their own practices while looking down upon other disciplines (namely the sciences) in disparaging terms – 'those blinkered scientists holed up in their labs' – because scientists are seemingly uncritical and unaware of their own positioning.[129] Steven Connor goes further, claiming that the discipline of English Literature 'has been converted into a factory for the detection and denunciation of various kinds of social sin, and the affirmation of various kinds of social good', a values-based discipline which has lost interest in the literary text itself.[130] This, he claims, is the opposite of what scientists do, since they 'do not spend their time wondering how or whether what they are doing does or does not constitute science'.[131] The implication is that literary scholars might adopt the approach which scientists apparently take to their work, and in so doing might 'accept their marginality' and refrain from 'mistaking epistemology for effect' when it comes to grand challenges such as climate change, which only science can solve.[132]

It is certainly true that neither literary texts nor literary scholarship is capable of single-handedly solving problems like climate change, or, for the purpose of this study, the effects of biofictional racial formations. Yet returning to a more positivist view of science as the answer to problems which have complex political, social and cultural origins as well as impacts, while suggesting that the job of the literary scholar is simply 'to protect and to care'[133] for their objects (texts) as well as science, rather than to critically apprehend the social and political import of them, implies that the relationship between the disciplines is one-way. Not only this, but as the approach of critical race scholars to contemporary genetics demonstrates, critique of science is clearly not the default mode of literary criticism. While, following Felski, I understand fiction to be an agent in the making of race, as an 'active mediator rather than passive intermediary'[134] in scientific contexts, and while *Biofictions* seeks to avoid automatic critique or any sense of literary superiority to science, I also believe that 'the defensive praise of science or the ritualized acknowledgement of the epistemological inferiority of the humanities'[135] is not the answer. For the latter stance is linked to a materialist, object-oriented form of analysis focused not on politics but on 'forging...links between things that were previously unconnected',[136] an interpretive mode which, when race is the object, flattens the possibility or desire for anti-racism. For example, Mitchum Huehls, in his book *After Critique*, argues that race in contemporary fiction does not mean or represent, but is an unknowable object: rather than requiring interpretation or defamiliarization, the contradictions of racial discourse within the contemporary neoliberal framework simply make race illegible, and contemporary writers are (as literary critics should be) only involved in describing this shifting object of race, rather than imagining futures yet unthought.[137] This deliberately non-radical stance presents itself as a form of radical thinking, the possibility for a new kind of politics located in the status quo, yet such ways of reading are the preserve of the privileged, and appear much like 'research processes that restrict their issues to those legitimated within the dominant forms of thought' rather than a more effective 'theory of knowledge that directs researchers to start off their thought from the lives of those marginalized or exploited by the dominant conceptual frameworks'.[138]

I am more interested in how an understanding that race is biofictional forces us to give up on the 'proper objects' that are biology and culture, and instead of either caring for or simply describing objects, to proceed on an anti-racist (and indeed feminist) critical basis that recognizes that what counts as biology and materiality is constantly in dispute.[139] Such an understanding opens up new ways of comprehending the effects of racism on the body and the impact of racist social environments on biology; recent research in epigenetics is uncovering how 'racialized taxonomies have real consequences upon biological functions, including the expression of genes'.[140] Such emerging insights into the nature of race guide this study as it explores how biofictional forms of race might 'reroute a racial hierarchy or disturb exclusionary boundaries'[141] as they cross between literature, science and politics. It is my hope that the chapters of this book will be of interest not only to literary scholars but to scientists, sociologists and others who are concerned not only to understand but also to actively address the often problematically racialized (and unconsciously racist) conceptions emerging from the contemporary genetic sciences of race. Each chapter acts as a case study which addresses a different genetic development in the context of wider social and political debates about race, connecting each genetic intervention chronologically from the 1980s to the present. While delving into the recent histories of racial ideas in science, this book is not a history of race in science, but an examination of how fiction investigates, actively contributes to, and might shape, the biofictional formation of race in genetics.

The first case study concerns the African Eve hypothesis (1987), the theory that all modern humans originate in Africa, which resulted from the first major attempt to apply DNA analysis to the study of human origins, which had previously been the sole province of palaeoanthropology. Having been the scientifically accepted (albeit contested) theory of the origin of modern humans for over twenty years, the hypothesis has been recently cast into doubt by the discovery that some contemporary human populations carry traces of Neanderthal DNA. This chapter asks why the hypothesis gained such credibility so as to become scientific orthodoxy. It argues that popularizers of African Eve were able to draw upon a widely known story of African origins, Alex Haley's novel *Roots*, which subtly shaped science writing on human origins published in the wake of Eve. Analysing in detail how Haley's novel enabled scientists to emphasize the anti-racist credentials of the hypothesis, the chapter demonstrates that it was ultimately the influence of anthropological scholarship on the composition of *Roots* itself which made it so appealing to genetic anthropologists. Haley portrayed Africans and their American ancestors conservatively, in a traditional form that was palatable to white readers and later audiences who watched the television adaptation of *Roots*. His tale thus provided a relatively safe model for writing on human origins in Africa, which was itself implicitly concerned to sell the idea that we are all from Africa to a white readership. Tracing how a fictional representation of race and racism has informed bioscientific fact, the chapter contends that Haley's novel assisted in the emergence of the highly influential, racially inflected conception of ancestry which predominates today: the idea that we can know ourselves through (selected) ancestors and that we can know them through genetic science.

Chapter 2 further explores this idea by examining the development of genetic ancestry tracing technologies in the 1990s within the field of population genetics, developments which drew upon the findings of the African Eve hypothesis. The study of differences between human populations under the auspices of the Human Genome Diversity Project (1991) was, like Eve, intended to be an anti-racist endeavour, focusing on geographical location, rather than race, as a means of identifying genetic differences. Yet rather than erasing racial distinctions, this study of human genetic diversity effectively re-named race as 'ethnicity', 'population' or 'geographical group' while claiming race and racism to be social phenomena distinct from scientific fact. The effects of this simultaneous erasure and re-inscription of race are explored by Kazuo Ishiguro in his 2005 novel *Never Let Me Go*, in which Ishiguro imagines the lives of a cloned population of humans, lives which bear many resemblances to those of people who are racialized and racially marginalized. The clones, apparently raceless, yet segregated on the basis of their genetic difference, are the product of a world without biological race, in which forms of racism nevertheless persist. As Ishiguro offers a critique of the post-racialism which population genetics superficially served to support, he presents an alternative vision of relatedness based on a non-genetic, non-racial affinity. The protagonist Kathy's narrative focuses on describing facial expressions in place of physical characteristics, enabling her to find recognition not in the face of a genetically similar other, but in the novel's only racially differentiated character, her teacher's Nigerian carer George. Evoking the logic of Darwin's theory of the universality of expression, and thus the common descent of different races, the novel's form challenges the idea that who you are can be discovered in tracing a (racial) genetic ancestry. Instead, Ishiguro offers a model of reciprocity grounded in an understanding of the imbrication of the biological body (facial expressions) and its cultural environment as a means of thinking beyond racial categorization and what the novel exposes as the false anti-racist strategies of population genetics.

The apotheosis of genetic science in the twentieth century was the HGP, an international effort led by the UK and the United States to identify all 25,000 genes in the human genome. When the completion of the draft of the genome was announced in June 2000, the implications for race were at the heart of the speeches given by the scientists and politicians assembled at the White House: as then President Bill Clinton put it, 'one of the great truths to emerge from this triumphant expedition inside the human genome is that in genetic terms, all human beings, regardless of race, are more than 99.9 percent the same'.[142] It was a moment with uncanny resemblances to a scene in Zadie Smith's debut novel *White Teeth*, which had been published six months earlier. Smith's tale of three London families, whose socially and racially varied backgrounds form the basis of their comic interactions, takes the new genetic science as one of its major themes: Marcus, head of the Chalfen family, is a geneticist whose experimental FutureMouse© has been designed to develop cancer and die on New Year's Eve 1999. Despite Marcus's assurances to the contrary at a grand unveiling of his genetic experiment, his science is not race free but has been developed from the work of a Nazi racial scientist, his mentor Dr Perret, the scientific links to which have been forgotten. Chapter 3 examines how *White Teeth* not only explores the consequences of the erasure of race, and subsequently the possibility of racism, from contemporary genetics, but demonstrates how the scientific 'reading' of the human body as non-racial is one of many complex and messy genetic narratives of race that make scientific discourse comparable to fiction. Drawing on Lionel Trilling's assertion that 'plot is to the novelist what experiment is to the scientist',[143] Smith sets up an extended comparison between the methods of the scientist and the writer of fiction as a means of testing this hypothesis. Smith uses the novel's comic form, a Forsterian mode characterized by coincidence, irrationality, humour, melodrama and 'artificiality', to highlight comparable qualities in genetic narratives, which, the novel suggests, create and transmit stories about race. In becoming itself a conduit for such stories, *White Teeth* underscores the importance of fiction to fully comprehend the intrinsically narrative qualities of race in science.

The complexities and indeed contradictions of genetic narratives of race come to the fore in Chapter 4, which examines how despite the Human Genome Project's rejection of the idea of genetic racial difference, only a few years later in 2005 the US Food and Drug Administration approved a new drug called BiDil, designed to treat heart failure exclusively in the African American population. The first ever 'ethnic drug', BiDil was supported by doctors and geneticists, and by the Association of Black Cardiologists, who saw the advent of the drug as placing a much-needed focus on the health of black populations. Tested only on 'self-identified' African Americans, BiDil's creators acknowledged that race was used as a proxy for an unknown marker and that the drug might be effective in non-black populations. However, the promotion and marketing of the drug obscured this fact, encouraging the public instead to view BiDil as a black drug in ways which made race into the condition to be treated, race the disease. Chapter 4 examines how this racialization of medicine is satirized in Colson Whitehead's 2006 novel *Apex Hides the Hurt*, in which the novel's unnamed protagonist, a nomenclature consultant, names a new range of plasters designed to match the skin-tone of their wearers. Using one himself after he stubs his toe, the plaster hides a more serious infection and he eventually goes on to have the toe amputated as a result. Whitehead's tale addresses how the market-driven personalization of medicine along racial lines relies not on biological explanations of race, but on the multiple ways race is signified in language; it examines how race operates, in Stuart Hall's terms, as a 'floating signifier', which determines how racial meaning can be created and exploited in science. The novel explores how, consequently, identifying with and accepting racialized medicine (which relies on language and linguistic signification to make race mean) result in the protagonist's illness: it is the protagonist's racialization as black which makes him ill because it has been leeched of any meaningful (historical) significance by the world of commerce and medicine. His recovery is only possible once he addresses the historical causes of pain and illness in the African American population, something which, it is implied, the new racial science and medicine also need to do. By drawing parallels between the protagonist's mysterious illness and the fictive disease Drapetomania invented by racist doctor Samuel Cartwright in 1851, Whitehead's novel demonstrates how pharmacogenetics' reliance on language and linguistic signification to make race mean has a precedent in the overtly fictional ways in which race was made disease in the racist medicine of the era of chattel slavery.

The final chapter investigates the role that fiction might play in the recent turn away from the gene-centric biology that was epitomized by the mapping of the human genome. Post-genomic biology, in particular epigenetics, has moved towards a more complex, non-deterministic conception of 'the gene' as plastic and interconnected with its environment, moving beyond older conceptions of genes as discrete entities with stable, determining effects. Epigenetics – broadly defined as the study of changes in gene function and expression that do not comprise changes in the DNA sequence – is revealing that genes can change, and that changes can be passed on to offspring, reconfiguring genetic inheritance and development as fluid and complex, rather than fixed, processes. This discovery has particularly far-reaching implications for the concept of race, as initial research has demonstrated that genes can carry a 'memory' of past environments and experiences (such as the experience of being enslaved), which may in part explain contemporary racial disparities in health. This chapter explores how contemporary fiction has already imagined the kinds of complexity that such post-genomic biology is beginning to uncover, and suggests that fiction might illuminate our understanding of these emerging scientific insights. The way experiences of racism become biologically embodied is explored in both Octavia Butler's *Kindred* (1979) and Salman Rushdie's *The Satanic Verses* (1988), each of which depicts the bodily transformations of their protagonists following exposure to racial violence. The chapter argues that what the novels' fantastical representations of the body highlight is the dynamic relationship between the imaginary and the real; the protagonists' transformations work to show the arbitrariness, absurdity, but also the ultimate power of the racist belief which shapes their reality. In the context of epigenetics, these depictions of the physiological impact of racism suggest that we might understand the relationship between the environment and genetics as the imaginary (such as slave owners' belief in the racial inferiority of their slaves) made biologically real through health disparities in the present.

In ending with an examination of epigenetics, a scientific development which is challenging the more usual ahistoricism of genetics by placing an emphasis on the significance of past environments, this book hopes to model how comprehending race as biofiction might empower geneticists, literary scholars and those for whom race is an inescapable force, to think differently about scientific narratives of race; to look to contemporary fiction as a source of knowledge, rather than simply understanding, of how race is formed and functions across scientific cultures. At a moment when the validity of scientific fact and the expertise of scientists are under attack from an emboldened right-wing global political movement, there might be a temptation, in defence of scientific expertise, to retreat into older, binary ways of thinking about fact and fiction as a means to defend against those who would dismiss science on the very grounds that scientists are themselves politically implicated and motivated. As Latour puts it (as he is thinking about climate change), 'dangerous extremists' are 'using the very same argument of social construction to destroy hard-won evidence that could save our lives'.[144] Yet to deny the ways in which the political, the social, the cultural and the literary are entangled with science (as tempting as such a denial might be in the face of an anti-science political sphere) would be as regressive and limiting as the attack on science itself. Far from undermining scientific knowledge and expertise, *Biofictions* aims to demonstrate how scientific approaches to complex, interdisciplinary ideas and problems like race might be bolstered, invigorated and enriched by engagements with fiction, which might play a key role in the creation of effective anti-racist scientific narratives and strategies in the future. Contemporary novels offer ways of comprehending how the apparently anti-racist consensus in science, reliant as it is (whatever the position on race taken) on maintaining the boundary between fact and fiction, can lead to the reproduction of the very racism it seeks to avoid. Instead the novels demonstrate how racial biofictions emerge at the very moments when race and racism are disavowed politically and scientifically, and offer alternative, anti-racist modes of understanding race; not only as the product of (racist) fictions made corporeal (as suggested in this book's final chapter), but as an idea co-produced across the disciplines of science and literature, the boundaries between which begin to dissolve when what is fact and what is fiction can no longer be easily aligned or equated with them.

1

The Roots of African Eve: Science Writing on Human Origins and Alex Haley's *Roots*

In January 1987, molecular biologists Rebecca Cann, Mark Stoneking and Allan Wilson sparked a major scientific controversy with the publication of an article entitled 'Mitochondrial DNA and human evolution' in the journal *Nature*. In the article they claimed that by analysing mitochondrial DNA derived from the placentas of 145 women representing five major geographic regions, they could infer that 'Africa is a likely source of the human mitochondrial gene pool',[1] and in addition, they offered a 'tentative time scale' which postulated that 'the common ancestor of all surviving mtDNA types existed 140,000–290,000 years ago'.[2] Mitochondrial Eve, or African Eve as she became more popularly known, was born. The controversy was immediate and intense. Palaeoanthropologists objected to what they saw as the complete dismissal of the fossil record by the Berkeley geneticists, whose study represented the first major attempt to apply the relatively new science of molecular biology to human origins, the study of which had previously been the province of palaeoanthropology. Palaeoanthropologists themselves had been split over what the fossil record revealed about the geographical origins of Homo sapiens: while multi-regionalists argued that modern humans had evolved from archaic homo populations in different geographical locations, others favoured an 'Out of Africa' model of the migration of modern humans from Africa to other parts of the world. However, whereas most traditional proponents of the Out of Africa model believed that once modern humans left Africa they interbred with premodern populations in other regions, the African Eve hypothesis stated that there had been no such interbreeding, that modern humans had simply replaced existing premodern populations.[3] Some 'Out of Africa' proponents, most prominently Chris Stringer and Robin McKie, wholeheartedly embraced the biologists' findings, and by the 1980s other evidence from within palaeoanthropology was pointing to Africa as the birthplace of modern humans.⁴ However the multi-regionalists only intensified their campaign. The leading multi-regionalist advocate Milford Wolpoff organized a symposium for anthropologists who opposed African Eve and described the hypothesis as consisting of the 'idea of killer Africans sweeping out across Europe and Asia, over-running everybody', genocidal terminology that had been carefully rehearsed and planned.⁵

Indeed, what was something of an academic battle over the question of human origins was also an ideologically and racially charged debate. Each side tried to accuse the other of being racist; the multi-regionalists were accused of exaggerating racial divisions while African Eve advocates were accused of implying a total and violent replacement of Homo erectus (or Neanderthals) by Homo sapiens.⁶ Much of what Venla Oikkonen has identified as the 'emotional tensions' in journal articles and scientific commentaries about African Eve in the 1980s and 1990s appears to be focused around the racial implications of the hypothesis.⁷ Proponents of the hypothesis were keen to seize the findings for anti-racist ends, to, in part, re-envision genetics as an anti-racist science which emphasized commonality and racial unity over difference, and their work was viewed favourably by black groups and commentators who seized upon the findings as positive evidence that 'all the world's people are Africans in disguise'.⁸ Yet others were uneasy about locating the source of all humanity in Africa, resulting in the 'hate mail, crank mail' and 'strange scrawling notes' that Rebecca Cann, lead author of the mitochondrial study, describes receiving after the publicization of her team's findings.⁹ Racist assumptions often surfaced in the discussions of those opposed to the hypothesis to the degree that, as Jason Antrosio argues, rather than celebrating Africa as the cradle of humanity, it is rather leaving Africa which came to be celebrated in certain academic and popular writing, a kind of celebratory attitude that the historian of science Robert Proctor has dubbed 'Out of Africa – thank God!'.¹⁰ The media response to the hypothesis similarly betrayed an unease about the racial implications of Eve: Newsweek's best-ever selling cover depicted an African Adam and Eve as mixed-race African Americans with chemically processed hair, an image which the illustrator claimed had originally been 'much more pure' but was changed at the request of the cover art director who wanted an illustration that would be 'more appealing to a wider variety of people'.¹¹

Yet despite threatening to unsettle racialized assumptions and hierarchies, the African Eve hypothesis became, by the 1990s, the academically accepted, dominant theory of human origins. Several scientists raised serious questions (that were not racially inflected) about the study at the time; some queried the team's statistical analysis, while others objected to the way Cann and Wilson had interpreted the racial origins of the women whose DNA they had studied.[12] Nevertheless, the theory took hold and has, since its inception, been taught to anthropology and biological science students alike. A slew of popular science writing on human origins was published in the wake of the hypothesis including Michael H. Brown's *The Search for Eve* (1990); Brian M. Fagan's *The Journey from Eden: The Peopling of Our World* (1990); Roger Lewin's *The Origin of Modern Humans* (1993); Richard Dawkins's *River Out of Eden* (1994); Richard Leakey's *The Origin of Humankind* (1994); Chris Stringer and Robin McKie's *African Exodus: The Origins of Modern Humanity* (1996); Bryan Sykes's *The Seven Daughters of Eve* (2001); Spencer Wells's *The Journey of Man: A Genetic Odyssey* (2002); John H. Relethford's *Reflections of Our Past: How Human History Is Revealed in Our Genes* (2003); Stephen Oppenheimer's *Out of Eden* (2003) and Norman A. Johnson's *Darwinian Detectives: Revealing the Natural History of Genes and Genomes* (2007) to name only some. Television documentaries such as *Children of Eve* (1987), *The Real Eve* (2002) and *Journey of Man* (2003) also embedded the story of the Eve hypothesis in the popular imagination.

However recent developments have called into question the validity of the hypothesis in ways which suggest that African Eve may be losing favour in the second decade of the twenty-first century. In 2011 scientists studying the genome of a Neanderthal skeleton revealed that interbreeding did take place between archaic and modern humans, disproving the replacement theory at the heart of the Eve hypothesis.[13] Human evolution is now thought to be more complex than previously thought; there is evidence that European and Asian populations contain some Neanderthal DNA, whereas African populations share nothing with Neanderthals, pointing to interbreeding either when humans emerged from Africa or at a later date. In 2010 scientists discovered a third hominin previously unknown to science –Denisovans – whose DNA matched neither humans nor Neanderthals, but traces of whose genomes were found in Australian aboriginal populations and in the Philippines.[14] African Eve is not yet dead, as continued references to her and to related discoveries attest, however there is now enough doubt around the hypothesis for scientists and sociologists of science to revisit the circumstances and context in which the theory took hold.[15]

The question that is raised by recent challenges to the hypothesis is why, given its scientifically contested foundations, the African Eve hypothesis was able to gain such credibility that it became scientific orthodoxy. Why did the reservations and questions raised about the study at the time it was published come to be dismissed and ignored in favour of a definitive narrative of an African Eve? Alexandra Hofmänner suggests that it was specifically the invocation of Africa, as an imaginative geography of otherness which has been projected onto the frontiers of science, which meant that an African Eve would always be more successful than a Russian, French or Korean Eve.[16] Such geographies motivate 'the collection and transport of empirical artefacts, information and ideas from elsewhere to sites of analysis where they are measured, mapped, qualified and interpreted against a Western epistemological order and its standards, concepts and theories'.[17] The hypothesis, in this sense, provides an example of the 'discursive conventions' operating within and privileged by anthropological science which 'determine which social categories will succeed in attaining significance in the constitution of the reward system of science'.[18] Another theory is that it was the Eve nickname itself which was responsible for the significant attention which the findings received and their eventual acceptance by both scientists and the public. As Kathleen Fuller contends, if Eve 'had been named mtMable, the rush to embrace her probably would not have occurred'.[19] The Eve sobriquet reportedly came from the paper's authors themselves, being 'casually bandied about the laboratory or raised at Wilson's weekly progress meetings', although both Cann and Wilson would later distance themselves from the name.[20] Fuller argues that 'the name "mtEve" fed into the creation stories many scientists were raised with; even if they no longer believed the stories, the concepts still manifested at an unconscious level'.[21] While providing a familiar and comforting way of conceptualizing human origins, the Eve nickname led to confusion in both public understanding and scientific circles where, as Roger Lewin has shown, 'captivated by the powerful images of an African Eve, many people naturally assumed that the Berkeley researchers were talking about a literal Ur-mother – the first modern human, with her Adam', when in fact Eve was simply one of many individuals in a population from which modern humans evolved.[22] For Lewin, Wilson's description of Eve as 'one lucky mother' muddied the debate, leading writers to describe her in ways that the evidence did not imply.[23] Nevertheless, Eve remained a popular point of reference for scientists writing about human origins. Richard Dawkins, as the title of his 1995 popular science book *River Out of Eden* suggests, embraced the biblical analogy wholeheartedly, although he was keen to point out that 'there is more poetry in Mitochondrial Eve than in her mythological namesake'.[24]

Yet there was another familiar origin story upon which proponents of this new tale of human ancestry were able to draw; Alex Haley's novel *Roots*, which had been published eleven years earlier in 1976 to immediate acclaim. Part autobiography, part fiction (Haley described it as 'faction'), *Roots* tells the story of Haley's African ancestor, Kunta Kinte, who lives a peaceful life in the Gambia, until he is captured by slave traders and taken to America on a slave ship. The narrative follows the lives of Kunta's descendants, enslaved people who keep the story of their African ancestor alive, until it eventually reaches Haley in the 1970s present. The book ends with Haley's account of how he came to write it and his trips to West Africa where he meets a griot (an oral historian) who verifies his tale. Haley's novel was extraordinarily popular, selling over 1.5 million copies within its first eighteen months and winning the National Book Award in 1976 and the Pulitzer Prize in 1977. *Roots* was made into a TV series which, when it aired in January 1977, made broadcasting history by becoming the most watched television programme ever in the United States, 130 million viewers (3 in 5 Americans) seeing all or part of the series, newspapers reporting the cancellation of night school courses, a huge drop in restaurant business and the emptying of bars on the night of the final episode.[25]

This chapter explores how Haley's novel and the search for African ancestors that it inspired among black populations provided scientists and science popularizers with a pre-existing narrative of African origins upon which to draw in their own storytelling about the origins of humankind in Africa. Haley's 'black family bible'[26] helped scientists to tell the story of African Eve in a way which would be both comprehensible and appealing to the public, lending their account – and genetics more broadly – power and plausibility by reinforcing what Keith Wailoo calls 'already existing cultural and political forms of imagining self and the past'.[27] *Roots* offered a narrative model for thinking about the relationship between African ancestors and present-day humans, a model taken up by Eve's proponents who were concerned to emphasize the implications of the hypothesis for individual identities in the present. *Roots* was an appealing intertext because Haley's tale of the struggle and survival of African Americans, and the ancestry tracing that it inspired, helped lend credibility to African Eve as an anti-racist hypothesis, the promotion of which had been partly based on a desire to distance anthropology from the race theories which had historically arisen within the discipline.[28]

Yet *Roots* ultimately appealed, I suggest, because it had itself been written somewhat anthropologically; Haley had been influenced by his reading of earlier African anthropologists, the influence of which partly accounts for the conservativism that many critics felt characterized Haley's portrayal of Africans and their American descendants. While the novel tells a story for all African

Americans prevented through the legacies of slavery from knowing their ancestries, it did so in a traditional form that was palatable to white readers and later audiences who watched the television show. Haley's traditional and to a degree non-threatening tale of African ancestry thus provided a relatively safe formal example for science writing on human origins in Africa. *Roots* was appealing because this science writing was itself implicitly concerned with promoting the idea that we are all from Africa to a white readership. The influence of *Roots* ironically racialized a theory which was intended to be anti-racist, and ultimately led to the emergence of the racially inflected conception of ancestry which predominates today: the idea that we can know who we are through selected ancestors and that we can know them through genetic science. This chapter offers an account of the narrative origins of this idea and of the significance of a literary text in the emergence of one of the most controversial theories of human origins of the twentieth century.

Finding *Roots* in genes

Roots is referenced directly in several popular science books about, or with sections concerning, human evolution and African origins that were published in the wake of the Eve hypothesis. Chris Stringer, a palaeoanthropologist who embraced the geneticists' findings, concludes his 1996 book *African Exodus: The Origins of Modern Humans* (co-authored with journalist Robin McKie) by quoting what they describe as the 'emotional climax' of Haley's novel, where Haley meets his lost ancestors in Africa in a ceremony which Stringer compares to humanity's relationship with its African kin.[29] The anthropological geneticist John Relethford opens the first chapter of his 2003 book *Reflections of Our Past: How Human History Is Revealed in Our Genes* by relating how as a graduate student he became captivated by *Roots*, both novel and TV series, which inspired his own interest in genealogy.[30] Geneticist Norman A. Johnson begins the section on mitochondrial DNA and African Eve in his book *Darwinian Detectives: Revealing the Natural History of Genes and Genomes* (2007) with a description of how 'Alex Haley traced back his ancestors to Africa'.[31] Steve Jones, however, viewed *Roots* in less inspirational terms, writing in his 1993 book *The Language of the Genes* that 'Alex Haley, by comparing his genes with those from Africa, would have learned much more about his forefathers than he could hope to uncover from the records'.[32] For Jones the 'ancestral voices' which 'are particularly fluent in telling the story of the past' are mitochondria, which are 'an accurate record of history'.³³ Jones typifies the attitude that many science writers have taken towards the historical record when writing about genes and ancestry – that is, as Deborah Lynn Steinberg puts it, to read genes as documentary evidence in a way that 'narrates social history as (a functional effect of) evolutionary biology'.³⁴ Discussing Jones's reference to Haley's novel, Steinberg contends:

> Jones's invocation of *Roots* as illustrative of the limits of social history and potentiality of genetics takes the textual metaphor to a number of disturbing conclusions. First is that genes enscribe a precise taxonomy of racial/ethnic origins... Second is the positivist notion that genetic profiling not only (accurately) traces racial, ethnic and national migrations but that these tracings are meaningful, indeed more meaningful, when they are stripped of political and economic context.³⁵

A similar dismissal of social and historical contexts is evident in Relethford's book in which (ironically, given that *Roots* provides him with a means to frame the opening questions of his book) he writes that 'our written and oral histories are incomplete and lack much time depth' and that genes are a much more authentic way of understanding the past.³⁶

While *Roots* may at first appear as simply a passing point of reference – whether emotionally embraced or dismissed – in such reflections on human origins, its influence goes deeper and can be discerned in the narrative organization and tone of this writing. This is perhaps most evident in the fusion of individual origins with wider human ancestries, and the narrative emphasis on the present as being the key to the past, which both *Roots* and science writing on human origins share. Haley's novel garnered such power and popularity, among African Americans and beyond, because he consciously conflated his own, individual search for ancestral roots with a wider tale of a collective ancestral past in Africa. The novel begins with an acknowledgements section in which Haley explains how the book arose from his 'intense wish to explore if my maternal family's treasured oral history might possibly be documented back into Africa where all black Americans began' before he goes on to write:

> Finally, I acknowledge immense debt to the griots of Africa (griots are storytellers) – where today it is rightly said that when a griot dies, it is as if a library has burned to the ground. The griots symbolize how all human ancestry goes back to some place, and some time, where there was no writing. Then, the memories and the mouths of ancient elders was the only way that early histories of mankind got passed along... for all of us today to know who we are.³⁷

From the outset, Haley presents his semi-autobiographical work as at once personal family saga, black history and human history, producing a work in the tradition of Afro-American autobiography which could be read, as Helen Taylor argues, not 'as personal statement or exploration, but as communal expression of the collective experience and unconscious'.[38] Haley knowingly wrote, as he explains at the end of the novel, a 'symbolic saga of all African-descent people',[39] and in so doing tapped into a desire among African Americans to re-connect with Africa as a source of both ancestry and pride, a desire that had been growing since Malcolm X had articulated the need for a history of the African origins of slaves told by their ancestors in his *Autobiography*, which Haley had co-authored. What made the wider, collective identification with Haley's story so easily possible, however, was the temporal structuring of his narrative. Through including in his acknowledgements section a partial statement of intent (as quoted above), Haley places himself, and the 1970s present, as the starting point for a narrative which otherwise begins, a page later, in 1750. The effect of this is that it is Haley himself (and by extension 'all of us') who becomes the hero of his epic tale, as it is Haley who begins and ends an otherwise linear narrative of which Kunta Kinte is undoubtedly the star. As Jerome de Groot argues, by the end of the novel, 'the author/researcher is the purpose of the research and the novel, the focal point of everything that has gone before'.[40] Distinctions between past and present are blurred in this narrative frame, where Haley, 'forever latent in the lives of his ancestors, emerges as heir to this past, the ready recipient of an uninterrupted lineage of strength and resistance'.[41] History functions as an extension of identity, a way of understanding both collectively and individually who we are in a present.

Relethford's reference to *Roots* at the beginning of *Reflections of Our Past* is immediately followed by an explicit link between his individual desire to know his family's ancestry and a much wider, scientific quest for knowledge of humanity's origins, the purpose of which is to draw the reader into his narrative as a potential protagonist of the epic tale he is about to narrate:

> Occasionally, a show would be aired that drew my primary attention away from my work and to the tube... One show that particularly captured my interest and attention, to the detriment of my studies for a week, was the mini-series *Roots*... I was captivated by both the miniseries and the book. In addition to the sheer drama, I found something very appealing about the idea of finding one's 'roots' and extending family history into the past. A number of years later, I acted upon this interest and contacted relatives on both my mother's side and my father's side of the family... Many of you may have similar interests in family

genealogy. It is natural to be curious about where you come from… My specific interest in family history grew into a broader interest in history and ancestry in general… much of my eventual professional research would ultimately revolve around 'roots' and human history.[42]

Relethford invites his readers to begin connecting the curiosity they might have about their own family history to the history of humankind, which become one and the same as he relates the focus of his book as being

on the evolutionary history of a population, or a group of populations… the scope of this book ranges from events that happened millions of years ago to events that occurred within the past few centuries. In a broad sense, this book deals with questions common to all humans – who are we, and where do we come from? In other words, what are our 'roots'?[43]

Relethford's direct, inclusive addresses to readers – 'we' and 'our' – signal his intention to tell a story which, much like Haley's, is in some sense a quest for self-knowledge, where 'we', 'our genes' can 'reconstruct the past' in a narrative which is otherwise structured 'in terms of a chronological journey'.[44] The effect, as Marianne Sommer identifies in her analysis of Relethford's book, is that 'the reader is led from thinking about his or her grandparents and great grandparents to the evolutionary history of populations, their migrations, and structural developments. The knowledge generated through population genetics is presented as a seamless extension of personal memories and family stories into humanity's deep past'.[45] Such a leap between past and present, family and humanity, is made possible because the genetic techniques which the team who 'discovered' African Eve introduced foregrounded the importance of individuals living in the present. Unlike traditional palaeoanthropological accounts of human evolution which relied on fossil evidence – human skeletons which are thousands of years old – to tell the story of human origins, the DNA analysis which led to the discovery of Eve involved deciphering the past from the present – from the placentas of living women.[46] These techniques stressed the primacy of present-day individuals in understanding human history in ways upon which science writers could draw in making the story of human origins in Africa relevant and exciting for contemporary readers; as Stephen Oppenheimer puts it in *Out of Eden*, 'we are participants in this genetic story, since 99 per cent of the work of reconstruction of our ancient gene trees was carried out using modern DNA given voluntarily by people living in different parts of the world today. This is a story of relevance to each and every one of us'.[47]

Haley's novel provided a literary model for how Eve's tale could be expressed in narrative terms. Haley not only positioned author and reader as the starting point of an epic history, but his prioritization of a single line of descent has echoes in the shape and even methodology of the hypothesis itself. As Norman Johnson explains:

> How did Wilson's group track back to the most recent common ancestor of our mitochondrial DNA, this Eve? They started with the idea that an Eve, a most recent common ancestor, existed, and then they worked backwards, both logically and chronologically. In this way, the method of Cann, Stoneking, and Wilson was not all that different from what traditional genealogical researchers do. Although the story of *Roots* was told chronologically from Africa circa 1767 to 1970s America, Haley's detective work was largely backwards. He started with the family he knew, and traced his way back generation by generation.[48]

Haley's research into his family history had originally been much wider: he had travelled to Ireland in search of his white ancestors, an experience he wrote up, but as his biographer Robert Norrell asserts, 'Over time, as his story became an exclusively African and black narrative, he deleted the passage about Ireland'.[49] The story that emerged is one which instead tapped into the desire of African Americans to know their African ancestry specifically, Haley creating a tale where Kunta's 'manhood and his Africanness united the family even in his absence' creating a 'harmonious reunion between an African past and an American present',[50] an emphasis designed to create a singular line of 'pure' African descent of which he and all African Americans could be proud. Yet, if conducting a comprehensive genealogy, Haley might have explored his ancestry along all lines, including his white European forebears that the novel itself makes explicit are part of his family; Kunta's daughter Kizzy is raped by her enslaver and much of the narrative focuses on the outcome of that rape, her son Chicken George.[51] This is an aspect of black American ancestry which Octavia Butler addresses in her 1979 novel *Kindred*, in which the novel's heroine travels back in time to save her white slave-owning ancestor and, by extension, herself. However, Haley's novel propounded a racialized politics of identity which consciously and symbolically prioritized a single (African) biological lineage as the root of identity and belonging, when any number of his ancestral lineages could have been explored with differing results.

The African Eve hypothesis similarly involved stressing the singularly African lineage of the African Americans from whom samples were taken, despite a forthcoming study which suggested there was up to 39 percent 'white' input into the black American mitochondrial gene pool.[52] Cann had used mitochondrial DNA mainly from African American women to stand for African populations (only two of the twenty 'African' samples were from women from Africa) which raised questions about how, given the history of slavery in the United States and mixing between black and white populations, these samples from African Americans could be considered indicative of a 'black' or African gene pool. Cann's defence was that sex had historically taken place between white men and black women, leaving the mitochondrial gene pool largely unaffected.[53] Yet Cann's controversial use of African American women's MtDNA to stand for African MtDNA did not lead to a discussion of the (genetic) legacies of American slavery (something that would later occur with the revelation, through Y chromosome analysis, that Thomas Jefferson had had children with his enslaved mistress Sally Hemings) or of the difficulties inherent in inferring racial or geographic origins from genes. Instead, the need to emphasize humanity's direct African lineage foreclosed this possibility, even though the Eve study relied on the contemporary prioritization of a singular characteristic (MtDNA) in order to construct a meaningful line of ancestry. As Daniel Dennett recognizes in his discussion of Mitochondrial Eve:

> Speciation can now be seen to be a phenomenon in nature that has a curious property: you can't tell that it is occurring at the time it occurs! You can only tell much later that it has occurred, retrospectively crowning an event when you discover that its sequels have a certain property…Mitochondrial Eve can only be retrospectively crowned.[54]

Such privileging of a singular ancestral line as representative of a definitive point of origin meant that advocates of Eve were able to emphasize the unity and similarity of human beings in the face of arguments from their multi-regionalist opponents. Indeed, what some scientists also appear to have borrowed from Haley was a way of narrating the story of human origins as a battle against all odds to tell that story in the face of adversity and racism. The triumph and achievement of the end of *Roots*, which is not only that Haley has been reunited with his Gambian kin but that he has been able to tell his story which 'can help to alleviate the legacies of the fact that preponderantly the histories have been written by the winners',[55] are replicated by Chris Stringer and Robin McKie when they quote Haley in the final paragraph of *African Exodus*. From the outset they frame their story as a fight to tell the truth of human origins in the face of 'a sustained programme of vilification by scientists who have spent their lives committed to the opposing view'.[56] Their book ends on a similar note where in the penultimate paragraph they describe how

> the scientific impact of the Out of Africa theory has already been enormous. Ten years ago, despite the best efforts of researchers like Chris Stringer, Gunter Brauer, and Desmond Clark, it would not have been possible to organise a scientific congress to discuss our recent African Exodus – there were too few supporters and too many influential opponents. But those days have gone. Its proponents now dominate the field... Our African Exodus, once a heresy, is today's orthodoxy... Two years after Chris last held the skull of that ancient forebear on the eve of its return to Ethiopia, Alex Haley – the black American author – told the story of the hunt for his own African 'Roots' (as his book was called). In his narrative's emotional climax, he tells how, reunited with his lost Gambian kin, the village women pass him their babies in an ancient 'laying on of hands' ceremony. Symbolically Haley was being told: 'Through this flesh, which is us, we are you and you are us.'[57]

Positioning themselves as heroically re-writing the history of science in the face of opposition to the Eve hypothesis, Stringer and McKie's triumph mirrors that of humans' African ancestors themselves. The interactive website that accompanies Oppenheimer's *Out of Eden* takes a similar tone: 'We are the descendants of a few small groups of tropical Africans who united in the face of adversity, not only to the point of survival but to the development of a sophisticated social interaction and culture expressed through many forms.'[58] Just as Haley fights to tell his true family story and his ancestor Kunta Kinte survives the physical and mental torture of slavery in order for him to do so, so African Eve's brave survival becomes embodied in us, and as a story to be told by a group of courageous scientists in the present wanting to uncover the truth about our human origins in Africa.

Clearly not all of this science writing concerning Eve makes direct reference to *Roots*, but the situation of contemporary African Americans and Black Britons seeking to trace their ancestries back to Africa – a phenomenon that can be traced back to the popularity of *Roots*[59] – also appears repeatedly in this writing and functions, as more overt narrative echoes of *Roots* do, as a means of reiterating the anti-racist credentials of this new approach to African origins. Stringer and McKie were keenly aware of the racial implications of the hypothesis: 'Already the story of our African Exodus has entered the maelstrom of American racial issues'[60] they write, citing the theory as a defence against attempts to link race and intelligence such as the infamous Bell Curve study. They ask readers to 'just consider the political implications' and note that 'our theory has made a great impact in black communities, particularly in the US. Pressure from organisations such as the Tu-Wa-Moja African study group recently led the Natural History Museum in Washington to close parts of its exhibition on human evolution because it did not reflect Out of Africa thinking'.[61] Such statements position genetic and anthropological science as righting the wrongs of the past, as helping in the fight against racism, much as Haley sought to do with *Roots*. Yet more than this, genetics is positioned as having a central role in enabling black people to tell stories of the kind that Haley set out. Bryan Sykes ends *The Seven Daughters of Eve*, a book about 'how the history of our species, *Homo sapiens*, is recorded in the genes that trace our ancestry back into the deep past',[62] with an account of working with a woman from Bristol with Jamaican parents who wanted to know more about her ancestry. His description of her reaction to his findings is one in which science enables the revelation of a history previously ignored, as the woman is transported through the generations back to Africa; 'the effect on her was overwhelming. She was literally lost for words ... It was as if the DNA was itself a written document from her ancestors, which in a sense it was; a document that had been handed down, one generation at a time, from the woman who had endured and survived that terrible voyage from Africa'.[63] Mitochondrial Eve once again collides with the example of an enslaved African ancestor who in turn connects to individuals in the present, in a moment in which the science of human origins liberates black people. However while the anti-racist sentiment behind connecting humanity's origins in Africa with the struggles of the living descendants of slaves is clear, this entanglement ultimately proves highly problematic for thinking about Eve. For rather than prompting a discussion about the legacies of slavery and racism, and their relationship to genetic science (a discussion which could have begun, for example, with the contested 'African' MtDNA samples), what African ancestry tracing and its precursor *Roots* helped to support in scientific narratives on human origins is a largely conservative mode of conceiving of race, kinship, ancestry and 'Africanness' which was familiar and acceptable to a white readership who needed to accept Eve as their ancestor and the methodology of genetics more broadly.

Anthropological *Roots*

Above all, *Roots* served as such a useful intertext in narratives on human origins in Africa because Haley represented race and ancestry in a traditional manner, drawing heavily upon anthropological and historical sources to produce a narrative which was itself, to a degree, anthropological in style and tone. According to Norrell, as part of Haley's research for *Roots*, he and his researcher George Sims studied anthropological works on West Africa to the degree that 'the first draft was a compendium of anthropological information on African life'.[64] Following the publication of an article entitled 'The African' in the *New York Times Magazine* in 1972, Haley received a letter from retired anthropologist Ina Corrine Brown praising his work and suggesting sources at which he might look.[65] Haley's novel became a 'patchwork' of 'pieces of anthropological scholarship incorporated whole, potted textbook histories, appropriated pieces of other writers' novels, folk memory, research, errors and epiphanies',[66] a patchwork that would eventually lead to two plagiarism lawsuits, the second of which Haley settled out of court with the anthropologist and novelist Harold Courlander. Haley conceded that several elements of Courlander's earlier novel *The African*, published in 1967, had made it into *Roots*, although Norrell has shown that the settlement was not intended by Haley to be an admission of guilt and that the judge in the case held racist views and doubted whether a black man like Haley could have written *Roots*, making a successful defence unlikely.[67]

Whether or not *Roots* did plagiarize *The African*, its indebtedness to anthropological writing was highlighted in a critical article written by Courlander, in which he argues that, setting aside the plagiarism issues, Haley 'derogated the ideal he sought to celebrate' in his characterization of Kunta Kinte and Africans in simplistic and, it is implied, potentially racist terms.[68] Courlander writes that 'the Mandinka, like the Bamana, Soninke and other peoples of the region, were far more sophisticated about Europeans and products of Europe than Haley suggests'[69] so that, for example, Kunta's inability to recognize horses in America doesn't ring true when 'horses had been a part of the scene in Sudanic Africa for centuries'.[70] Yet simultaneously, Courlander contends, Kunta takes on the ethnological perspective that is implied by such characterization: Haley has 'placed in Kunta's mind the observations and knowledge of generations of scholars' as Kunta observes in detail 'what Bell, the cook in the Big House, like an academic Africanist calls "Africanisms"'[71] of the American-born enslaved people he lives alongside. Courlander provides the following example from the novel as evidence:

> These heathen blacks wouldn't understand drumtalk any better than the toubob. Kunta was forced to concede, though – if only with great reluctance – that these pagan blacks might not be totally irredeemable. Ignorant as they were, some of the things they did were purely African, and he could tell that they were totally unaware of it themselves. For one thing, he had heard all his life the

very same sounds of exclamation, accompanied by the very same hand gestures and facial expressions. And the way these blacks moved their bodies was also identical. No less so was the way these blacks laughed when they were among themselves –with their whole bodies, just like the people of Juffure.[72]

For Courlander, Kunta's ethnologically detached, snobby, attitude towards his fellow slaves discredits the novel in literary terms, but we might also view Kunta's almost scientific gaze not as the result of extensive borrowing from anthropological sources, but as part of a strategy (if crude and limited in its success) on Haley's part to write a hero who is the intellectual equal of the whites who enslave him. Kunta's observations of white people in particular seem to deliberately reverse colonial anthropological discourses on Africans as Haley turns the language of the (racist) white observer onto the whites themselves. For Kunta, the white slave raiders 'had a peculiar stink', the white deck hands on ship had 'faces pitted with the holes of disease, their peculiar long hair in colours of yellow or black or red, some of them even with hair around their mouths and under their chins' and 'a kind of paleness without features that he knew would never leave his mind'.[73] The first white woman he sees in America astounds him because 'after seeing the hungry way the toubob on the great canoe had lusted after black women, he was amazed to see the toubob had women of their own; but looking at this specimen, he could understand why they preferred Africans'.[74] When he later encounters more poor white indentured labourers, Kunta is astounded because 'even the wild animals of his homeland, it seemed to Kunta, had more dignity than these creatures'.[75] Kunta's dehumanizing observations of the white people he encounters are at one level a response to the inhuman ways in which they are behaving; but his observations are also an attempt to reverse the pseudoscientific, anthropological narratives through which Africans had so frequently been viewed. By making the whites the 'specimens' to be viewed in this way, Haley goes some way to undermining the dominance and truth status of these discourses.

Indeed, Haley's exposure to scientific, and pseudoscientific, ideas about Africa extended beyond anthropological scholarship. Haley had begun work on what was to become *Roots* at the same time as he was writing the *Autobiography of Malcolm X* – an account of Malcolm X's life and political beliefs published in 1964 which was Haley's first real commercial and critical success.[76] Whilst Haley is often portrayed as having been keen to distance himself from what were considered to be Malcolm X's radical and controversial views, it seems clear that much of what Malcolm X articulated about African Americans' ignorance of their history and ancestry inspired Haley to uncover this history in *Roots*. In one episode Malcolm X describes his conversion to the Nation of Islam while in prison, which was prompted by his brother Reginald, who tells him 'you don't even know who you are... You don't even know, the white devil has hidden it from you, that you are a race of people of ancient civilisations, and riches in gold and kings. You don't even know your true family name',[77] a sentiment echoed in Kunta's observation of his fellow American-born slaves in *Roots*; 'how ignorant of themselves they were; they know nothing of their ancestors, as he had been taught from boyhood'.[78] For Malcolm X, the solution lay in the core teachings of Elijah Muhammad, founder of the Nation of Islam, which he describes thus:

> 'The true knowledge,' reconstructed much more briefly that I received it, was that history had been 'whitened' in the white man's history books, and that the black man had been 'brainwashed for hundreds of years'. Original Man was black, in the continent called Africa where the human race had emerged on the planet Earth... The devil white man cut these black people off from all knowledge of their own kind.[79]

Muhammad preached that blacks were the first race on earth and that the white race was genetically engineered by a disaffected black scientist called Yacub, who, having been exiled, 'decided, as revenge, to create upon the earth a devil race – a bleached-out, white race of people'.[80] This origin story led Malcolm X to read *Findings in Genetics* by Gregor Mendel, from which he concluded that 'the white gene is recessive', and to develop an interest in the work of archaeologists and anthropologists in Africa: he cites British anthropologist Louis Leakey's fossil and bone findings as triumphant proof of humanity's origins in Africa, likely one of the 'white men's books' he was forced to use in educating his fellow inmates about the African origins of slaves, who 'wouldn't believe it unless they could see that a white man had said it'.[81]

The tension Malcolm X felt in employing the findings and writing of white scientists to locate human roots in Africa is also felt by Haley, who not only aimed to provide black Americans with knowledge of their African origins (and was clearly influenced by X in this regard[82]) but saw his writing process as a counterpoint to white writing. Explaining how he came to write *Roots*, Haley stated:

> Most of what I'd read so far had been written by outsiders, predominantly white missionaries and anthropologists, and even among the most knowledgeable and well intentioned of them, the tone was somewhat paternal and condescending. Their insights and observations were inevitably limited by the cultural chasm separating them from their subjects.[83]

Haley didn't subscribe to the idea that white people had been created by a scientist called Yacub, but he clearly wrote with the knowledge that humanity originated in Africa. While he had reservations about 'white missionaries and anthropologists', in writing *Roots* Haley describes how he 'began to devour books about Africa, especially about the slave trade',[84] many of which were undoubtedly written by them.

The result is that the while Haley attempted to undermine the (pseudo) scientific anthropological and historical discourses that he recognized as problematic in their representation of Africa and Africans, this was embedded, in *Roots*, within a narrative which reproduced, without irony, the traditional modes of narration to be found in those texts. As Philip Curtin has shown, historians of Africa in the mid-twentieth century who were concerned to overturn the racist idea that 'Africa had no history' initially approached this task by taking 'the argument on the opponent's "terms"', that is, by reproducing an elitist style of history which drew on the same roots as Eurocentric history.[85] Selecting some segments of African history and ignoring others, such historiography produced, Arnold Temu and Bonaventure Surai contend, a teleological, glorified account of the African past.[86] This approach is evident in *Roots*, where there is a tension between Haley's desire to redress the absence of black history, to counter the fact that 'histories have been written by the winners' and his own approach to (re) writing that history. Narrative time moves linearly from Kunta's birth through to Haley's triumph, portraying all the while the greatness and exceptionality of the Kinte clan. That theirs is a history worth telling because the family command a high level of respect in Juffure and beyond is an unsettling reproduction of the kind of history that Haley, at the end of the novel, claims to be writing to overcome. Yet Haley's treatment of gender and class reveals his own narratorial alignment with these winning histories. Haley consciously highlights Kunta's sexism and the patriarchal values of Juffure throughout the novel: Kunta 'intended to put Binta in her place as a woman' and 'he would deal firmly with her if she ever made it necessary. After all, she was a woman'. The women are painfully stereotyped as coming to village meetings only 'if a case held the promise of some juicy gossip'. Later when married to Bell, Kunta would 'listen with one ear while he thought about something else'.[87] While a charitable reading might situate these moments as part of Haley's characterization of Kunta, this patriarchal dominance is reinforced by the narrative itself which is focalized almost exclusively through Haley's male ancestors. Approximately half the book is given to Kunta's life and Haley uses free indirect narration to ensure that other points of view are rarely experienced. When Kunta's daughter Kizzy is sold away and the story moves with her, there are only a couple of chapters dedicated to her experience before the narrative moves on to the perspective of her son, Chicken George, for the greater part of the second half of the book. Ironically, given that it is Haley's grandmother and great aunt through whom he hears about his ancestral history, women are problematically side-lined in Haley's tale in a way that undermines the mission of his book.

Something similar can be said for Haley's treatment of class. Class stereotypes abound: where Kunta's first enslaver is a rich doctor who treats the people he has enslaved comparatively well, Kizzy's master is poor and (concomitantly) rapes her and treats his slaves badly. On seeing some white indentured labourers, 'it was easy for Kunta to understand why plantation-owning massas and even their slaves scorned and sneered at them as "lazy, shiftless, no-count white trash" ... in fact, as far as he was concerned, that was a charitable description'.[88] Kunta's view is in direct alignment with the plantation owner, a kind of elite conservatism that is carried over in his attitude towards rebellion and organized resistance,

> as much as he hated slavery, it seemed to Kunta that no good could come of the white folks giving guns to blacks. First of all, the whites would always have more guns than the blacks. And he thought about how in his own homeland, guns and bullets had been given by the toubob to evil chiefs and kings, until blacks were fighting blacks.[89]

Despite all his suffering and bravery, Kunta's political stance is unthreatening and pragmatic; he 'didn't believe that a rebellion could ever succeed' yet criticizes his fellow slaves, 'their own worst enemy was themselves... never did more than a handful so much as protest, let alone resist'.[90] The kind of resistance that Kunta (and by extension Haley) advocates is cultural: it is the maintenance of Africanness, of African culture, language and identity, which is upheld as more powerful and effective than militant resistance or organized group action – the kind of action being taken by the Black Panthers when Haley was writing the novel in the late 1960s and early 1970s.[91]

Haley's relentless focus on the life of one heroic and exceptional individual and the life of his descendants certainly fulfils the role of the griot as Kunta understands it – to tell of 'great deeds of the ancient kings, holy men, hunters and warriors who came hundreds of rains before us'.[92] Yet it is a telling of history in which many remain losers despite its being told from the perspective of an enslaved person, a history which depicts African Americans through the frame of a family saga which led critics to dub the novel a black *Gone With the Wind*.[93] Indeed the novel faced criticism, according to Helen Taylor, from black critics who located it within the tradition of plantation novels from *Uncle Tom's Cabin* onwards, texts known for their 'patronising, racist or exploitative presentation of black history and experience'.[94] Haley's apparent blindness to how his blending of historical fact and fiction might in fact challenge traditional forms of historical narrative also resulted in criticism of the novel both for its lack of historical accuracy and for its unacknowledged borrowing from other sources.[95] Several contemporaneous responses sought to challenge the historical accuracy of the narrative Haley set out, yet rather than argue that 'he was part of an intertextually rich black tradition'; Haley was, according to Taylor, 'reluctant to see himself as part of a black continuum'.[96] The result is that Haley has largely remained, since *Roots*, an understudied if not ignored author in literary terms. While the novel was an undoubted commercial success, its credibility was undermined to the degree that it is often absent in contemporary studies and anthologies of African American slave narratives.[97]

Yet it was the conservatism with which Haley approached slavery and the African roots of African Americans which undoubtedly accounted for the novel's popularity among white readers, including, ultimately, the science writers who refer to it in their accounts of humanity's origins in Africa. Haley's tale of suffering and triumph stressed the plight of Kunta and his family, but did so in a non-threatening way, through a form with which white readers were familiar. This familiarity was amplified when it came to the television adaptation of *Roots*. White critics praised the novel not only because it was being read by whites but also 90 per cent of the audience for the television miniseries was white.[98] The relative appeal to America's white population was something that was taken into account during the production of the miniseries. Norrell has shown that 'the producer's first concern in casting *Roots* for television was how whites would receive the show. Wolper said he was "trying to appeal to whites"'.[99] This was achieved as 'The ABC executive Brandon Stoddard said the network used actors whom white viewers had seen a hundred times before, "so they would feel comfortable"'.[100] The television script went further than the book by introducing more white characters and making 'some white characters "good", whereas in the book there are almost no admirable white figures'.[101] The anti-racist message of the novel, designed to foreground the history of African Americans which had hitherto been largely ignored, was thus, when adapted for television, overtaken by the need to make palatable the role that white people had had in the slave trade, for the benefit of the contemporary white American population who might, it is assumed, feel uncomfortable in beginning to make their own connections as to whom their ancestors might have been.

Thus, despite the progressive and anti-racist intentions of the authors of popular science writing on human origins in Africa, their direct and indirect invocations of *Roots* served to reinforce the often traditional and conservative ways in which they represented Africa and Africans. To take one example: just as Kunta Kinte and the village of Juffure are represented by Haley as more 'primitive' than they would have been at that time, so narrative and visual representations of the Eve hypothesis often rely on stereotypical portraits of contemporary Africans in 'primitive' terms, as a way of evoking Africans living in the era of Eve. The covers of both editions of Stephen Oppenheimer's *Out of Eden* (or as it is titled in the United States, *The Real Eve*) typify this conflation. Each portrays the head of a young black woman next to a group of Africans in traditional dress, walking across a barren-looking landscape. Similar images crop up in the television documentary *The Real Eve* (based on Oppenheimer's book) where images of Africans hunting with spears are interlaid with multiple close-up shots of silent African faces that create an anthropological, Western gaze.[102] While it might be argued that these images are designed to be evocative of an ancient time, rather than indicative of contemporary African lives, a consistent emphasis on imagining contemporary Africans as rural, simple and almost timeless (and thus living much like Mitochondrial Eve would have done) is also scattered casually throughout this writing. Spencer Wells, in *The Journey of Man: A Genetic Odyssey*, explains in his endorsement of Eve that 'you are more likely to sample extremely divergent genetic lineages within a single African village than you are in the whole rest of the world', before going on to explain why the racist notion that Africans are less evolved than other populations is wrong:

> One of the interesting corollaries of inferring a single common ancestor is that each descendant lineage continues to change at the same rate, and therefore all of the lineages are the same age. The time that has elapsed between my mitochondrial DNA type and Eve's is exactly the same as that of an African cattle herder.[103]

While declaiming the racial theories of earlier anthropologists such as Carleton Coon, Wells's contemporary Africans do not live in cities and are not modern, but herd cattle, as Mitochondrial Eve might have done 200,000 years ago. As Priscilla Wald has shown in her analysis of Wells's film which accompanied the book, 'a familiar developmental hierarchy pervades the language and images', where the San Bushmen are constructed as 'relics from whom the rest of humanity has evolved' and are frozen 'in genomic time'.[104]

Figure 1 Front cover of *Out of Eden: The Peopling of the World* by Stephen Oppenheimer. London: Constable and Robinson, 2003. Reproduced with the permission of Little, Brown Book Group.

A similar image of timeless Africans emerges in Michael Brown's comprehensive account of the development of the African Eve hypothesis, *The Search for Eve*. Brown discusses at length the implications for race that surrounded the hypothesis and the problems which the metaphors used to promote it caused, yet he ends his book with a description of a trip to Africa in which modern-day Africans are represented as one and the same as their ancient ancestors:

> There were groups of twenty or so natives in the tiny settlements, just like in olden times, and warriors in red capes approached with spears trying to sell us ostrich eggs.
> I thought: Eve must have used ostrich eggs for something.
> And the Masai women, in sackcloth and doing a lot of heavy lifting, carrying huge loads of firewood at the same time they tended straggling offspring: how tired Eve must have been, how absolutely pooped, that star-laden night so long ago![105]

While Brown's book received terrible reviews for its 'clumsy phrases',[106] for being 'relentlessly tabloid in its language'[107] and for its 'many clichés and unappetizing images',[108] here, he does what nearly all the writers discussed so far do; directly compares Mitochondrial Eve to Africans and/or African Americans living in the past couple of hundred years. In fact, this is what is implicit in references to *Roots* in this science writing. Not only does Haley's representation of Africans somehow legitimize simplistic representations of Africans in these narratives, but the very comparison made between Haley's novel and the search for humanity's roots in Africa encourages the collapsing of distinctions between Africans of 200,000 years ago, a couple of hundred years ago and the present.

The problematic effect of this convergence is that it ironically recalls the idea which typified earlier anthropological and scientific writing about Africa: that Africans are not as 'evolved' as Europeans or whites, because they are in fact a different species. Polygenism – a precursor to the multi-regional hypothesis – was propounded by American anthropologist Josiah Clark Nott in his 1855 publication *Types of Mankind*, in which he describes Africans of the Cape Colony as 'the lowest and most beastly specimens of mankind... but little removed, both in moral and physical characters, from the orang-outan'.[109] Ranking some African groups above others, Nott proclaimed them all to be 'without a history' and stated that 'Negroes in Africa must remain substantially in the same benighted state wherein Nature has placed them, and in which they have stood, according to Egyptian monuments, for at least 5000 years'.[110] Africans' supposed primitiveness was evidence of their failure to evolve forward in time and while Nott's views were controversial in the mid-nineteenth century, representations of Africans as primitive and timeless have continued. That science writers on human origins in Africa find it almost impossible not to compare recent black history with the evolutionary history of humans thus undermines the more overt anti-racist intentions of their writing. Their anti-racist intentions are sincere, as Wald notes, but racism is 'intricately interwoven in the language, images and stories – the representational conventions – that have developed with centuries of oppression… the narratives that inform the science and its applications can perpetuate the very inequities they seek to address'.[111]

The griot called MtDNA

The African Eve hypothesis represented one of the first instances when new genetic techniques of analysis were used to make a definitive pronouncement on race. The idea that all humans are descended from Africa refuted older bioscientific emphases on racial types and biological racial difference in favour of an explicitly anti-racist stance designed to foreground human similarity and relatedness. Although the hypothesis called into question the foundations upon which much scientific racial thinking had been based, it still asserted genetic science to be a practice which could make such declarations on race; put differently by Wald, 'implicit in the very conviction that genetics can refute the logic of racism is an assumption about the authority of genetics… to establish definitive terms of relatedness'.[112] African Eve re-established genetic science as an authority on race which, whether it was argued to be biologically real or not, was a concept whose meaning and parameters could be ultimately determined by science.

Yet African Eve was a scientific fact which, as this chapter has argued, was shaped by fiction in such a way that the popularization of what was supposed to be an anti-racist hypothesis became racialized. The hypothesis was of significance for all humanity, regardless of race, because as Stringer and McKie put it, 'our variable forms mask an essential truth – that under our skins, we are all Africans',[113] a sentiment reiterated by Rebecca Cann, who, interviewed in 2012, claimed that 'I tell my students they should all celebrate black history month, since they are all Africans genetically'.[114] However references to *Roots*, and to the experiences of black people attempting to trace their ancestries back to Africa more broadly, meant that the implications of the hypothesis were invariably seen to have most significance for black people. The conflation of Eve's tale with the search for African ancestors by the descendants of enslaved people racialized the findings so that the white population could view African ancestors from a distance through the familiar narrative frames of Haley's tale (and thus through older anthropological conventions), while the emotional import of the findings was reserved for black populations still grappling with the recent history of transatlantic enslavement.

What *Roots* helped to establish in those black populations and in genetic science is a way of thinking about relatedness, race and identity as a question of biology, genealogical thinking which created a 'stable epistemology for rootedness' based on blood ties, reproducing and embedding a heteronormative understanding of identity and kinship.[115] This way of thinking had not always been the norm: for example, in *Dusk of Dawn: An Essay toward an Autobiography of a Race Concept* (1940), W.E.B. Du Bois contemplated what might constitute a tie to Africa and, while acknowledging it as the place where a large portion of his ancestors lived, wrote:

> The physical bond is least and the badge of color relatively unimportant save as a badge; the real essence of this kinship is its social heritage of slavery; the discrimination and insult; and this heritage binds together not simply the children of Africa, but extends through yellow Asia and into the South Seas. It is this unity that draws me to Africa.[116]

This is a political and social sense of belonging and cross-racial kinship which is absent from *Roots*, where instead Haley reinforced the 'rules that govern relatedness'[117] in his singular vision of familial relationships and a racially black line of descent recognized at the time by one reviewer as 'playing its part in the reaffirmation of ethnicity'.[118] For, as Louis Kushnuck contends, 'if the present is unsatisfactory and, indeed, dangerous to the political/economic ruling class because of the possibility of growing class consciousness, a renewed and largely artificial ethnic identity is just what the capitalist ordered'.[119] The impact of the political conservatism of *Roots*, published at a time of black radicalism and anti-racist activism, was that knowing 'who you are' became individualized, something to be discovered through ancestry and biology rather than collective affiliations in the present. This idea was by no means widespread in biological science of the time either: writing about Haley's *Roots* in an exchange of letters in the journal Bioscience in 1978, biologist Gairdner Moment countered that 'whether you are black, white, or any other color, you do not need to know anything whatsoever about your biological ancestors to "know who you are"'.[120]

Yet this is the very idea which would become central to the technology which the application of genetic techniques to human evolutionary history made possible – genetic ancestry tracing.

The following chapter explores the development of genetic ancestry testing in the 1990s, the appeal of which, as Alondra Nelson contends, cannot be understood without considering the social transformation in the public's interpretation of the past occasioned by *Roots*.[121] Marketed primarily at African American populations, genetic ancestry tracing has gained enormous support from those who, like Haley, wish to recover family histories erased and disrupted by the Atlantic slave trade. Literary scholar Henry Louis Gates has made several TV series including *African American Lives* (2006–2008), *Faces of America* (2010) and *Finding Your Roots* (2012), which employ genetic technologies to trace the ancestries of (black) American celebrities, and he offers genetic ancestry testing through his own company AfricanDNA. This contested technology has not only reinforced the importance of knowing biological ancestors to individual identity, but made more explicit what was latent in science writing on Eve; the idea that the body is a more significant source of historical information than material evidence or writing. Writing on human origins, geneticist Bryan Sykes contends that 'within the DNA is written not only our histories as individuals but the whole history of the human race' and that 'our DNA does not fade like an ancient parchment; it does not rust in the ground like a sword of a warrior long dead'.[122] Writing is used as a metaphor but dismissed as a medium, to be replaced by the genes which go 'way beyond the reach of written records or stone inscriptions'.[123] As Richard Dawkins puts it, 'We can use DNA archives to reconstruct history',[124] through what Spencer Wells terms the 'historical language of the genes'.[125] It is an idea not out of step with Haley's stress on oral storytelling and embodied knowledge over the written word: recounting his visit to Gambia at the end of *Roots*, Haley meets griots who criticize the Western 'crutch of print' as he is reminded that 'every living person ancestrally goes back to some time and some place where no writing existed; and then human memories and mouths and ears were the only ways those human beings could store and relay information'.[126] Haley's novel and science writing on human origins together present a vision of the body as supreme in creating and storing a knowledge which is the foundation of identity, a vision which would have a great influence on the racial developments in genetics to come. But it was a vision which would be challenged – not least in the realm of fiction where, as I will argue in Chapter 2, the significance of writing itself is tested against the idea that the search for biological origins, for 'who we are' and where we come from, is something of great importance for individuals, racialized communities and humanity more broadly.

2

Race, Genetic Ancestry Tracing and Facial Expression: 'Focusing on the Faces' in Kazuo Ishiguro's *Never Let Me Go*

In 1998 a group of scientists led by retired pathologist Eugene Foster published an intervention into what they termed the 'long-standing historical controversy over the question of US President Thomas Jefferson's paternity of the children of Sally Hemings, one of his slaves'.[1] They had compared the Y-chromosomal DNA of the male descendants of Jefferson's uncle and the male descendants of Hemings's sons, and concluded Hemings's youngest son, Eston Hemings Jefferson, was the son of Thomas Jefferson. Supporting their finding with historical claims that Eston 'is said to have borne a striking resemblance to Thomas Jefferson' while noting some historians' belief that Eston was in fact the son of one of Thomas Jefferson's nephews, the scientists claimed that the presence of a rare haplotype which had never been observed outside of the Jefferson family meant that the 'simplest and most probable explanations for our molecular findings are that Thomas Jefferson, rather than one of the Carr brothers, was the father'.[2] The study unsettled what many historians had previously believed and while its findings were dismissed by some, they were taken as a starting point by others for a re-evaluation of Jefferson and his attitudes towards slavery. The findings contradicted the oral history known to the descendants of Hemings – that it was her first son whom Jefferson fathered – thus also unsettling long-standing family stories of the kind upon which Alex Haley had relied.[3] Making genes act as a 'new kind of historical evidence',[4] the Jefferson study was one of the first instances that brought to wider public attention the use of DNA analysis to trace ancestral history.

It is no coincidence that questions of race and racial mixing were central to what would become one of the catalysts for a public boom in genetic ancestry testing at the turn of the new millennium. The techniques that the Jefferson study employed – namely Y-chromosome analysis – had been developed alongside and as part of a much larger initiative premised on making distinctions between human population groups, the Human Genome Diversity Project (HGDP).[5] Proposed in 1991 by the population geneticist Luca Cavalli-Sforza and Allan Wilson (the lead scientist behind African Eve) as a response to the larger Human Genome Project (HGP), the HGDP set out to 'study the genetic richness of the entire human species' in order to 'show both humanity's diversity and its deep and underlying unity'.[6] The project's method was to take blood samples, saliva and hair from populations around the world from which DNA could be extracted and made available to scientists globally.[7] Populations were defined as 'ethnic groups defined by a self-imposed name' and prioritized according to anthropological interest, cultural and linguistic uniqueness, and those in danger of 'losing their identity as genetic, cultural, or linguistic units'.[8] The Y chromosome was 'the star of the project'[9] providing 'the male perspective'[10] on human evolution, the genetic study of which had been dominated by (female) MtDNA and African Eve. It was argued that in addition to enabling scientists to understand the evolutionary history of humanity, the information gathered could help in the fight against disease worldwide, including in the indigenous populations to be sampled where, for example, the incidence of recessive diseases could be estimated.[11]

The HGDP was, much like African Eve, presented as an anti-racist endeavour: for Cavalli-Sforza the project represented an 'attack on racism', an example of population genetics demonstrating that the genetic differences between populations were much smaller than superficial physical differences might imply, and he suggested that thinking about humans in terms of 'groups' and 'populations' based on geography was more productive than using the hard-to-define term 'race'.[12] As Jenny Reardon has shown, Cavalli-Sforza believed that what genetics undermined was 'popular' constructions of race, which were based on superficial phenotypic (physical) differences and were separate from genotypic differences which were, in contrast, real.[13] Thus, dismissing the significance of physical appearance, Cavalli-Sforza could join with anthropologists, social scientists and government officials in the late 1980s to argue that race, as phenotypical difference, was meaningless in science and society, replacing it with a genetic definition of difference which reconstructed the meaning of race to be molecular, and therefore distanced from ideological agendas.[14] As such, Cavalli-Sforza argued that the HGDP should be funded precisely because it could be used to combat 'social problems such as racism' for which, he contended 'there is no scientific basis'.[15] Relegating race, as commonly understood, to the realm of fiction, science was asserted as an authority on (the non-existence of) race and as separate from the sociocultural sphere from which race was deemed to have emerged.[16]

Such assertions on Cavalli-Sforza's part were necessary because despite his claims to the contrary, the HGDP was accused by many indigenous and ethnic groups as constituting a racist, colonial, exploitative attempt to extract and make money from the biological material of people whose fates and lives were otherwise of no interest to the scientists involved. Dubbed by critics as 'The Vampire Project', a problematic rhetoric of alarm about vanishing populations from which DNA needed to be urgently collected was central to the project's launch.[17] The team claimed that 'isolated human populations contain much more informative genetic records than more recent, urban ones. Such isolated human populations are being rapidly merged with their neighbors, however, destroying irrevocably the information needed to reconstruct our evolutionary history'.[18] Focusing on groups deemed to be 'uncontaminated' by European expansion, the HGDP appeared to act as a continuation of nineteenth-century anthropology, classifying non-Westerners as distinctive tribes stuck in the past.[19] As a result, the project stalled as debates about its ethics continued into the late 1990s, the scientists involved forced to begin addressing in far greater depth issues of ownership, consent and consultation with participating populations.[20]

Yet aside from significant concerns about whether scientists would profit from the collection of the biological material, and whether it would be used for racist ends, the project also participated in what Troy Duster has called 'the molecular reinscription of race'.[21] For while the project emphasized 'the importance of human population genetics for a feeling of panhuman kinship', including, as part of its sampling, Y chromosomal DNA, which was considered not to correlate with any racial markers of old,[22] it ultimately did constitute a search for population differences which could be mapped on to older divisions between races. As several critics have pointed out, in his 1994 co-authored book *The History and Geography of Human Genes*, Cavalli-Sforza published maps showing genetic differences which in some cases divided populations into geographical ethnic regions; Africans, Caucasoids, Mongoloids and Australian Aborigines.[23] A map presented in 2005 grouped the fifty-two populations included in the HGDP in less racialized terms, but still categorized them as Africans, Europeans, Asians, Oceanians and Native Americans.[24] What Cavalli-Sforza's search for population differences amounted to was the re-labelling of race as geographic ancestry, his insistence that science could be separated from society, ignoring the 'mutual constitution of natural, social, and moral orders'[25] which, rather than society alone, had produced ideas of race based upon phenotype. Although Cavalli-Sforza was acutely aware of the history of racial science and vehemently denied that his project was in any way associated with it (accusing those who made such connections as lacking understanding of human population genetics),[26] he was unable to comprehend the role that science played, and would continue to play, in the formation of the sociocultural understandings of race upon which it also drew.

The result is that as the term 'race' was being erased from human population genetics, scientific discussion of population differences continued to evoke races in all but name. This is perhaps no more evident than in genetic ancestry testing technologies, the commercial arm of population genetics, which has seen geneticists set up businesses which draw upon genetic data from indigenous communities to offer their customers individual maps and analyses of ancestral origins.[27] Analysing MtDNA, Y chromosome and autosomal DNA, companies such as 23 and Me, Oxford Ancestors, Roots for Real and African Ancestry promise to give their customers information about their 'family history',[28] 'a clear view of your ancestry, your people and your heritage'[29] and to 'estimate the location of your ancestral origins'.[30] While all are careful not to use the term race, it nevertheless remains a central way in which the services are to be understood and sold: Roots for Real, for example, recognizes that African Americans and British African Caribbean clients have 'special requirements' due to the history of slavery, and warns them that 'to trace your paternal line, you can select the Y-DNA test, but beware that 25% of American blacks and Caribbean blacks have a European Y chromosome due to historical admixture with plantation owners'.[31] Racial terminology ('black') is conflated with the geographical 'European' as a particular group of people defined by race is directed to think about their test results in those terms. Similarly, another company, African Ancestry, asserts that it is 'committed to providing a unique service to the black community' by determining individuals' 'specific ethnic groups of origin with an unrivalled level of detail, accuracy and confidence'.[32] The differences between race, ethnicity, clan, tribe, group or population – to name only some of the terminology employed in this industry – are unclear and unexplained.[33] Instead, consumers of this technology are largely left to create their own interpretations of what 'a single population or ethnicity'[34] means. That it is black people who are, as sociologists have shown, most interested and influenced by DNA ancestry tests,[35] and at whom many of the services are marketed, suggests that the technology has done little to change public understanding of race. It has rather served to underscore what Alondra Nelson terms 'a classificatory logic of human types that compounds, rather than challenges, social inequality',[36] because, as Anders Nordgren and Eric Juengst argue, 'the identity categories that customers tend to seek to confirm, discover, or reject through DNA testing are usually social categories' which 'genomic testing can powerfully reinforce'.[37] As in the Hemings case, DNA testing operates to confirm or deny particular 'racial' lineages, rather than to raise questions about the validity of the concept of race itself.

This chapter examines how the simultaneous denial and re-inscription of race in population genetics and genetic ancestry testing are addressed in one of the most popular and successful novels of the early twenty-first century, Kazuo Ishiguro's *Never Let Me Go*. A tale of the relationship between three human clones, Kathy, Tommy and Ruth, who have been brought up and educated in a kind of boarding school, Hailsham, the novel charts their lives as they grow from children into adults. As teenagers, the clones are sent to live in 'the Cottages', a complex which functions as a half-way house where they prepare for their future roles as both the carers of organ donors and donors themselves; each clone will donate three or four organs until they 'complete', being cared for between donations by other clones who have yet to begin their own donations. It is only once Kathy, Tommy and Ruth leave Hailsham that they realize that they have been brought up in exceptional circumstances compared to other clones and start to hope that there may be a way to escape their fate. *Never Let Me Go* is not a novel that engages with science, race or the relationship between the two in any overt way. Ishiguro provides little scientific detail about how human cloning has arisen and sets his novel in the recent past when human cloning did not exist in order to avoid interpretations of the novel as, in his words, 'a chilling warning about the way we're going with cloning and biotechnology'.[38] Instead the novel appears to reprise the themes and concerns of Ishiguro's previous fiction, only in a different guise: the idea of growing up without parents explored in *When We Were Orphans* (2000) and the narrative of an individual looking back over a career, who has acquiesced to a system that represses them, depicted in *The Remains of the Day* (1989). Reviewers and critics have, as a result, tended to conclude that *Never Let Me Go* is not about human cloning, instead interpreting the novel variously as referring to class,[39] the holocaust,[40] the relations between humans and animals,[41] 'the neoliberal state',[42] 'vulnerable actors in our modern economic order'[43] or more generally as a 'disquieting look at the effects of dehumanization on any group that's subject to it'.[44]

The novel is clearly not a comment on the dangers of cloning (something which was being publicly debated in the years immediately preceding its publication[45]), nor can it be classified as science fiction, yet the critical evasion of its biotechnological premise has obscured the ways in which it does engage with another strand of genetics – ancestry testing – and the role of that science in shaping contemporary ideas about race and racial identity. I argue that *Never Let Me Go* draws a subtle analogy between the lives of the clones and people who are racially marginalized, as a means of exploring the ways in which race is erased from population genetics on the basis that it is a social rather than biological category, yet continues to be evoked in that science through the use of other, euphemistic terminology and forms of classification.[46] Identifying correspondences between the exploitation of the clones and the marginalization of Britain's non-white immigrants and migrant workers, as well as similarities between the clones' functional education and the education of the colonized, I demonstrate that despite appearing post-racial, the world of the novel is saturated in racialized forms of discrimination. The clones, apparently raceless yet segregated on the basis of their genetic difference, reflect the internalization of race that is enacted in Cavalli-Sforza's denial of race's phenotypic significance in favour of the genotype – an invisible marker of difference. The clones' condition reveals the ironic outcome of the claim that race has no biological (only social) meaning, which is that 'any exploitation of non-white workers is expiated symbolically through the scientific admission of their human equality'.[47] Rather than helping in the fight against racism, the claim that race is not biological can serve to shore up colourblind ideologies which remove race without removing racism, ideologies which result from the attempt to separate biology from culture, the separation of which the novel's clones are a product.

However the chapter contends that as *Never Let Me Go* explores the paradoxes of the post-racialism which population genetics served to support, it also presents an alternative vision of a form of kinship based on a non-genetic, non-racial affinity. I identify an emphasis in Kathy's narrative on describing and interpreting facial expressions in place of physical characteristics. Kathy's privileging of looks and faces not only enables her to achieve a level of emotional comprehension not possible through her education but it is also particularly significant in relation to her search for a 'possible'.[48] Searching for recognition in the face of a genetically similar other, Kathy instead finds the recognition she has been seeking in the facial expression of the novel's only racially differentiated character, Miss Emily's Nigerian carer George. Evoking the logic of an older biological science, Darwin's theory of the universality of expression, and thus the common descent of different races, I argue that *Never Let Me Go* explores the capacity of facial expressions to disrupt racial thinking and challenges the idea promoted by genetic ancestry tracing companies that the question of who you are can be answered genetically, that tracing your (racial) genetic ancestry is a way of discovering an authentic, lost identity. Instead, the non-racial recognition between Kathy and George suggests a way of moving beyond the genetic assumptions that underpin much contemporary, racialized identity politics, towards a model of reciprocity that recalls the insights of an earlier Darwinian biology. It is ultimately through the novel's emphasis on facial expression that Ishiguro undermines the artificial division of biological fact and sociocultural fiction which Cavalli-Sforza upheld. Kathy and George's mutual recognition eschews genetic or racial similarity as it embraces their common experience of exclusion in a culture of racism which distinguishes their bodies along racial/genetic lines; yet it is a recognition grounded in biological similarity, a physiological unity brought to the fore by a socio-scientific fiction of difference. The world of the novel is one in which the idea of racial difference is reinforced through the combined effort of the scientific and sociocultural spheres, but it is also a world in which the entanglement of the biological body with its cultural environment provides the means for thinking beyond race.

The racial aura of *Never Let Me Go*

Writing about the paradox of contemporary genetic science, in which the idea of race is at once erased and reinvigorated, Alys Weinbaum suggests the implication of this paradox for art that takes biotechnology as its subject is that race is always inevitably present in such art.[49] Weinbaum applies Walter Benjamin's idea – that the aura of the singular artwork is lost in mechanically reproduced art, but that the aura of art is also 'that which is artificially produced to replace or fill-in where a loss of "authority" or "authenticity" is identified'[50] – to the use of race in biotechnology. She argues for 'an uncanny correspondence between aura, as Benjamin develops it, and the concept of race that circulates in our supposedly post-racial times: the present denial of the biological existence of race shapes all invocations of race, effectively making biological race auratic each and every time it appears'.[51] Thus, in art that engages with biotechnology, 'in a supposedly post-racial age even genomic art without overt racial content is paradoxically haunted by racial aura ... the denial of the existence of the genetic reality of race is in fact accompanied by racial aura; or put differently, that in the context of post-racialism, race is always already present'.[52]

Although *Never Let Me Go* is not quite 'genomic art' in that cloning is not its central concern, Weinbaum's analysis is instructive for understanding the peripheral or indeed 'auratic' emergence of race in the novel and for comprehending the novel's capacity to perform a 'critical assessment of our supposedly post-racial moment'.[53] As a novel without 'overt racial content', the world of Never Let Me Go appears post-racial. There is no discussion of race or ethnic differences in England; the only kind of difference is that between the clones and normals, who are not represented as being physically different from each other. It is as though race has been effaced in the manner that Paul Gilroy imagines might be made possible by the new genetics, its signification moving from the visual level of skin colour to an internal 'cellular' level.[54] However, the result is a post-racialism premised on a kind of whiteness where, as Shameem Black has suggested, 'the world of Hailsham is a world of cultural sameness, a normative ideal of white, middle class culture', which suggests 'the triumph of a white, fascistic racial ideal that effectively obliterates the markers of multicultural Britain so common in the late 1990s'.[55]

Yet despite the apparent absence of race, the idea of racial difference nevertheless emerges in the predetermined roles that the genetically differentiated clones fulfil. As bodies that have been created to serve the needs of the 'normal' population, the clones' experience appears little different from the contemporary exploitation of the black and minority ethnic workers who are often reduced simply to bodies that carry out various forms of undesirable and poorly paid labour. In addition to evoking the increasingly racialized trade in organs for transplantation, where human organs are illegally bought by people in the West from the impoverished in countries such as Turkey, Iraq and Brazil,[56] the lives of the clones echo those of the largely unseen populations of poorly paid migrant workers in Britain. Once the students leave Hailsham and live independently in 'the Cottages', which are 'the remains of a farm', they spend 'a lot of the time…being chilly' and 'huddled around half-dead fires in the small hours'.[57] Their only contact with the outside world is Keffers, 'this grumpy old guy who turned up two or three times a week in his muddy van to look the place over',[58] who operates much like a gang-master, providing only the bare minimum the clones need to survive. Following their donations they are sent to 'recovery centres'[59] located in peripheral locations such as Dover, which are reminiscent of the detention centres in which asylum seekers are often detained for long periods (including the notorious Dover Immigration Removal Centre). At Hailsham they are given 'Culture Briefing' classes where 'we had to role play various people we'd find out there – waiters in cafes, policemen and so on',[60] preparing them, in the manner of contemporary citizenship tests that immigrants are required to take, for what is essentially the foreign culture that they are about to enter following their isolation at Hailsham. As with the largely unseen, usually unreported populations of poorly paid migrant workers who often live and work in dire circumstances, the clones' existence in Ishiguro's imaginary Britain is shielded from the mainstream society of the normals, who 'didn't want to be reminded how the donation programme really worked'.[61]

The correspondence between Britain's non-white immigrant populations and the experiences of the clones is most explicitly drawn, however, at the end of the novel in its first and only portrayal of racial difference. Kathy and Tommy track down their former guardians, Madame and Miss Emily, in the mistaken belief that as Hailsham students they might be able to defer their donations for a year or so by proving that they are genuinely in love. The only time that the clones are given a clear, unambiguous understanding of their situation, this moment is the most dramatic of the novel. Yet Kathy's confrontation with her guardians is repeatedly interrupted by the presence of another character, whose existence is first indicated by Kathy's observation as she enters the guardians' house that 'it was like a servant of some sort had got the place ready for the night-time', then by 'a gruff male voice', which 'called something from upstairs'.[62] The character is George, a nurse and carer to the wheelchair-bound Miss Emily, and his presence might be unremarkable were it not for the fact that he is described as being Nigerian. Although we are only presented with a brief glimpse into George's life, there are clear parallels between his situation and that of Kathy. Like the clones, George is a carer and as the only character differentiated by race in the novel, his ethnicity seems linked to the social role that he inhabits. As Philomena Essed and David Theo Goldberg have argued in an essay on the cultural contexts which have made cloning conceivable:

> One can also imagine the cloning of non-white, able-bodied, good-natured, caring, docile, moderately smart but not too intelligent bodies to do the service work that those more privileged seem to demand more and more. Whereas biological cloning is still for the most part a fiction waiting to be realized, the cultural cloning of preferred types to inhabit segregated spaces is everyday practice, especially among social elites.[63]

George is the culturally cloned equivalent of the genetically cloned Kathy; he is not only a carer but a servant forced to respond to the barked orders of his mistresses: 'I've told you what to do. Just do as I explained' and 'George! George!'.[64] Where Kathy must care for her fellow clones as they slowly die through donating before sacrificing her own body, George, circumscribed by his racial difference, is destined to serve and care for Miss Emily. Ann Whitehead has noted how the novel portrays a system of care analogous to Britain's care homes, which are often staffed by migrant workers without citizenship.[65] George represents this underclass of Britain's migrant workers. His shadowy, voiceless presence in Kathy's narrative – a 'faint thump', 'muffled', the 'footsteps',[66] answering the door – reflects not only his peripheral status in the world of the normals, but also the increasingly peripheral nature of race itself. George's condition exposes the pitfalls of the post-racialism that the biological disavowal of race enables: removing the concept of race, as Goldberg argues, does not remove the material conditions of race or racism.[67] The near absence of racial difference in the novel only serves to highlight the presence of racial discrimination as the model for the clones' subjugation and oppression.

The novel's critique of the erasure of race is extended in its allusion to the historical racisms and exclusionary modes of humanism that provide a precedent for the contemporary forms of dehumanization that the denial of race enables. If the inescapability of the clones' situation corresponds to the contemporary exploitation of migrant workers, the way in which their humanity is queried and judged during the course of their education recalls the experiences of the colonized. Albert Memmi writes of the schooling of the colonized child that the 'memory which is assigned him is certainly not that of his people. The history which is taught him is not his own ... Everything seems to have taken place out of his country',[68] and it is this sense of alienation and externally acquired habits of memory that characterize the educational system of the 'colony' of Hailsham. The clones are taught about the different counties of an England they have never seen through romanticized 'picture calendars', which consist of images of 'little villages with streams going through them, white monuments on hillsides, old churches beside fields' that Kathy holds on to once she has left Hailsham: 'it's amazing, even now, after all these miles I've covered as a carer, the extent to which my idea of the various counties is still set by these pictures Miss Emily put up on her easel'.[69] Given Kathy's familiarity with an alternative England in which she is more likely to be 'having coffee in a service station, staring at the motorway through the big windows',[70] her preservation of the former image reflects the gap between expectation and reality that has often characterized the immigrant experience of the mother country, the result of an education designed to serve the needs of the colonizer.

The functional role of the students' education is particularly apparent in the emphasis placed on their ability to be creative and to produce art, again recalling the experience of colonized or enslaved people. At the beginning of the novel Kathy explains the young students' preoccupation with the arts, 'paintings, drawings, pottery; all sorts of "sculptures",[71] upon which they are encouraged by their guardians to focus their attention. Their creations are then sold at 'Exchanges' where the work of all the students is displayed and bought by other students, with the best pieces being taken away for the mysterious Madame's 'Gallery'.[72] In her school days, Kathy reveals that 'how much you were liked and respected, had to do with how good you were at "creating"'.[73] The clones come to attribute great significance to their art, convincing themselves that it might be a qualification for getting their organ donations deferred because, according to Miss Emily, 'things like pictures, poetry, all that kind of stuff, she said they *revealed what you were like inside.* She said *they revealed your soul*.'[74] It is not until the end of the novel that the real purpose of the gallery is explained by Miss Emily: 'We took away your art because we thought it would reveal your souls. Or to put it more finely, we did it to prove you had souls at all'.[75]

The guardians' reduction of the students' art and creativity to functioning as evidence of their humanity echoes the artificial relationship between art and humanity that historically characterized Europeans' judgement of the non-European subject. Discussing the way that the humanness of black Africans was assessed by Europeans during the Enlightenment, Henry Louis Gates, Jr. writes:

> Since the beginning of the seventeenth century, Europeans had wondered aloud whether or not the African 'Species of Men', as they most commonly put it, could ever create formal literature, could ever master 'the arts and sciences.' If they could, the argument ran, then the African variety of humanity and the European variety were fundamentally related. If not, then it seemed clear that the African was destined by nature to be a slave.[76]

Gates goes on to give the example of George Moses Horton, an African American slave poet in the 1820s whose master promised him his freedom in exchange for an adequate return on sales of his poetry.[77] As Gates explains, 'Writing, for these slaves, was not an activity of mind; rather, it was a commodity which they were forced to trade for their humanity'.[78] Such limited criteria for what constitutes art, and therefore what constitutes the human, is little different to the function performed by the clones' art.[79] Far from proving their humanity, the hope the students invest in art and education only reveals their subjection to a debased liberal ideology premised on a limited idea of what constitutes the human. Yet while the clones' art is unable to liberate them, *Never Let Me Go* might itself be considered 'art that paves the way for liberation' in critically apprehending racial aura and making its spectral presence visible.[80] In recalling the historical ways in which the colonized and enslaved have been excluded from the human and the contemporary figurative cloning of a racialized underclass, Ishiguro's portrayal of the clones exposes the ambivalent nature of race in genetics and in British society more generally. The seemingly post-racial world of the novel reveals itself to be a world saturated in forms of racial differentiation and discrimination, displaced onto the genetically differentiated clones whose condition reflects the 'paradoxical persistence of geneticized racial thinking in our supposedly post-racial moment'.[81]

Identifying with the other: Race versus face

As *Never Let Me Go* explores the paradoxes of a seemingly post-racial genetics, it also presents a vision of how human relations, and what it means to be human, might be understood without allusion to racial difference. This is achieved through Kathy's narrative style. For a number of critics, the banality and repetition of Kathy's narration challenges the (falsely) humanist education and artwork that the clones are brought up to revere.[82] I suggest that the challenge of Kathy's narration does not reside solely in its apparent inhumanity but that her emphasis on descriptions of facial expressions (in place of physical characteristics) enables her to challenge the conventions of the art and education that have ultimately contributed to, rather than ameliorated, her oppression. Significantly, this style of narration places an emphasis on a universal human trait – facial expression – above physical attributes including racial differences. In so doing it recalls Darwin's emphasis on the unity of man over racial distinctions and difference outlined in *The Expression of the Emotions in Man and Animals*, which, published in 1872, sought to show that the origins of human facial expressions could be found in the expressions of animals, an argument which formed part of his response to the continuing debates on evolution sparked by the *Origin of Species* (1859). In making this argument Darwin was able to conclude that 'all the chief expressions exhibited by man are the same throughout the world', and that 'the young and the old of widely different races, both with man and animals, express the same state of mind by the same movements'.[83] Darwin's theory thus had implications not only for man's relationship to animals, but also for the relationship between different human races; the universal facial expressions of man proved that all races had evolved from the same species and not, as the polygenists of the time argued, that races had evolved from different origins. Although there has since been much discussion of whether expressions and emotions are universally human,[84] Darwin's thesis remains a powerful indictment of scientific racism and demonstrates that, as Sarah Winter contends, 'prior to modern genetics, the biological species unity of humanity can be clearly defined – and the biological status of race refuted'.[85] It is the logic of Darwin's thesis upon which Ishiguro draws in the alternative form of non-racial and non-genetic kinship that the novel proposes.

Kathy's narration represents her experience in a way that evades the codes, conventions and expectations of the traditional education she has been given and that has contributed to her oppression. The kind of writing that Kathy has been taught to do is at the forefront of her mind as she narrates her life story in the present:

> Sometimes I'll be driving on a long, weaving road across marshland, or maybe past rows of furrowed fields, the sky big and grey and never changing mile after mile, and I find I'm thinking about my essay, the one I was supposed to be writing back then, when we were at the Cottages... When I think about my essay today, what I do is go over it in some detail: I may think of a completely new approach I could have taken, or about different writers and books I could have focused on... Just lately, I've even toyed with the idea of going back and working on it, once I'm not a carer any more and I've got the time.[86]

Although Kathy is thinking about her former writing and reading as she composes her narrative, there is little evidence in her writing of the intellectual training she received at Hailsham. Despite revealing her familiarity with *The Odyssey*, *1001 Nights* and the novels of Thomas Hardy, George Eliot, Edna O'Brien, Margaret Drabble and James Joyce, Kathy does not adopt the techniques for storytelling or stylistic innovation represented in these wide-ranging literary texts. Instead, as John Mullan argues, 'for all her earnest reading, Kathy H.'s narrative voice feels deprived of resources'.[87] From the first line of the novel – 'My name is Kathy H. I'm thirty-one years old, and I've been a carer now for over eleven years'[88] – to the last – 'I just waited a bit, then turned back to the car, to drive off to wherever it was I was supposed to be'[89] – Kathy writes in a mundane style that would seem to suggest a limited capacity for creativity and critical thinking.

Yet it is creativity that has been functionalized in Kathy's experience. She recounts how the essays the students were told to write were designed to 'absorb us properly for anything up to two years', and that 'how well you were settling in at the Cottages – how well you were *coping* – was somehow reflected by how many books you'd read'.[90] Distracting the students from their impending deaths, their essays and reading are merely an extension of an education that has prevented them from reaching a true understanding of their situation. Denied the possibility of freedom through art of the kind given to the slave poet George Moses Horton, Kathy produces an artwork that challenges the conventions of the canonical, European literature she has studied. Specifically, her description of faces challenges the emphasis in much Victorian literature (the topic of her essay) on physical features as representative of character, the product of the contemporaneous science of physiognomy.[91]

Kathy rarely describes the physical characteristics of the people she presents in her narrative and never refers to race or ethnicity. No information is given about what Kathy and her closest companions, Ruth and Tommy, look like. Only the physical features of the guardians and the veterans at the Cottages are described and then only in very basic terms. Kathy describes the same traits, height and hair, each time: Madame 'was a tall, narrow woman with short hair', Miss Emily 'wasn't especially tall…she wore her silvery hair tied back', 'Chrissie was a tall girl who was quite beautiful when she stood up to her full height' and Rodney 'went around with his hair tied back in a ponytail'.[92] These repetitive, unimaginative physical descriptions highlight the limited importance of the physical body in Kathy's psyche. Awaiting the harvesting of their organs, Kathy and the other clones are emotionally detached from their own bodies, which are merely functional rather than individual, an attitude reflected in their emotionally disconnected approach to sex: 'sex had got like "being creative" had been a few years earlier. It felt like if you hadn't done it yet, you ought to, and quickly'.[93] Devoid of meaning, bodies do not provide or add to an understanding of character.

Rather than describing physical features, Kathy instead describes facial expressions. Her narrative abounds with descriptions of people's countenances and her interpretation of the thoughts and feelings that these looks express. Typical of this is Kathy's recollection of an encounter with Miss Emily: 'I remember when I went to tell Miss Emily my chosen topic was Victorian novels, I hadn't really thought about it much and I could see she knew it. But she just gave me one of her searching stares and said nothing more'.[94] Kathy 'sees' in order to understand the thoughts of others. Having been brought up being 'told and not told'[95] about the true purpose of her life, she learns to interpret facial expressions, which reveal more than what is said. When the students joke among themselves about electric fences in Second World War prison camps, Kathy is initially alerted to the possibility that Hailsham's fences could be electrified through Miss Lucy's look: 'I went on watching Miss Lucy through all this, and I could see, just for a second, a ghostly expression come over her face as she watched the class in front of her'.[96] Kathy's inability to articulate her own feelings (for example 'I wasn't keen on Ruth going with them to Norfolk, though I couldn't really say why'[97]), which is evident everywhere in her narrative, is the product of an upbringing in which words mask, or cannot convey, the full picture of what someone is feeling. As a result, in place of dialogue Kathy meditates on facial expressions which, for Kathy, are a more reliable and honest marker of emotion. As she humiliates and mocks Ruth about her belief in the potential of her possible, the humans the clones are copied from, she monitors Ruth's face for a reaction: 'I glanced at Ruth beside me. There was no anger in her eyes, just a kind of wariness. There was even a sort of hope, I thought, that when the poster appeared, it would be perfectly innocuous – something that reminded us of Hailsham, something like that. I could see all of this in her face, the way it didn't quite settle on any one expression, but hovered tentatively'.[98]

Although she is somehow conditioned to see what is not said, Kathy also privileges this form of non-verbal communication because it brings her closer to an understanding of the human soul than any of her art or writing. Ultimately it is her ability to interpret facial expressions (rather than words or texts) that gives her a reliable and honest understanding of human emotion. Darwin privileges the facial over the verbal in this way when he writes: 'We readily perceive sympathy in others by their expression; our sufferings are thus mitigated and our pleasures increased; and mutual good feeling is thus strengthened. The movements of expression give vividness and energy to our spoken words. They reveal the thoughts and intentions of others more truly than do words, which may be falsified'.[99] As Ruth lies dying after a donation, Kathy observes:

> Just for a few seconds, no more, she looked straight at me and she knew exactly who I was. It was one of those little islands of lucidity donors sometimes get to in the midst of their ghastly battles, and she looked at me, just for that moment, and although she didn't speak, I knew what her look meant. So I said to her: 'It's okay, I'm going to do it, Ruth. I'm going to become Tommy's carer as soon as I can.' I said it under my breath, because I didn't think she'd hear the words anyway, even if I shouted them. But my hope was that with our gazes locked as they were for those few seconds, she'd read my expression exactly as I'd read hers.[100]

It is through reading expressions and locking gazes that Kathy attempts to form a relationship with another based on a reciprocity of feeling, emotion and understanding in which words are insignificant. She draws on this capacity at the end of the novel when she encounters Madame and they discuss the moment at Hailsham when Madame catches Kathy singing 'Never Let Me Go' while cradling a pillow. Attempting to break the barrier between clones and normals, Kathy tells Madame, 'I think I know what you're thinking about,' and notes that 'Madame's expression didn't change as she kept staring into my face'.[101] Although Madame initially resists Kathy's attempt to establish a mutual interpretation of the moment by mocking Kathy's attempt to read through seeing, 'a mind-reader. You should be on the stage', their meeting ends when Madame, overcoming her fear of the clones, empathizes and physically connects with Kathy by looking: 'She reached out her hand, all the while staring into my face, and placed it on my cheek. I could feel a trembling go all through her body, but she kept her hand where it was, and I could see again tears appearing in her eyes'.[102]

Kathy's looking is tied to, and perhaps also derived from, another kind of looking that she performs in her search for a possible. Throughout the novel, Kathy's sense of alienation from the world of the normals is linked to her inability to find a reflection, a lack caused by the absence of a genetic parent or ancestor. From a young age Kathy senses this difference:

> So you're waiting, even if you don't quite know it, waiting for the moment when you realise that you really are different to them; that there are people out there, like Madame, who don't hate you or wish you any harm, but who nevertheless shudder at the very thought of you – of how you were brought into this world and why – and who dread the idea of your hand brushing against theirs. The first time you glimpse yourself though the eyes of a person like that, it's a cold moment. It's like walking past a mirror you've walked past every day of your life, and suddenly it shows you something else, something troubling and strange.[103]

It is a moment which has been compared to the experience of alienation brought about by racism; Martin Puchner describes this scene as 'a recognition scene, a standard feature in novels about racism and other forms of discrimination'.[104] Searching for recognition and familiarity in a world that deems them to be less than human, Kathy and the other clones look for their possibles, who they believe could be discovered at any moment. Kathy looks in pornographic magazines, explaining how 'I hardly saw the contorted bodies, because I was focusing on the faces. Even in the little adverts for videos or whatever tucked away to the side, I checked each model's face before moving on',[105] and it is during this time at the Cottages that the students take a trip to Norfolk after a sighting of a possible for Ruth. Kathy explains that 'we all of us, to varying degrees, believed that when you saw the person you were copied from, you'd get *some* insight into who you were deep down, and maybe too, you'd see something of what your life held in store'.[106] Once again, seeing is understanding for Kathy, whose search for reciprocity and recognition in the faces of others is caught up in her search for genetic recognition.

However, instead of discovering who she is by finding a possible, the only person in whom Kathy can find a likeness is George. It is through a comment made by Miss Emily that the reader learns of George's racial difference and Kathy's reaction to it. In describing her first post-Hailsham encounter with Kathy, Miss Emily says: 'I recognized you, but you may well not have recognized me. In fact, Kathy H., once not so long ago, I passed you sitting on that bench out there, and you certainly didn't recognize me then. You glanced at George, the big Nigerian man pushing me. Oh yes, you had quite a good look at him, and he at you'.[107] Instead of recognizing Miss Emily, the guardian for whom she has been searching, Kathy recognizes herself in George. Through their silent face-to-face looking Kathy gains access to a sense of kinship that goes beyond the confines of the genetic connection she has hitherto been seeking in a possible. The recognition between Kathy and George is based on their mutual exclusion on the basis of their genetic and racial alienation, yet it is also a recognition that negates the significance of these differences. Privileging facial expression over physical appearance enables Kathy to recognize that understanding who she is might be achieved in the recognition of shared human experience, in a non-biological and non-racial affinity.

In this way *Never Let Me Go* offers an alternative view of kinship that challenges the idea that understanding who you are can be achieved through the genes, in tracing a (racial) genetic ancestry.[108] This has been the claim of genetic ancestry tracing companies, a claim popularized in television programmes such as the 2003 BBC2 documentary *Motherland: A Genetic Journey*, in which the scientists behind the company Roots for Real were featured. Billed as a 'quest to recover lost identity', the documentary followed three Black Britons as they traced their ancestries, through DNA analysis, to specific parts of Africa, exploring their emotions as they confronted their African 'distant cousins' in order to discover 'who they are and where they came from'.[109] One participant, Mark Anderson, described how 'the question of who my ancestors were and what my past was like was one that always needed answering for me. I was never comfortable describing myself as a Black Briton. I always felt that something was missing from my story'.[110] Not only have serious questions been raised about the accuracy of genetic ancestry tests which, while claiming to offer individualized results, present results which would likely apply to large populations (and in the absence of historical information could be explained by any number of scenarios),[111] but the focus on Y chromosome and MtDNA analysis as ways of understanding ancestry is also misleading because these only represent two 'corridors of ancestry', excluding many others.[112] It is on this basis that Richard Dawkins criticized the *Motherland* documentary, of which he writes:

> They used Y-chromosomal and mitochondrial DNA because, for the reasons we have seen, they are more traceable than genes in general. But unfortunately, the producers never really came clean about the limitations this imposed. In particular, no doubt for sound televisual reasons, they came close to actively deceiving these individuals, and also their long-lost African 'relatives', into becoming far more emotional about the reunions than they had any right to be.[113]

For Dawkins, the *Motherland* documentary was 'sentimental rubbish' because 'different genes tell different stories' and 'at any given time in the past we have a huge number of genealogical ancestors' meaning 'a single chunk of DNA, such as from a mitochondrion or Y chromosome, gives as impoverished a view of the past as a single sentence from a history book'.[114]

However beyond his methodological objections, Dawkins does not challenge the idea that, as he puts it, 'ancestors hold the key to understanding life itself',[115] a claim which is central to the appeal of genetic ancestry testing. The tests make ancestry key to identity, to which race is also key; as biologist Fatimah Jackson contends, ancestry testing companies have exploited a vulnerable market in African Americans where 'identity is disproportionately linked to phenotype, and in ethnic minority groups is associated with levels of self-confidence, performance, and overall positive life outcomes'.[116] Put differently by Stuart Murray, 'Because genomic vocabularies have so pervaded the public sphere, it is impossible not to understand the self as a problem in these terms.'[117] The silent bond between Kathy and George resists the naturalization of genetic explanations of kinship, the prevailing conception that DNA is the key to the self. Instead, they embrace the kind of ethics of care that Murray argues is needed in an era in which genetic technologies have recast family relationships in genetic terms. They eschew 'a self that uncritically does the bidding of those ideologies we call family, nation, or race ... however "naturalized" or "biologized" these terms may become' in favour of an ethical care which 'will mobilize these as the tropes that they are, and seek new relations, new modes, and new terms by which we might once again ask the question of the good life'.[118] The seemingly natural connection between race and identity is broken in the non-racial recognition between Kathy and George, creating a post-racial vision that, rather than being based on a denial of racial inequality, gestures towards the kind of affinities that Donna Haraway imagines might emerge from a unity between social relations, science and technology: 'a self-consciously constructed space that cannot affirm the capacity to act on the basis of natural identification, but only on the basis of conscious coalition, of affinity, or political kinship'.[119] While Black argues that 'the students' loss of cultural specificity signals one tactic by which they lose their purchase on human identity',[120] it is rather the belief that such cultural or ethnic forms of identification are self-evidently human that Ishiguro's portrayal of Kathy and George confronts. Who you are, the novel suggests, is determined not in the promise of a recovered genetic ancestry (in this case by the discovery or identification of a 'possible'), but by your interactions and affiliations in the present and the shared experiences on which such affiliations are built.

Reading faces, reading literature

Kathy's emphasis on a universal, biological means of expressing emotion has, however, implications beyond repudiating the primacy of racial and genetic forms of identification. Her emphasis on facial expression overrides the articulation of emotion in words, apparently calling into question the efficacy of the novel's own communicative means. This tension is explored at various points in the novel where the value of words, writing or literature is undermined. One such moment is when Kathy is at Hailsham and catches Miss Lucy

> leaning over in concentration, forehead very low, arms up on the surface, scrawling furious lines over a page with a pencil. Underneath the heavy black lines I could see neat blue handwriting. As I watched, she went on scrubbing the pencil point over the paper, almost in the way we did shading in Art, except her movements were much more angry, as if she didn't mind gouging right through the sheet.[121]

Miss Lucy scrawls over the students' work in anger at the false ideals they have developed through their education; their writing is a sham that reduces, rather than proves, their humanity. Kathy, who assesses the situation in her usual way – 'I could see her face was flushed, but there were no traces of tears' – narrates how she was confused and upset by what she had seen but adds, 'if you'd asked me to define just what I was so upset about, I wouldn't have been able to explain'.[122] It is precisely because their writing leaves the students unable to express their true feelings in words that Miss Lucy reacts against it; Kathy at some level understands this, which is why she responds emotionally to Miss Lucy's 'flushed' face.

Another such incident occurs when Kathy describes the experience of reading *Daniel Deronda* at the Cottages, around the time that she and the other students are struggling to make sense of their origins and look for their possibles. She makes no explicit connection between this discussion of possibles, of genetic ancestors or parents, and her reading of *Daniel Deronda*, the tale of a young man adopted at birth who becomes involved with a Jewish family only to discover that he is Jewish himself, giving a sense of purpose to his hitherto directionless life. Instead, she simply remarks that she had 'not been enjoying it very much'.[123] For Kathy, reading *Daniel Deronda* is part of the competitive reading the students are forced to do in order to prove how well they are coping; its meaning, the way that it might relate to the human condition (in this case Kathy's) or how Kathy as a reader might empathize with its characters is erased, despite the fact that the resonances are clear: when Eliot describes how Deronda's 'own face in the glass had during many years been associated for him with thoughts of someone whom he must be like – one about whose character and lot he continually wondered, and never dared to ask',[124] we are immediately reminded of how Kathy's looking in a mirror provokes similar questions about who she is.

These moments draw attention to the assumptions embedded in the act of reading and the expectation that literature and writing will signify something to the person reading it. That Kathy's reading of faces is more significant than her reading of books is not an indication that the significance of literature is diminished; it is, rather, part of an alternative mode of interpretation that might act as a model for our own reading. Derek Attridge is instructive here: he writes of a 'parallel between creativity and responsiveness' in literature and argues that 'creatively responding to the other ... involves the shifting of ingrained modes of understanding in order to take account of that which was systematically excluded by them'.[125] Kathy's responsiveness to others, particularly George, is enabled by her creative method of describing facial expressions in place of physical characteristics, involving a 'shifting of ingrained modes of understanding'. In this, Ishiguro provides an example of how we, as readers, might creatively respond to and interpret the novel. It is in looking and seeing beyond ingrained assumptions about how literature should work, seeing beyond what appears as a banal and unremarkable narrative mode, that the reader, like Kathy, is able to read differently and see how Kathy reads differently in interpreting what is written on the face. Attridge argues that literature is effective even if it 'solves no problems and saves no souls',[126] a moot point in the case of Kathy and her fellow clones; although literature itself cannot save them or prove they have souls, it remains effective as a means through which Kathy can challenge and subvert the very idea that it can save them.

Yet the novel also moves beyond the more abstract responsiveness espoused by Attridge towards a biologically grounded conception of recognition and human similarity that reveals literature's ability to apprehend the human experience of facial expression. In the concluding sections of *The Expression of the Emotions in Man and Animals*, Darwin reflects on the difficulty of describing specific expressions, which, in the context of the novel, reminds us of Kathy's limited mode of description:

> M. Lemoine argues that, if man possessed an innate knowledge of expression, authors and artists would not have found it so difficult, as is notoriously the case, to describe and depict the characteristic signs of each particular state of mind. But this does not seem to me a valid argument. We may actually behold the expression changing in an unmistakable manner in a man or animal, and yet be quite unable, as I know from experience, to analyse the nature of the change... It has often struck me as a curious fact that so many shades of expression are instantly recognized without any conscious process of analysis on our part. No one, I believe, can clearly describe a sullen or sly expression; yet many observers are unanimous that these expressions can be recognized in the various races of man... If, then, great ignorance of details does not prevent our recognizing with certainty and promptitude various expressions, I do not see how this ignorance can be advanced as an argument that our knowledge, though vague and general, is not innate.[127]

The lack of specificity in Kathy's descriptions of faces reflects her lack of 'any conscious process of analysis'; hers is an innate, human reaction that would seem to prove Darwin's point that a 'great ignorance of details' (which arguably defines Kathy's experience) does not prevent the recognition of expression. Kathy's sparse language thus highlights her human ability to respond, feel and recognize, so that as readers we feel more than empathy towards Kathy, as she feels more than empathy towards George: we recognize ourselves in the life of a clone. Rather than providing a warning about the dystopic potential of new genetic technologies, or simply critiquing formations of race in genetic science, *Never Let Me Go* acknowledges our human biological commonality and develops a biofictional narrative form which harnesses the power of facial expressions to suggest a way of moving beyond both the dismissal of biology and its separation from cultural context in debates about the meaning of race. As it speaks to such contemporary debates about race and science while drawing on the logic of an older, Darwinian science of facial expression, the novel recalls an insight from Eliot's *Daniel Deronda*, which, in this case, does signify that 'often the grand meanings of faces as well as of written words may lie chiefly in the impressions of those who look on them'.[128]

3

'One Part Truth and Three Parts Fiction': Race, Science and Narrative in Zadie Smith's *White Teeth*

In June 2000 US President Bill Clinton joined with British Prime Minister Tony Blair (via satellite), Francis Collins, Director of the National Human Genome Research Institute, and Craig Venter, Chief Officer of Celera Genomics Corporation, at a White House press conference to announce that the first-ever draft of the human genome had been completed. The Human Genome Project (HGP), begun fifteen years earlier, had identified all 25,000 genes in the human genome and sequenced the 3 billion base pairs in human DNA. The culmination of international scientific collaboration, as well as public and commercial scientific work (represented by Collins and Venter respectively), the project came to symbolize half a century of rapid developments in the biological sciences and placed the new scientific discipline of genomics at the forefront of twenty-first-century scientific endeavour. In pronouncing on the significance of the completed first draft, and the scientific knowledge and subsequent medical benefits that would be made possible by this major achievement, the scientific and political figures at the White House meeting described the genome variously as a book, language or writing, which scientists would now be able to read. Collins explained that the genome was 'the human book of life', arguing that we must now 'learn how to speak the language of the genome fluently',[1] Clinton claimed it was 'the language in which God created life',[2] while Venter declared that 'for the first time our species can read the chemical letters of its genetic code'.[3] The book metaphor had first developed from genetic scientists' use of the initial letters A, C, G and T to stand (metonymically) for the names of the four base molecules (adenine, cytosine, guanine and thymine) that make up DNA.[4] From this, a whole set of equivalences developed in genetic discourses; a gene was a sentence, a chromosome a chapter, DNA a language and the genome the book.[5] By the time it was used by Clinton, Venter and Collins to announce the completion of the draft, the book metaphor was more than what Brigitte Nerlich, Robert Dingwall and David D. Clarke describe as 'a conventional means of articulating a shared understanding of the biological phenomena being discussed';[6] it provided a way for the speakers to convey a sense of profundity about the project in language which would be readily understood by the public.

However, describing the genome as a book also had wider implications for books more traditionally conceived, an issue of which both scientists involved in the announcement seemed peripherally aware. Collins stated: 'We are here today to celebrate a milestone along a truly unprecedented voyage, this one into ourselves. Alexander Pope wrote, "Know then thyself. Presume not God to scan. The proper study of mankind is man." What more powerful form of study of mankind could there be than to read our own instruction book?'[7] In quoting from a literary source, Collins appears unaware of the irony of his analogy; while using Pope's words to explain the importance of sequencing the genome, of studying man, he then asserts the genome to be the ultimate book, there being no 'more powerful' way to understand human life than reading it. Reading other books which may grapple with the study of mankind, such as Pope's, appears less significant. The question of the place of the literary in a world where the genome is proclaimed to be the definitive book of life is taken up more directly by Venter, who ended his speech thus:

> Some have said to me that sequencing the human genome will diminish humanity by taking the mystery out of life. Poets have argued that genome sequencing is an example of sterilizing reductionism that will rob them of their inspiration. Nothing could be further from the truth. The complexities and wonder of how the inanimate chemicals that are our genetic code give rise to the imponderables of the human spirit should keep poets and philosophers inspired for the millenniums.[8]

Venter imagines a productive future for literature inspired, rather than threatened, by the genome, yet the meaning and mysteries of life remain grounded in the 'genetic code', which in his brief account of the direct linkage between 'inanimate chemicals' and 'the imponderables of the human spirit' leans towards the reductionism he describes poets as fearing. Science has often provided poets with inspiration but, in Venter's account, literature is framed as merely responsive to science, capable of expressing a form of humanity which has already been delineated by science.

These comments by Collins and Venter, the 'book of life' metaphor, demonstrate how the sequencing of the genome presented an implicit challenge to the literary. If the genome was a book, then scientists were the new literary critics, interpreting the meaning of an array of different genes by 'reading' them, making 'the body a text for interpretation'.[9] As Patricia Waugh contends, 'the idea that the human self is written was hardly news to anyone who had spent the past twenty-five years in the literary academy',[10] yet the kinds of readings of the genes being conducted by scientists were somewhat different to the mode of reading and interpretation which characterized contemporaneous literary criticism. Deborah Lynn Steinberg has argued that while the language metaphor 'would seem to democratize, to open up the expert conceptual terrains of science and to invite a familiar, interpretive mode of address to the non-scientific reader', what it actually signified was a fixed mode of reading where 'the genetic scientist as "reader"; decodes, but significantly does not produce; is a discoverer rather than mediator of meanings construed as already embedded'.[11] Rather than understanding genes as being open to multiple kinds of interpretation and analysis, the meaning of which is dependent on their context (in the way that a literary critic might understand language), in genomics at the turn of the new millennium 'the phenomenon of language itself is essentialised in structuralist, positivistic terms. The denotive properties of *genes* as *words* – their "claims" as it were – emerge as naturalized, as equivalent certainties'.[12] Such an understanding of language (and thus of genes) was rooted in the origins of the book/writing metaphor which Lily E. Kay identifies as 'historically specific and culturally contingent'.[13] The metaphor reflected the culturally dominant modes of thought of the early twentieth century, and became embedded in the very structure of science itself: Judith Roof, for example, has shown how the emphasis on the double helix structure of DNA was in part the product of structuralism and theories about the binary nature of language prevalent at that time.[14] Therefore at the completion of the draft of the HGP, the scientific reading and interpretation of genes led their meanings to become relatively fixed and singular despite the complexity that the sequencing uncovered, enabling geneticists to present their claims about the genome in definitive and certain terms.

Indeed one of the only things that those gathered at the White House were able to be immediately definitive about – as discoverers rather than mediators of genetic meaning – was one of the project's most significant findings about humanity; that race has no biological meaning. Clinton's speech is famous for his assertion that 'one of the great truths to emerge from this triumphant expedition inside the human genome is that in genetic terms, all human beings, regardless of race, are more than 99.9 percent the same'.[15] This point was reiterated later in the proceedings by Venter who, describing the different ethnicities of the people whose genomes he had sequenced, claimed that they could not be distinguished from one another genomically and that the results showed 'the concept of race has no genetic or scientific basis'.[16] Francis Collins received a long round of applause following his statement 'I am happy that today the only race we are talking about is the human race'.[17] Geneticists only had one reading of the human body when it came to race, its genetic non-existence put forward as a hard fact that it was no longer possible to dispute. Yet reading genes, as Steinberg contends, is not the neutral and definitive act it may be presented as; 'the power to "read" genes is, in part, embedded in the power to manipulate them … *editorial* decisions about which genes are meaningful; which genes can or should be deleted, are predicated on the inequalities and dependencies that shore up the boundaries of professional expertise, authority and authorship'.[18] Put differently, scientists' readings of genes at the turn of the second millennium were perhaps not only more contingent and provisional than they appeared, but rather than simply reading genes geneticists were also in part authors of the genome. As Waugh notes, 'as science grows more theoretical' (and in the case of the genome its objects of study less visible) 'so it becomes more dependent on narrative presentation and the use of rhetorical tropes such as metaphors'.[19] The book of life metaphor itself evinced geneticists' reliance on language and narrative in ways which suggest that their subsequent readings of the gene were anything but straightforwardly factual or definitive. Writing and reading occurred simultaneously, and just as the powerful and shaping language metaphor was the product of the wider cultural discourse of the moment, in the case of race, scientists' readings of the gene should themselves be read and understood in the context of wider socio-political discourses about race which ultimately became part of the narrative of race which emerged from the HGP.

For it is clear that the announcement that race had no biological meaning occurred at a time when in the wider political sphere race was being minimized as a meaningful subject of public concern. As discussed in the Introduction to this book, the anti-racist movements of the 1980s and 1990s, which drew their impetus from struggles against racism such as the anti-apartheid movement, had begun to give way to the disappearance of race from political and social dialogues.[20] In the United States, political conservatives were advocating the removal of the concept of race from law and politics, and advocating colourblind policies, often employing genetic reasoning as evidence that race was no longer valid, as a means of attacking affirmative action programmes.[21] In the UK, anti-racist legislation came into force in 2000 in the wake of the racist murder of Stephen Lawrence and the finding of the MacPherson enquiry that the police were institutionally racist. The Race Relations Amendment Act placed a duty on public bodies to eliminate discrimination and promote equality, but the effect of this move was in fact a quieting of discussions of race and racism, as David Theo Goldberg contends, 'formal public admissions also slide into absolutions, dissolving the energy of the insurgent into the modest, quieting force of the law, reducing resistant antiracist anger each time to the formalisms of antiracial insistence. "We will not tolerate racism" invariably and quite quickly becomes "We cannot speak the language of race".'[22] This was certainly the turn taken by the leaders of the HGDP, who, as discussed in the previous chapter, saw the solution to accusations of racism as being to deny the biological reality of race itself.

It was in this context that those gathered at the White House stressed that they would ensure that the mapping of the genome would not result in discrimination of any kind, a public affirmation of the anti-racist credentials of the project. But it was their assertions about the genetic non-existence of race which were put forward as the project's ultimate contribution to anti-racism; what they announced was the end of race itself, a biofictional 'reading' and narrative of race which both fed into and drew upon the political and social discourses of the moment as well as preceding scientific statements of race. There is little doubt that the anti-racist intentions of the scientists involved in the HGP were genuine, and their findings found favour with the views of many in the humanities that race as concept was nothing more than a social fiction made biological by bad science. The year 2000 was also the year in which Gilroy published his influential text *Against Race*, in which he argued that developments in genetics had caused a crisis in racial thinking which presented the opportunity to move beyond race. However, as Waugh asserts, 'a science that threatens to impinge on human life not merely in the form of technology but also in the shaping of values and public policy, needs to be as vigilant as possible about the status of its evidence and the effects of narrative transmission.'[23] For the effect of the transmission of the anti-racist reading of the gene was a narrative which could be used to support a wider erasure of race and de-prioritization of the need to tackle racism. While 'commitments to do away with race ... have long been associated with social movements to end racism', as Goldberg contends, 'the end of racism is confused with no more than being against race, the end of race substituting to varying degrees for the commitment to – the struggles for –ending racism. The refusal of racism reduces to racial refusal; and racial refusal is thought to exhaust antiracism.'[24] Ending genetic race was – as in the case of the HGDP – posited as enough to end racism (rather than anti-racist action), but this position risks silencing populations historically discriminated against because the basis of that discrimination is no longer thought to apply.

Zadie Smith's debut novel *White Teeth*, published in the same year that the draft of the HGP was announced, examines the consequences of the removal of race – and thus the possibility of racism – from genetic science. The novel tells the story of the Iqbals and the Joneses, two working-class, multi-racial north London families, in which the fathers, Samad Iqbal and Archie Jones, met as soldiers during the Second World War. Their children, Irie Jones and twins Magid and Millat Iqbal, grow up together, before meeting the Chalfens, a middle-class family to whom they are sent by their school to be mentored. Marcus Chalfen is a geneticist whose experiments have led him to engineer the genome of a mouse (his FutureMouse© bears a close resemblance to Oncomouse®, a genetically modified mouse predisposed to contracting cancer, created in the 1980s by a group of Harvard scientists). Both Irie and Magid become interested in his science and the Chalfens' 'scientific' approach to life more generally. Marcus is insistent that his science has nothing to do with racial classification or racism, but as the novel progresses it is revealed that the creation of FutureMouse© has been possible only through the work of his predecessor and mentor Dr Perret, who is revealed to be the Nazi racial scientist that Archie and Samad had encountered during the Second World War. This is one of several moments in the novel at which Smith suggests that the removal of race from science leads to both cultural and scientific amnesia about historical racisms and to the reproduction of past structures of racial thinking in the present. Arguing against critical assessments of the novel which read Smith's engagement with genetics as linked to a post-racial message about the blending, mixing and hybridity which are seen to make race increasingly redundant in postcolonial London,[25] this chapter contends that it is Smith's portrayal of genetic science which destabilizes the notion that contemporary London is post-racial. For the novel uncovers how the science upon which such conclusions often rely is the product of not only historical and contemporary political currents but of narrativization – it is a story which cannot be reduced to a singular or definitive meaning.

White Teeth explores how genomic science, far from being neutrally objective in its 'readings' of the body and of genes, creates and transmits stories which, like those of fiction, are complex, messy, multiple and contradictory. Smith sets up an extended comparison between the methods of the scientist and the writer of fiction as a means of testing this hypothesis, drawing on Lionel Trilling's claim that 'plot is to the novelist what experiment is to the scientist'[26] to offer a metafictional consideration of the similarities between the science the novel addresses and the narrative form of the novel itself. *White Teeth* is written in a Forsterian comic mode characterized by coincidence, irrationality, humour and melodrama, designed, in the vein of Forster's novels, to convey the 'messy human concoction'[27] of life and the muddle of human nature. That this understanding of life can only be fully realized through the 'artificial' imposition of these forms by the novelist to test human nature is what makes her practice, Smith imagines, comparable to the experiment of a scientist. However her comparison also opens up space for a consideration of how, conversely, science is like writing, and how the messiness of the human in fiction might be closer to that of science than those who announced the mapping of the genome imagined it to be. This chapter examines how in highlighting the narrative qualities of genomics, rather than simply being passively inspired by that science, *White Teeth* becomes one of the 'stories that expose the stories that are told to us, by the scientists "for our own good"'.[28] Rather than upholding the anti-racist story told by the Human Genome Project 'for our own good', the novel's examination of the stories told by science leads us to the questions posed by Steinberg; 'can there be a genetics divorced from its own history?...how is an anti-racist genetics possible?'.[29] The beginnings of an answer, the novel suggests, lie in interrogating the nature of scientific narrative and its transmission. For it is in science as narrative that race is variously latent, fictionalized and varied in meaning, an emblem of the instability of scientific 'reading' and an indicator of shifting (scientific) interpretations of the genes themselves.

Genetics, race and the comic novel

In 1943, long before his intervention in the two cultures controversy between C.P. Snow and F.R. Leavis, Lionel Trilling published an essay on E.M. Forster's first novel *Where Angels Fear to Tread* in which he offered a comparison of the methods of the scientist and the writer of fiction. In defence of Forster's melodramatic plots, from which, Trilling suggests, 'contemporary taste draws back, insisting that life is not like that', he writes:

> Plot is to the novelist what experiment is to the scientist, which is exactly what Zola did not know when he wrote his essay 'The Experimental Novel'; Zola's defense of scientific naturalism in fiction has nothing at all to do with experiment. The science he had in mind as analogous to novel writing was medicine as practised by the great physician Claude Bernard; that is to say he had in mind an empirical, not an experimental science. And Zola's novelistic 'science' was a science of observation, and precisely not of experiment. He condemned plot as artificial, but experiment is artificial too – nature does not exist in test-tubes and

retorts and under controlled conditions, and to conclude that what happens in the laboratory is what happens in the universe requires a leap of the imagination. But experiment, with its artificiality, is our best way of making things act so that we can learn about their nature. And plot in the novel does the same for human nature.[30]

Interviewed in 2002 about her short story *The Trials of Finch*, Zadie Smith refers to Trilling's scientific analogy as she reflects on the construction of character and plot in her own writing, coming to a similar defence of artificiality:

> Real character gives itself away, I think, in the quiet moments, and, for me, it's a great effort to write the quieter bits, to not always explicate through plot. The objection, again, with Finch was this: life is not like that! But I'm still not sure what's meant by that idea. That's sort of why I'm studying the novel again. I do believe in the uses of plot – Lionel Trilling talked about it as a sort of laboratory of ideas. What happens in a lab is an artificiality that sets us up for an experience of the world. The scientist begins with a thesis he wants in some way to prove – he may not get the results he expects, but his experiment is tangential to the world, it has a place there. I think the intention is the same in fiction.[31]

It seems likely that Smith came to Trilling's essay through her self-professed 'love' of E.M. Forster, 'to whom' she has stated, 'all my fiction is indebted'.[32] Smith has written of and, similarly to Trilling, defended Forster's melodrama, recognizing its influence on her own work.[33] Following the publication of *White Teeth*, Smith was criticized for the artificiality of her style: James Wood branded the novel part of an emerging genre which he dubbed 'hysterical realism', novels characterized by improbable plots in which novelists 'clothe real people who could never actually endure the stories that happen to them'.[34] For Wood – espousing the kind of objection to melodrama that Trilling identifies – 'they are stories which defy the laws of persuasion'.[35] Yet Smith's reflections, via Trilling, on the use of plot suggest that the 'artificial' elements of her writing are strategic and considered, rather than indicative of the out of control postmodernism that Wood considers them to be.

Indeed they are the product of her emulation of the characteristics of the Forsterian comic novel, of which she has both written and spoken extensively. Asked in an interview about what appeals to her in Forster's work, Smith stated that 'Forster represents one of the earliest loves of my reading life and the first intimations I ever had of the power and beauty of this funny, artificial little construction, the novel'.[36] Smith identifies two characteristics of the Forsterian comic novel which have influenced her writing; the artificial and, related to this, the funny, which is characterized, for Smith, not only by humour but by the peculiarity, inconsistency and muddle of the human condition. She writes that:

> there is a lot in Forster that fails, is both cloying and banal: his Pantheism, his fetish for the exotic, his idealisation of music. The mystic will occasionally look the fool. Forster took a risk, opening the comic novel to let in the things it was not designed for; small patches of purple prose were the result. But Forster's innovation remains: he allowed the English comic novel the possibility of a spiritual and bodily life, not simply to exist as an exquisitely worked game of social ethics but as a messy human concoction. He expanded the comic novel's ethical space (while unbalancing its moral certainties) simply by letting more of life in.[37]

For Smith, Forster's strength lies in the fact that he 'suggested there might be some ethical advantage in not always pursuing a perfect and unyielding rationality', and that he 'wanted his people to be in a muddle: his was a study of the emotional, erratic and unreasonable in human life'.[38] The influence of this Forsterian comic muddle on *White Teeth* is clear: from Samad's decision to send one of his twin sons to Bangladesh to remove him from the 'corruption'[39] of English culture in response to his own affair with the twins' teacher Poppy Burt-Jones, to Archie's coin tossing to decide whether or not to commit suicide or later, whether to shoot Dr Perret, or Irie's decision to sleep with both twin brothers Magid and Millat within hours of each other, the novel is full of people who behave in emotional, unreasonable and funny ways. However there has been a critical tendency to overlook the comic form of *White Teeth*, despite the fact that it was the novel's comedy which was arguably responsible for its almost instant popularity: the novel's back cover attests to the fact that Smith's humour was celebrated (and marketed) above all else: reviewers described the novel as 'funny, generous, big-hearted', 'swooping, funny', 'relentlessly funny', 'hilarious', 'extremely funny'.[40] Literary critics have instead focused more on articulating the postcolonial themes of the novel, on Smith's portrayal of race relations in late twentieth-century London and of the inevitable hybridity and cultural mixing which the presence of immigrant populations has brought about.[41] Where the novel's comedy is commented upon, it is interpreted as a tactical strategy through which Smith avoids being overtly political: for Claire Squires the comic deflation which characterizes Smith's portrayals of racism works to show that racism is out of date,[42] while for Susie Thomas, Smith's comic mode more problematically evades painful questions about race and multiculturalism.[43]

Yet Smith's comic style does not consist simply of the whimsical, the light-hearted or even the funny treatment of her subjects, but in emulating a Forsterian 'messy human concoction', Smith is able to present an altogether more complex understanding of race and racism in relation to science. For while the novel explores the racial implications of contemporary genetics through Marcus's science to offer what Ashley Dawson calls a 'timely warning that the history of "race" is by no means over',[44] it does so in a comic mode in which science is subject to the irrational and misguided interpretations of the novel's characters. Smith makes popular misunderstandings about genetics part of the comic fabric of the novel, depicting the ways in which Marcus's genetic ideas infiltrate the thoughts of the other characters, where they become muddled and confused. Alsana's nightmare vision of the 'dissolution, *disappearance*' that the immigrant fears is expressed through her comic misunderstanding of the process of genetic inheritance, her anxieties about the behaviour of her children merging with broader, cultural anxieties about the meaning of genetics:

> Even the unflappable Alsana Iqbal would regularly wake up in a puddle of her own sweat after a night visited by visions of Millat (genetically BB; where B stands for Bengali-ness) marrying someone called Sarah (aa where 'a' stands for Aryan), resulting in a child called Michael (Ba), who in turn marries somebody called Lucy (aa), leaving Alsana with a legacy of unrecognizable great-grandchildren (Aaaaaaa!), their Bengali-ness thoroughly diluted, genotype hidden by phenotype.[45]

Cultural, racial and genetic forms of inheritance become conflated in a kind of reductionism that Roof has identified as characterizing popular understandings of DNA: 'When we imagine genes as agents, they become literal representatives of our bodies, our wills, and our desires. We become our genes and our genes become us, so that we imagine that we, too, somehow survive from generation to generation.'[46] Millat's attempt to shoot Dr Perret at the end of the novel comically becomes a mission determined by his genetic inheritance from his revolutionary great-great-grandfather Mangal Pande; 'his is an imperative secreted in the genes and the cold steel inside his pocket is the answer to a claim made on him long ago. He's a Pandy deep down. And there's mutiny in his blood'.[47] The genes become the ultimate carriers of historical meaning; history is 'made to appear materially in the present, carried with us always … We are what we are because they were who they were.'[48] Patterns of behaviour are repeated from generation to generation, the past lives on in the present, through the genes. Thus Samad's 'sins' – his affair with Poppy – will be passed on to his sons 'stored up in the genes',[49] while the Chalfens comically consider the success of their extended family in terms of the '*good genes* which were so often referred to'.[50] In an analysis of film comedies about science, Roof suggests that 'science comedies take over and amplify cultural beliefs as part of their generic working. Popular misconceptions about science become part of the stuff of the comedy so that comedies are much more symptomatic readings of myth than more "serious," or even fantasy, genres might be'.[51] Such an amplification of cultural belief is evident in the comic misconceptions of genetics presented in *White Teeth*: making science the stuff of comedy and, specifically, the stuff of the comic novel, Smith uncovers the myths about genetics which circulate in contemporary culture.

Yet the novel suggests that science itself is part of the human muddle and mocks the attempts of scientists to extricate themselves from the unreasonable and irrational human behaviour which contributes to such popular misinterpretations of their science. Marcus, explaining his FutureMouse© experiment to Irie, emphasizes the precision, predictability and rationality of his science, everything that the novel's muddled and impassioned characters are not: 'if you *re-engineer* the actual genome, so that *specific* cancers are expressed in *specific* tissues at *predetermined* times in the mouse's development, then you're no longer dealing with the *random*. You're *eliminating* the random actions of a mutagen'.[52] However, no amount of explaining can prevent the public's misunderstanding of his work. Waiting for Magid at the airport Marcus encounters an Asian girl reading his popular science book, whose interpretation of his science, 'where are we going here? Millions of blonds with blue eyes? Mail order babies? I mean, if you're Indian like me you've got something to worry about, yeah?' leaves him bemused;

> It was exhausting just to listen to her. Nowhere in the book did Marcus even touch upon human eugenics – it wasn't his field, and he had no particular interest in it. And yet this girl had managed to read a book almost entirely concerned with the more prosaic developments in recombinant DNA – gene therapy, proteins to dissolve blood clots, the cloning of insulin – and emerge from it full of the usual neo-fascist tabloid fantasies.[53]

What might otherwise be a sympathetic portrait of a scientist struggling to communicate the truth of his science is undermined, however, by the fact that in his desire for a straightforward and rational understanding of his science, a desire reflected in the design brief for the 'white/chrome/pure/plain ... uncontaminated cavity'[54] of the Perret Institute, Marcus has ignored the truth of his science's history; the fact that his work on FutureMouse© is the direct result of the racial scientific research of the Nazis. Dr Perret's photograph hangs on Marcus's wall alongside those of Watson and Crick, and at the launch of FutureMouse© at the Perret Institute, Marcus describes his mentor as 'elemental and inspirational. Not only is he a personal inspiration, but he laid the foundations for so much of this work'.[55] The racial aspects of Perret's science have become obscured in the present, their trace to be found only in small details, in the fact that FutureMouse© is programmed to lose its pigmentation and turn from brown to white, and in the ironically blank yet racialized space of the Perret Institute, which is 'pared down, sterilized, made new every day by a Nigerian cleaning lady with an industrial Hoover and guarded through the night by Mr DeWinter, a Polish nightwatchman'.[56] Science, Smith suggests, cannot exist in an empty, purified space, separate from the complexities and entanglements of its history; it is, unavoidably, part of the popular interpretations the public attribute to it, part of the muddle that the comic novel strives to represent.

It is the scientific approach to race in the novel which exposes precisely the ways in which science can be muddled and unreasonable, as Smith calls attention to the contradictions and inconsistencies in geneticists' comprehension of both race and racism. While Marcus's denial of the significance of race in his work is undermined by history, it is also shown to be dubious given the attitudes towards the Iqbals and the Joneses displayed by the Chalfen family. Irie is sent to the home of Marcus and his wife Joyce by the headmaster of her secondary school Glenard Oak Comprehensive. The headmaster makes Irie part of a 'guinea-pig project', with the aim of 'bringing children of disadvantaged or minority backgrounds into contact with kids who might have something to offer them'.[57] The educated, middle class liberals Joyce and Marcus are the modern-day heirs of the school's colonialist founder, Edmund Glenard, who set up the school as an experimental workhouse for Jamaicans, because 'the natives required instruction, Christian faith and moral guidance'.[58] Indeed scientists Joyce and Marcus, from an extended family characterized by 'the *good genes* which were so often referred to: two scientists, one mathematician, three psychiatrists',[59] have something of the colonialist about them as they interact with Irie and the twins. This is an attitude first hinted at when Smith introduces Joyce through an extract from her book on plants, *The New Flower Power*, which is full of language common to racial science:

> Yes, self-pollination is the simpler and more certain of the two fertilization processes, especially for many species that colonize by copiously repeating the same parental strain. But a species cloning such uniform offspring runs the risk

of having its entire population wiped out by a single evolutionary event ... cross-pollination produces more varied offspring that are better able to cope with a changed environment[60]

The way in which Joyce writes and thinks about her science spills over into her interaction with the teenagers, whom she calls 'brown strangers'.[61] Millat is 'Beautiful', 'gorgeous',[62] 'exotic'[63] and Joyce comically theorizes about the children using a combination of her preconceptions about race and her knowledge of plants; 'Joyce paused and looked at Irie and Millat the way she had looked at her Garter Knight delphinium ... There was a quiet pain in the first one (Irieanthus negressium marcusilia)'.[64] Thinking of herself as someone who is helping the troubled teens, Joyce's interventions only serve to comically highlight her own prejudices and her own, inevitable muddled mixing of scientific ideas with non-scientific ones;

> She had read up on the subject. And it appeared Millat was filled with self-revulsion and hatred of his own kind; that he had possibly a slave mentality, or maybe a colour-complex centred around his mother (he was far darker than she), or a wish for his own annihilation by means of dilution in a white gene pool, or an inability to reconcile two opposing cultures.[65]

Marcus takes a comparable approach, deciding to educate Irie yet continually treating her as an exotic object of sexual fascination; he describes her as a 'big brown goddess' who 'has the most tremendous breasts'.[66]

It is not only the Chalfens who are characterized in this way. The novel is full of white middle-class professionals who largely see themselves as non-racist yet who perpetuate racial stereotypes and racialized ways of thinking which impact people of colour. At the twins' primary school the Parent Teacher Association makes it clear that they have gone out of their way to consider cultural diversity, celebrating 'a variety of religious and secular events; amongst them, Christmas, Ramadan, Chinese New Year, Diwali, Yom Kippur, Hanukkah, the birthday of Haile Selassie, and the death of Martin Luther King',[67] although Smith shows that this has resulted from a fear of being racist as much as anything else. The chairwoman of the PTA, in arguing with Samad, 'wanted to check that it was not her imagination, that she was being unfair or undemocratic, or worse still racist (but she had read *Colour Blind*, a seminal leaflet from the Rainbow Coalition, she had scored well on the self-test) racist in ways that were so deeply ingrained and socially determining that they escaped her attention'.[68] While well-meaning, Smith suggests that such neuroticism about race is ultimately an inadequate way to recognize the impact of racism.

The teachers, like the Chalfens, cannot help but espouse a continual stream of subtle, racial microaggressions: teacher Poppy Burt-Jones who attends the meeting assumes Samad is Indian, compares him to Omar Sharif, his good looks explained because 'they say dark skin wrinkles less'.[69] The novel suggests that racism and racial thinking, rather than having disappeared or been reduced to the preserve of 'a few rotten folks'[70] as post-racialist politics would have it, are endemic and only reproduced when their possibility is denied. This is the social backdrop to Marcus's genetic experiments and it has the important role of highlighting how the cultures in which scientists live and work impact upon their scientific thinking. In a study of the ideology of colourblindness in genomics, sociologist Johnny E. Williams found race to be deeply embedded in scientists' socio-political belief systems because scientists are a part of a society in which everyone is racially socialized.[71] Williams contends, however, that 'the ideology of color blindness as a rhetorical mechanism conveniently enables genomicists to position their research as being beyond the influence of "race" and systemic racism', enabling racial ways of perceiving and interacting with genes to go unacknowledged.[72] In an example which strongly echoes the justifications of the fictional Marcus Chalfen quoted above, Williams cites a scientist who claims 'I'm very much a scientist [who] believes in fact, not opinion. The interpretation is very simple. I know which mutation caused the disease, and the severity of the mutation determines the severity of the disease and how much treatment [I] have to give... As far as I'm concerned, race plays no part in the kind of work I do'.[73] Williams's point is that the scientific removal of the significance of race from genetics comes from a position of (often white) privilege which does not recognize the ways in which racism is deeply ingrained in all parts of society, precisely the point that Smith makes in her portrayal of the Chalfen family. Marcus's denials about the connection of his science to eugenics only produce muddle because he has failed to ask himself Goldberg's question, 'what residues of racist arrangement and subordination – social, economic, cultural, psychological, legal and political – linger unaddressed and repressed in singularly stressing racial demise?'[74] The novel provides an answer, identifying and uncovering the 'residues of racist arrangement' in everyday social interactions which feed into institutions and professions such as science which have placed themselves beyond race. Far from trivializing racism through the novel's comic form, Smith uses that form to demonstrate the pitfalls of removing race from science; namely, the failure to recognize the residues of racial thinking which remain operative when race itself disappears.

The science of fiction

In making scientific rationality and truth the stuff of the comic novel, Smith appears to present what might be deemed a typically literary or deconstructive view of science, the kind of critique to which scientists began to object during the culture wars of the 1990s. Waugh outlines how the questioning of scientific knowledge at the end of the twentieth century led to

> constructivist claims that objectivity and rationality are culturally produced systems, that science cannot arrive at knowledge of a mind-independent natural reality, that its methods are always relative to shifting and heterogeneous theoretical frameworks, and that the 'objects' of scientific knowledge are therefore as 'intentional' as those of a literary text ... In other words, scientific knowledge and language are no more exact than aesthetic knowledge and language.[75]

Smith does not fall into a constructivist trap, but instead satirises the incomprehension of scientists towards literary critiques of their work while self-consciously addressing the status of her own novel as a literary representation of scientific endeavour. Marcus consistently identifies literature as the antithesis of scientific rationality and reason, the Chalfens espousing a traditional belief in 'the truth' which, for them, is the opposite of humanistic study:

> If you were arguing with a Chalfen, trying to put a case for these strange French men who think truth is a function of language, or that history is interpretive and science metaphorical, the Chalfen in question would hear you out quietly, then wave his hand, dismissive, feeling no need to dignify such bunkum with a retort. Truth was truth to a Chalfen.[76]

For Marcus, science and fiction have little to say to each other; 'science and science fiction were like ships in the night, passing each other in the fog';[77] his popular science collaboration with the novelist Surrey T. Banks, which is a 'split level high/low culture book, whereby Marcus wrote a "hard science" chapter on one particular development in genetics and then the novelist wrote a twin chapter exploring these ideas from a futuristic, fictional, what-if-this-led-to-this point of view, and so on for eight chapters each', is motivated purely by 'pecuniary reasons'.[78] Factual, high-culture science is pitted against fiction, which is culturally 'low', as Smith pokes fun at both Marcus's polarized view of the two cultures and her own portrayal of genetics, as the novel itself becomes the target of Marcus's objection to the 'great ocean of idiots, conspiracists, religious lunatics, presumptuous novelists, animal-rights activists, students of politics, and all the other breeds of fundamentalists who professed strange objections to his life's work'.⁷⁹ Perhaps anticipating a criticism of the novel that never actually materialized, Smith acknowledges the limitations of novelists' attempts to represent complex scientific ideas, something of which she was conscious when writing the novel. Christina Patterson, interviewing Smith, reports that Smith 'read one "incredibly boring" book about onco-mice and cancer genes in mice and talked to "a lot of bright friends" in order to write the scientific stuff, but is still, with characteristic modesty, convinced that the science in the book is "incredibly bad"'.⁸⁰

Yet the novel demonstrates that its own literary, comic representation of science has value by showing that, contrary to Marcus's view, science does have similarities with fiction, and that the novel's inevitable representation of partial, plural and multiple truths about science simply reflects the fact that science itself consists of both the truthful and the fictional. Smith thus rejects the idea put forward by Magid when he writes to Marcus, that 'when you delve into the mysteries of inherited characteristics, surely you go straight to the soul of the human condition as dramatically and fundamentally as any poet, except you are armed with something essential the poet does not have: the truth'.⁸¹ Smith would not disagree with Magid's characterization of the literary as being inaccessible to a singular truth: she has written of writers' ability to 'speak simultaneous truths',⁸² and has said that the aim of her writing is 'truth without generalization, without cliché, and without simplification – which is almost impossible. But that's the nice thing about the novel. The aim is way out of everybody's reach, so you keep on writing them just in case'.⁸³ Indeed the status of writing as a source of 'the truth' is questioned everywhere in *White Teeth*: Irie, 'sick of never getting the whole truth',⁸⁴ turns to her grandmother's schoolbooks from Jamaica to try to discover the truth of her heritage, but the colonial books she reads '*Dominica: Hints and Notes to Intending Settlers*' and '*In Sugar Cane Land*' give her a false picture of 'dashing Capt. Durham',⁸⁵ the Englishman who impregnated her great-grandmother Ambrosia Bowden. The history of Glenard Oak School is reconstructed inaccurately through a booklet written by the PTA, who decide to remember the school's founder, Edmund Glenard – the English colonialist who tried to rape Ambrosia – as 'their kindly Victorian benefactor'.⁸⁶ Samad is incensed by the way historians have written of his great-grandfather as a drunkard rather than a revolutionary, 'the truth mutating, bending, receding'.⁸⁷

Smith demonstrates, however, that this might also be a description of Marcus's science, which frequently takes narrative and fictional forms that disrupt any straightforward access it may claim to 'the truth'. Marcus ironically recognizes the slippery nature of narrative as a source of 'the truth' when he dismisses the Iqbals' history, 'a great revolutionary. So I've heard. I wouldn't take any of that seriously, if I were you. One part truth and three parts fiction in that family, I fancy',[88] yet is unable to recognize that his science is also part truth and part fiction. The boundaries between science and fiction are certainly more porous than Marcus is willing to admit: when Irie reads the FutureMouse© press release to a journalist, 'though she had repeated the words many times, they still seemed fantastical, absurd – fiction on the wings of fantasy – with more of a dash of Surrey T. Banks in them'.[89] The communication of science to the public relies on the use of narrative, but this imaginative strain also becomes part of the science itself. Marcus inadvertently hints at this when he contradicts his earlier assertion about science fiction when introducing Dr Perret, whom he describes as 'pushing the envelope, when work in this area was seriously underfunded and looked to remain in the realms of science fiction'.[90] However it is through FutureMouse© itself that his science becomes fiction: the hyperbolic promotion of FutureMouse© means that it becomes, in the public's eyes, a version of the cartoon character Danger Mouse; the mouse is a '*cartoon* of an idea' where 'one expected the damn mouse to stand up and speak by itself'.[91] Roof has argued that 'representations of science render scientific facts less "true" (or more culturally relative) while the figures of their representation become scientifically operative'.[92] This is a paradox which *White Teeth* goes some way to uncovering: the science behind FutureMouse© is elided by the mouse itself, the mouse transformed into a fiction, which then becomes a kind of truth, as the novel ends with FutureMouse© escaping, Danger Mouse style, from its display case at the Perret Institute.

Suggesting points of similarity between Marcus's genetics and the fictional, Smith not only offers a comment on what happens to science in culture, on the biofictional nature of science and the representation of science, but also draws attention to the relationship between the novel itself and the science which it represents. If the comic novel conveys a Forsterian 'messy human concoction'[93] it does so, for Smith, through its portrayal of irrational, messy characters and, in the case of *White Teeth*, the entanglement of those characters with an equally as unreasonable science. However the comic novel is also characterized by its artificial form: writing of Forster's muddled characters, Smith states that 'what interests me is that his narrative structure is muddled also; impulsive, meandering, irrational, which seeming faults lead him on to two further problematics: mawkishness and melodrama'.[94] As I have already touched upon, both Smith and Trilling recognize that Forster's plots, which consist of 'all the old devices of recognition scenes, secrets, letters that prove something, stolen babies, destroyed wills, long-lost brothers, hidden sins, shocking revelations and even physical conflict',[95] tend to melodrama, leaving his writing open to the charge of artificiality. Yet such artificiality of plot is justified, and has value, because it is the novelist's way of examining human nature, 'of making things act so that we can learn about their nature',[96] in the manner of a scientist. Trilling's comparison between scientific experiment and novelistic plot is a means of defending Forster's art but in *White Teeth* it becomes a means for Smith to further interrogate the relationship between science and the (comic) novel. For while Smith considers the ways in which science is like fiction, she also imagines how fiction is like science.

The artificiality and melodrama of the plot of *White Teeth* cannot be disputed. James Wood incredulously summarizes what is arguably the novel's most melodramatic point – its ending – thus, '*White Teeth* ends with a clashing finale, in which all the novel's characters – most of whom are now dispersed between various cults and fanatical religious groups – head towards the press conference which the scientist, Marcus Chalfen, is delivering in London, to announce the successful cloning of his mouse'.[97] The finale connects all of the novel's groups and characters together improbably in the same place, to which Smith adds the shocking revelations, recognition scenes and physical conflict of the Forsterian novel: Archie recognizes Dr Perret as the Dr Sick whom he failed to kill during the war, Samad realizes Archie's lie, Millat tries to shoot Dr Perret and FutureMouse© escapes. The muddle is complete, resolved with further, unresolvable muddle: it is unclear to the authorities which twin is responsible for the shooting, while it is also unclear which is the father of Irie's baby, a plot device too far for Wood; 'near the end of *White Teeth*, one of the characters, Irie Jones, has sex with one of the twins, called Millat; but then rushes round to see the other twin, called Magid, to have sex with him only moments after. She becomes pregnant; and she will never know which twin impregnated her. But it is really Smith's hot plot which has had its way with her'.[98]

However Smith's 'hot plot', like Forster's 'hot melodrama',[99] is more controlled than Wood imagines it to be. Smith self-consciously turns her plot into part of the experiment around which it revolves. In a kind of literalization of Trilling's analogy, Smith imagines the manoeuvring of her characters through plot as a scientific experiment, inviting the reader to recognize the novel as a fiction, as artificially constructed and contrived as Marcus's FutureMouse©. Smith gestures towards this at various points in *White Teeth* where the novel's fictive, constructed nature is made explicit. For example, when Irie is employed by Marcus to organize his filing cabinet and is arranging the letters between Marcus and Magid, she 'split the filing system in two, choosing to file by author primarily, then chronologically, rather than let simple dates rule the roost. Because this was all about people. People making a connection across continents, across seas'.[100] This is how Smith has structured each of the novel's four sections – by character and date, two dates for each section: Archie 1974, 1945; Samad 1984, 1857; Irie 1990, 1907; Magid, Millat and Marcus 1992, 1999. That the novel is organized in the same way as Marcus's filing cabinet is funny, but it also draws attention to the possibility of an experimental exchange between what science does and what the novel does, an idea Smith develops more fully at the novel's end, where she imagines, in the manner of a scientist or social scientist, how people would react to the scene at the Perret Institute. Although initially referring to the imaginary 'focus group' which has chosen the décor of the institute, the people Smith imagines as wanting to know about different strands of the plot become her readers, as Smith reveals how they too have been subject to the novel's experiment:

> and there is surely a demographic pattern to all those who wish to see the eyewitness statements that identified Magid as many times as Millat... And it is young professional women aged eighteen to thirty-two who would like a snapshot seven years hence of Irie, Joshua and Hortense sitting by a Caribbean sea... And it could be that it is largely the criminal class and the elderly who find themselves wanting to make bets on the winner of a blackjack game... It would make an interesting survey (what kind would be your decision) to examine the present and divide the onlookers into two groups: those whose eyes fell upon a bleeding man, slumped across a table, and those who watched the getaway of a small brown rebel mouse.[101]

The Perret Institute is transformed into a kind of laboratory in which, as with the design and engineering of FutureMouse©, there is 'no question about who was pulling the strings':[102] Smith has, like a scientist in the lab, engineered the scene to see what results she gets, creating 'an artificiality which sets us up for an experience of the world'.[103]

The 'scientific' aspects of Smith's plot are also evident in the novel's emphasis on cause and effect. Marcus demonstrates complete mastery over FutureMouse© by being able to determine how and when the mouse will die; he creates 'mice who year after year expressed more and more eloquently Marcus's designs... planting instructions and imperatives in the germ line to be realized in physical characteristics. Creating mice whose very bodies did exactly what Marcus told them'.[104] His science is characterized by examining the consequences of actions in time, as he explains to Irie, looking at photos of the mouse with a progressively bigger tumour in each picture, 'what you really want to know is how a tumour progresses in *living tissue*',[105] 'I plant a cancer and a cancer turns up precisely when I expect it'.[106] Marcus's science is based on predictability and precision, on being able to determine exactly how a tumour will progress in time, a precision which, I have shown, the novel undermines in its emphasis on the unpredictable and the irrational. Yet it is such causality which gives structure to the novel's melodramatic plot. For Trilling, the Forsterian plot 'represents the novelist's interest in causality' and 'because it is concerned not only with states of being, but with consequences, gives the greatest reality to social forces'.[107] Smith accords a similar importance to causality, writing that 'it seems that if you put people on paper and move them through time, you cannot help but talk about ethics, because the ethical realm exists nowhere if not here: in the consequences of human actions as they unfold in time, and the multiple interpretive possibility of those actions. Narrative itself is the performance of that very procedure'.[108]

The plot of *White Teeth*, like Marcus's FutureMouse©, consists of the consequences of actions as they unfold through time: Archie, having saved Dr Sick during the Second World War, is not only destined to save him once again at the Perret Institute but his actions enable the rest of the plot to unfold in the existence of Marcus, his science and the relationship between Archie's daughter, Irie, and the Chalfen family. The consequences of Archie's coin flipping resonate throughout the novel, his predictable fate underscored by the repeated mantra that 'every moment happens twice: inside and outside, and they are two different histories'.[109] The uncertainty of repetition, the possibility of difference in the predictably repeated which this phrase encapsulates, is what makes the novel different to Marcus's science: Marcus's concern to 'eliminate the random'[110] allows no room for chance, whereas Smith recognizes, as Alsana does when she understands that Magid (having been sent to Bangladesh) is more English than Millat, that 'you can't plan everything'.[111] An element of chance must also be factored into the plot, hence the escape of FutureMouse© at the end of the novel, and the fact that Archie's decisions rest on the toss of a coin. Trilling writes that 'one thing to say is that certain kinds of unmotivated events in fiction represent what happens in life. Life is not only a matter of logic and motivation but of chance. The storyteller may –perhaps should – suggest this element of life'.[112] *White Teeth* celebrates chance, placing it in opposition to Marcus's scientific rationalism, but at the same time Smith self-consciously demonstrates that such chance is part of the artificial and constructed nature of the novel's plot and is, in this sense, comparable to the artificial experiments of the scientist (Marcus) in the laboratory.

Narrativizing the genetics of race

In articulating the ways in which the novelist's engineering of plot is comparable to a scientist's engineering of a mouse, Smith moves beyond a defence of melodrama, beyond Trilling's analogy, to consider what fictional writing about science entails, which, the novel suggests, is a degree of reciprocity: in uncovering the narrative aspects of genetics as part of her wider critique of science's claims to rationalism, objectivity and neutrality, the novelist must also reflect upon her own claims to represent human messiness, the irrational, unreasonable and uncertain. Smith demonstrates that the fictional representation of the messy human concoction requires a degree of artificiality and, by making the novel's fictive, constructed nature explicit, reminds readers that what the novel does is only another form of what science does – both are practices which artificially test and experiment with (human) nature. Reflecting on the stories told by science through an examination of its own forms of storytelling, *White Teeth* demonstrates that the contemporary novel can do more than simply explore the science of race in the manner of Marcus's collaborator Surrey T. Banks, 'from a futuristic, fictional, what-if-this-led-to-this point of view'.[113] It does examine the claims, forms of representation and cultural reception of contemporary genetics, but also thinks through its own relationship to the science which it represents, thus throwing into doubt Dominic Head's claim that

> the dominant transnational forces of globalization are promoted through developments in science and technology, and this has become an area of human experience that is especially difficult for the novel to register. To engage with rapid technological change, an instantaneous response is demanded, and this is beyond the capabilities of a literary form that is, rather, cumulative in its procedures of reflection and commentary.[114]

White Teeth not only registers the rapid developments which led to the completion of the human genome sequence in the year of its publication, exploring the impact of the public prominence of genetics on conceptions of race, but Smith demonstrates that the novel's form, far from being the cumulative commentary to science's rapidity, is a reflexive form with the capacity to suggest points of confluence between science and fiction, shedding light on both practices at the beginning of the twenty-first century.

White Teeth suggests that we might approach the racial pronouncements of the HGP differently, viewing what was promoted as a definitive, anti-racist statement on the non-biological nature of race as anything but definitive.

Indeed, as the following chapter will investigate, the findings of the HGP did not put a stop to the use of racial categorization in genetics, which has, if anything, increased in a number of strands of genetic investigation since the mapping of the genome. *White Teeth* exposes the inconsistencies around race in science in the twenty-first century by demonstrating how such uncertainties inevitably arise from the narrative exposition and transmission of science combined with a politics of colourblindness which have together worked to obscure experiences of racism. If, as Roof writes, 'genetic sameness' is being acknowledged by science 'at the very moment conservative factions pressure for the end of programs that help disadvantaged citizens',[115] then Smith suggests that understanding such pronouncements as scientific stories is one way of beginning to unpick the assumed anti-racist tenor of contemporary science which often ironically enables, rather than forecloses, the possibility of socio-political racisms.

4

'The Sick Swollen Heart of This Land': Pharmacogenomics, Racial Medicine and Colson Whitehead's *Apex Hides the Hurt*

In the summer of 2015, a worldwide media storm erupted after the parents of Rachel Dolezal, a civil rights activist and Professor of Africana Studies in Washington State in the United States, gave an interview in which they claimed that their daughter had been posing as a black woman when she was in fact white. Wearing tanning lotion and afro hair weaves, Dolezal had presented as black to her colleagues, students and fellow officers at her local chapter of the National Association for the Advancement of Colored People, of which she was president. Following a television interview in which she was asked whether she was African American, Dolezal appeared on NBC news and confirmed that she identified as black and with 'the black experience'.[1] The case garnered international attention as commentators and critics argued over whether choosing a race was something that it was ethical, or indeed possible, to do. A minority supported Dolezal as a 'transracial' woman who had proved that race is ultimately a fiction, but most condemned her as participating in a form of black-face, pointing to the fact that the idea of being transracial and the ability to choose a racial identity are options only really open to white people. Among the many debates and discussions about Dolezal which occurred across various fora, a meme appeared which pictured Dolezal with the caption 'But doc we black people need Bidil'.

Designed as a humorous comment on the case, the meme references a drug, BiDil, which was approved by the US Food and Drug Administration (FDA) in 2004 for the treatment of congestive heart failure exclusively in the African American population. The invention of the first-ever racially targeted drug (a combination of two pre-existing heart failure drugs isosorbide dinitrate and hydralazine) was reported widely in the media upon its approval, but the drug failed to gain widespread acceptance in the medical community in large part due to the controversy which surrounded its development. Based on a contested

Figure 2 Rachel Dolezal Meme. Anonymous, http://www.quickmeme.com/p/3w42zi.

statistic that heart failure rates were twice as high in black people as in white, the drug's developers located the cause of this disparity in biology, rather than taking account of what an editorial in *Nature Biotechnology* called the 'host of factors, including genetics, diet and lifestyle, social discrimination, economic inequality and even geographic location'[2] that a greater part of the medical community recognized as the cause of health inequities between black and white populations. While only a few years earlier the HGP had asserted that race had no genetic meaning, BiDil seemed to affirm the opposite; that race was in fact a medically verified genetic reality. Indeed, its appearance in the Dolezal meme ten years after its approval reveals not only widespread public knowledge of the drug, but a public understanding of race as a genetic and medical fact. The joke of the meme works through appealing to the 'common sense' of its viewer, who knows that BiDil is a drug only for African Americans and therefore not one that Dolezal could possibly take: her blackness is not real because it is not biological and so her identification as black is revealed to be not only a sham, but a potential danger to her own health. Anyone can look black, the meme suggests, but race is really an internal property, something which cannot necessarily be seen and, therefore, claimed by anybody, even if the social conditions were to be such that a white person might want to become black.

It is therefore somewhat ironic that it was in fact self-identification with a race which lay at the heart of the method used to develop BiDil. The original study, which re-examined data from existing clinical studies, was based on patients 'self-identified as black (defined as of African descent)'.[3] An earlier linked study on the methodology of the BiDil trial noted that 'although ethnicity may not be accurately determined or have a true biologic basis, identifying patients by ethnicity does select a group of individuals who have some characteristics in common'.[4] The researchers identified 'African-American ethnicity by patient self-identification' because this was 'the method used in other studies in which the impact of ethnicity was analyzed'.[5] BiDil thus emerged from a medical understanding of race not as biological essence, but as a proxy for unknown genetic markers which, its proponents argued, were clustered in self-identified black populations but might well also be found in white populations. Until researchers could 'identify genotypic and phenotypic characteristics that would transcend racial or ethnic categories',[6] BiDil, it was argued, should be prescribed on the basis that 'the drug is saving lives in a large and clearly identifiable black population'.[7] The pitfalls of using such a loose and ultimately 'unscientific' methodology have been well-documented. A 2003 study found that prospective patients of race-based medicine do not have complete knowledge of their ancestry and that 'the ability to identify one's geographic ancestry in a way that rules out recent admixture and provides a homogeneous background for drug prescription or diagnosis is not reliable with a proportion of the population that is large enough to be of relevance in designing medical policy'.[8] As Jonathan Kahn contends, the relationship between skin colour or physical appearance and genetic ancestry is unstable, and while self-reporting – a fundamentally subjective social practice – may capture valuable social variables that affect health, it is something which changes over time as people age and may fail to capture significant variation in biological ancestry.[9] Dolezal's identification as black is a case in point.

The Dolezal meme looks different in this light: what was no doubt intended as an off-the-cuff joke about race reveals a chasm between the public understanding of BiDil and the scientific reasoning upon which its development was based. Dolezal could, in fact, be a viable candidate for BiDil because there was no genetic basis for the drug. Despite being presented as a 'path-breaking example of the coming age of pharmacogenomics … [BiDil] is not a pharmacogenomic drug', Kahn notes, as 'the mechanism of action by which it appears to have a beneficial effect on heart failure patients is unknown'.[10] Far from being based on specific genetic markers, which might correlate to a particular racial group, there were no definitive biological traits that BiDil could be linked to. Yet the public's (mis)understanding that BiDil is based on a genetic understanding of race is unsurprising, given that the original acknowledgement by the drug's developers – that race does not have a true biologic basis – was largely erased once BiDil was approved by the FDA. Instead, the connection between race and genetics was, as Sarah Blacker has argued, 'taken up in the social world untranslated'.[11] This lack of translation was something of a deliberate strategy on the part of NitroMed, the pharmaceutical company which developed BiDil, because their marketing of the drug relied on obscuring the complexities and ultimately incoherence of race in pharmacogenetics in favour of a narrative which represented racial health inequalities as what Blacker describes as 'naturalized biological categories that are understood as inevitable'.[12] Kahn has shown in detail how BiDil was transformed from a drug presented as suitable for patients of all races (which failed to gain the approval of the FDA because the statistics on which it was based did not meet FDA standards) into a black drug because 'race continues to have a commercial value in differentiating products in a crowded biomedical marketplace' and 'racial identity itself is becoming a patentable commodity'.[13] Locating BiDil as part of a wider revolution in personalized medicine, NitroMed harnessed the support of black organizations including the Association of Black Cardiologists and the NAACP, to target African Americans and present the drug as a means of empowering a community historically exploited and left behind by medicine.[14] Celebrated in trade magazines as a racially targeted marketing success story,[15] this marketing strategy presented BiDil as an anti-racist invention, a drug which gave black patients power, and, as was argued at the FDA meeting at which it was approved, a drug which could act as a sign of the American government's intention to right racial wrongs.[16] This anti-racist framing made some scientists uneasy; it was argued that the drug represented 'the primacy of political correctness over science' and that the FDA might have 'felt it should take the path of affirmative ethnic drug approval in the face of political pressure'.[17] Yet BiDil's advocates used similar reasoning to defend it: for Jay Cohn, one of the lead medical researchers involved in the study, opponents of the drug who objected to it on the basis that it re-inscribed race as biological were using 'political correctness' to deprive black patients of effective therapy.[18] As in the case of the HGDP, those advocating for a racialized understanding of genetics through BiDil invoked anti-racist reasoning to support their views, leading to a degree of public acceptance and support for the drug which could be used for commercial ends.

However BiDil was a commercial failure: costing seven times more than the two generic drugs of which it consisted, medical insurance companies were reluctant to pay for it while many doctors remained unconvinced about the rationale and motivations behind it.[19] NitroMed, in focusing its marketing on winning over black patients and communities, also failed to recognize that doctors might not listen to their black patients in the same way as they did their white patients.[20] Yet despite its lack of commercial success, which eventually caused NitroMed to fold (NitroMed ceased operations in 2011, selling BiDil to Arbor pharmaceuticals through which the drug is still available as of May 2019), BiDil left a significant legacy. It legitimized the use of racial categories in medicine and the idea that specific genetic markers could be linked to particular races, while simultaneously underscoring how fragile, unstable and incoherent race becomes in that context where it is accepted and worked with even though there were no justifiable medical or scientific grounds for doing so. In some ways the attempt to racialize heart disease that BiDil represented was not new. As Anne Pollock has shown, racial thinking had been present in cardiology since the discipline's founding, and the idea of race itself has been shaped by medical practice across a long period of time.[21] Another recent study of race in medicine, Lundy Braun's *Breathing Race into the Machine*, has demonstrated how, in the case of lung capacity, the idea of racial difference became embedded in the machinery used to measure lung function, with predictably negative results for the health of black populations.[22] What distinguished BiDil, however, was its branding. BiDil not only suggested that there was an association between race and genetic difference but branded race itself as the condition to be treated, and made race the disease; as drug companies began to strategically brand certain medical conditions, in the case of BiDil, race itself became a condition to be addressed through targeted intervention and advertising.[23]

Colson Whitehead's 2006 novel *Apex Hides the Hurt* satirizes the racialization of medicine in the United States as it explores the consequences for African Americans of the conflation of business interests and medical science in the name of racial justice. The novel's protagonist is an unnamed African American man who works as a nomenclature consultant – his job is to name or to re-brand commercial products, anything from drugs developed in the pharmaceutical business to children's toys, a job he does very successfully, winning many awards. His crowning achievement is the name he gives to a new range of bandages – Apex – which have been designed in a range of colours to match the skin-tone of their wearers, marketed with the tagline 'Apex Hides the Hurt'.[24] Increasingly disillusioned with his profession, the protagonist stubs his toe in his apartment, and uses one of the plasters he has named, obscuring his wound which continues to fester due to repeated and unexplained toe stubbings and which eventually develops into a serious infection after he steps in some mud near a pig farm on an away day with his colleagues. Unaware of its seriousness due to the Apex, he eventually collapses and is forced to have his toe amputated in hospital. The novel's narrative moves between the before and after of the amputation. After a long and lonely convalescence, the protagonist agrees to take on a new job, the renaming of a small town, to which he travels in order to talk to its residents and to determine what it should be called.

Whitehead's novel is about the creation of meaning through naming, the power that naming wields, and *Apex Hides the Hurt* explores how things from commercial products, to towns, to people themselves are variously made to signify in relation to the names they are given. Whitehead has said that the inspiration for the novel came from his reading of an article in the mid-1990s in the *New York Times* about the naming of Prozac and the profession of pharmaceutical naming,[25] and has also stated that the novel is about 'certain forms of multicultural cheerleading [which] are as susceptible to corruption as capitalist boosterism and frontier idealism, two other systems I talk about in *Apex*'.[26] This chapter argues that *Apex Hides the Hurt* examines the commercialization both of medicine and of multiculturalism through the novel's imaginary medical aid Apex, the marketing of which relies on the fact that, as in the case of BiDil, the meaning of race and racial identity is nebulous, and the many ways it signifies can be employed to create an aura of certainty and legitimacy where none exists. What Whitehead demonstrates is that where once race was widely held to be grounded in biology, new developments in genetics (most prominently the Human Genome Project), which have asserted that race is not genetic, mean that race must now be signified through language, and this is something that medical science and its marketing rely upon. The novel explores how race is, as Stuart Hall theorized, a floating signifier, and its lack of a fixed signified, the inability for it to be grounded in genetics (as was demonstrated in the case of BiDil), means that it is language, in particular naming, which becomes the primary mode through which racial meaning can be created and exploited.

Making naming the new 'science' of race, the novel works as a kind of allegory about racial medicines such as BiDil, as it considers what happens when people are encouraged by medical science to self-identify with something which has no clear or comprehensible meaning, with a proxy for the unknown which is, in essence, biofictional – race. Buying into the racial identities signified by the words and images of medical marketing results, in the novel, not in better health but in illness; race literally becomes the disease in *Apex* as the protagonist's mysterious physical and mental illness manifest as a response to his gradual realization that his blackness has been leeched of any meaningful significance by the world of commerce. Recovery from his illness is only possible by restoring the links between race, racism and American history, by acknowledging the historical origins of names and language and their power to signify in the present. While this process of restoration is most overtly carried out in the protagonist's investigations into the black history of Winthrop, the town he is sent to rename, this chapter explores how Whitehead also suggests that a comparable form of historical recovery might also be necessary in medicine. The protagonist's illness bears striking resemblance to the imaginary disease Drapetomania which was hypothesized by doctor and racial scientist Samuel Cartwright in 1851. The novel Signifies, in the tradition of African American writing as theorized by Henry Louis Gates, on this earlier racial science, intertextually evoking and revising Cartwright's theory as it links that theory to modern racial medicine. In this way Whitehead satirizes the purportedly anti-racist import of medicines such as BiDil, but also underscores how pharmacogenetics' reliance on language and linguistic signification to make race mean has a precedent in the overtly fictional ways in which race was made disease in the racist medicine of the era of chattel slavery. By invoking Cartwright's ludicrous Drapetomania hypothesis, Whitehead not only parodies white scientific racism, through the tradition of black Signification, but foregrounds the long history of the biofictional constructions of race which have shaped, and continue to shape, the public understanding of blackness.

The science of marketing race

The marketing, operation and effects of Apex, the 'multicultural bandage'[27] that is named by the protagonist of *Apex Hides the Hurt*, bear many resemblances to BiDil. Invented by a pharmaceutical company wanting to sell more bandages, Apex, like BiDil, re-purposes an existing treatment by racializing it in such a way as to make race a matter of consumer choice: 'The boxes didn't say Sri

Lankan, Latino, or Viking. The packages spoke for themselves. The people chose themselves and in that way perhaps he had named a mirror. In pharmacies you started to see *that motion* – folks placing their hands against the box to see if the shade in the little window matched their skin.'[28] Invoking racial difference without explicitly naming it, Apex capitalizes on social understandings of race as it encourages people to essentially choose their own medicine on the basis of how they self-identify – exactly the move encouraged by the makers of BiDil. Such self-identification is encouraged through a marketing campaign which is targeted at particular racial communities; 'at Oglivy and Myrtle they knew the neighborhoods ... They knew the colors of clientele and zip codes and could ship boxes accordingly.'[29] The marketing campaign cynically situates Apex as a force for social good, its invention framed as a step towards inclusivity and diversity, as Whitehead comically shows how the language and imagery of multiculturalism come to be used for corporate ends; 'in the advertising, multicultural children skinned knees, revealing the blood underneath, the commonality of wound, they were all brothers now, and multicultural bandages were affixed to red boo-boos. United in polychromic harmony, in injury, with our individual differences respected, eventually all healed beneath Apex.'[30] Racial difference becomes a branded, corporatized story to be told as a way of personalizing medicine while maintaining a broad, commercial appeal. Apex is a product which everyone, from people in 'poor countries' to 'school nurses of integrated elementaries' can use so not, as the protagonist puts it using his typical wordplay, to add 'insult to injury.'[31] While Apex makes clear that the pink flesh tones of standard plasters reflect a medical system which by default caters to whiteness, the solution it creates is not one interested in addressing inherent racisms or inequalities within medicine. Rather, just as the social and environmental causes of heart failure and differential rates thereof between white and black populations were overlooked by those emphasizing genetic difference through the promotion of BiDil, the advertising of Apex decontextualizes pain and makes it a universal experience, something processed by everyone in the same way despite the racial difference for which it also caters. This is ultimately a move which fails to address the causes of pain and illness, instead covering them over, hiding, rather than confronting, the hurt: 'the deep psychic wounds of history and the more recent gashes ripped by the present, all of these could be covered by this wonderful, unnamed multicultural adhesive bandage. It erased. Huzzah.'[32]

While the protagonist's firm works on behalf of pharmaceutical companies, there is no discussion of medical science in the novel as Whitehead suggests that medicine and marketing have become one and the same, medical science subsumed by, if not indistinguishable from, the marketing strategies of the drug companies which often fund it. In the world of the novel it is marketing which is now scientific, and the protagonist understands his job in scientific terms: describing how 'he came up with the names' on the first page of the novel, we are told that 'he exposed them to high temperatures for extended periods of time. Sometimes consonants broke off and left angry vowels on the laboratory tables. How else was he to know if they were ready for what the world had in store for them?'[33] The scientific method which matters is not that which creates the product itself but the method by which it is named. When names go wrong and start to lose their intended significations, 'it was time for the neologists to return to their laboratories',[34] and after he becomes ill and is no longer able to work, 'he had this suspicion that all he had inside himself now were Frankenstein names, lumbering creatures stitched together from glottal stops and sibilants, angry unspellable misfits suitable only for the monstrous. Names that were now his kin'.[35] Like Frankenstein, he takes little responsibility for releasing 'the logos, his former charges'[36] into the world; naming and marketing are not enterprises concerned with human consequences, something underscored by the colonial imagery in which the protagonist also conceives of himself and his 'science'. He imagines his inspiration to come from 'his interior' composed of 'rocks and mountain ranges ... strange flora, saplings that curtsied eccentrically, low shrubs that extended bizarre fronds', 'a territory within himself' from which 'he would bring back specimens to the old world. These most excellent dispatches. His names'.[37] The invention of Apex is 'a terrain so far uncharted. Pith helmets necessary'.[38] Multinational commerce and to a degree medicine, Whitehead suggests, are neo-colonial in so far as their promise of anti-racist liberation is simply a meaning created by the marketing of products which ironically reproduce the very things they disavow. Yet the protagonist can think of his work in these terms, apparently without any irony, precisely because his job is to control the meanings of imagery and phrases so that they only signify in particular, ahistorical and ultimately superficial ways.

For the protagonist's science is semiotics, 'the science of communication studied through the interpretation of signs and symbols as they operate in various fields, esp. language'.[39] His job is to manipulate the meaning of signs by coming up with signifiers (names like Apex) which can be attached to referents (in the case of Apex, multi-coloured plasters) to create signifieds which go beyond the denotive: Apex does not simply signify a particular kind of plaster, but a benign form of multiculturalism and celebration of diversity, a connotation which is used to sell the product.[40] As he explains to a man he meets in a bar,

'I name things like new cars and toothbrushes and stuff like that so that they sound catchy. You have some kind of insurance policy to reassure people or make them less depressed so they can accept the world. Well you need a reassuring name that will make them believe in the insurance policy'.[41] The names he gives must signify the objects or products themselves but also a particular feeling; the actual meaning of words is less important than how they sound, the associations they convey and the emotions they provoke. Pondering on the name 'New Prospera' that has been suggested by his old firm as the new name for the town he is tasked with naming, the protagonist thinks that Prospera 'Had that romance-language armature, he was pretty sure it was a Spanish or Italian word for something. What it meant in those languages was unimportant; what was important was how it resonated here. The lilting *a* at the end like a rung up to wealth and affluence, take a step. A glamorous Old World cape draped over the bony shoulders of prosaic *prosperity*'.[42] While the relationship between the names and their objects is very clearly arbitrary in a Saussurean sense – the name Apex and bandages have no intrinsic relationship to each other – at the same time the protagonist recognizes that once established as signs the signifier/signified relation has long-lasting cultural power and significance; 'some might say a rose by any other name but he didn't go in for that kind of crap … A rose by any other name would wilt fast, smell like bitter almonds, God help you if the thorns broke the skin'.[43]

Whitehead's novel suggests that semiotics is not only responsible for the commercial success of medicines but that, in the case of Apex (and following from this BiDil), language is integral to the way race functions and signifies in medicine itself. Whitehead's protagonist exploits but also grapples with the fact that race is, in Stuart Hall's terms, a 'floating signifier', a term which has no fixed or definitive signified. Noting how biological definitions of race have been debunked, and how black is not a genetic category, Hall explains that these associations nevertheless remain because

> *race works like a language.* And signifiers refer to the systems and concepts of the classification of a culture to its making meaning practices. And those things gain their meaning, not because of what they contain in their essence, but in the shifting relations of difference, which they establish with other concepts and ideas in a signifying field. Their meaning, because it is relational, and not essential, can never be finally fixed, but is subject to the constant process of redefinition and appropriation. To the losing of old meanings, and the appropriation and collection on contracting new ones, to the endless process of being constantly re-signified, made to mean something different in different cultures, in different historical formations, at different moments of time.[44]

There is nothing fixed that is signified by the signifier 'race' with the result that the meaning of race is always slippery, shifting and changing; race 'cannot be secured in its meaning', which is what, traditionally, science has attempted to achieve. For Hall, understanding race as operating primarily like a language is the opposite of a scientific, physiological understanding of race – 'to say that race is a discursive category recognizes that all attempts to ground this concept scientifically, to locate differences between the races, on what one might call scientific, biological, or genetic grounds, have been largely shown to be untenable'.[45] Yet what Whitehead suggests is that, ironically, it is an understanding of race as floating signifier (rather than as biologically grounded reality) which is now being utilized in the interlinked development and promotion of racial medicine. Tacitly recognizing the pitfalls – social, political and scientific – of explicitly claiming race as genetic, Apex exploits the lack of a concrete signified for race by invoking the ideas associated with and clustered around it; mainly bodily and physical appearance, in particular skin colour, but also difference, diversity, identity, biology and language. The result is that 'it was hard to argue against the utility of an adhesive bandage and in those early days of Apex, he, like many citizens, found it near impossible to contradict the reasoning of the multicultural bandage'.[46] Its reasoning cannot be contradicted because there is nothing definitive or fixed against which it can be measured or judged; always being re-signified and made to mean something different, Apex ironically capitalizes on race's lack of concrete biological grounding by making race a floating signifier.

The protagonist slowly begins to recognize that not only is race a floating signifier, but that it is a signifier which itself takes many forms and has gone through many iterations precisely because its signified is not fixed. He begins to understand that the names he gives to things obscure more than they reveal, a revelation which crystalizes around the idea of what Apex does, 'a name that got to the heart of the thing – that would be miraculous. But he never got to the heart of the thing, he just slapped a bandage on it to keep the pus in'.[47] This is the work of racial categorization: it attempts to name and identify people but can only ever do so in crude and ultimately harmful ways because identity cannot be contained or defined by a signifier that has no definitive signified. As he digs deeper into the history of Winthrop, the shifting nature of racial signifiers themselves is brought directly into view:

> Colored. The sliver of himself still in tune with marketing shivered each time Gertrude used the word colored. He kept stubbing his toe on it. As it were. Colored, Negro, Afro-American, African American. She was a few iterations

behind the times. Not that you could keep up, anyway. Every couple of years someone came up with something that got us an inch closer to the truth. Bit by bit we crept along. As if that thing we believed to be approaching actually existed.[48]

These attempts to name something that does not really exist – racial difference – underscore the linguistic, rather than biological, ways in which race is brought into being, and thus ultimately the fictional nature of the concept of race itself. The novel suggests that racial marketing exploits this, with the result that medicine comes to be more reliant on language and signification to establish racial meaning, than on genetics. This was certainly the case with BiDil where, having acknowledged there to be no genetic basis for race, the drug's developers then utilized the slipperiness of signifier and signified to obscure the fact: the language of the patent for BiDil used the terms 'black' and 'African American' interchangeably,[49] and its reliance on self-identification operated as a 'fig leaf that covers a broad array of implicitly biologized conceptions of race'.[50] *Apex Hides the Hurt* suggests that recognizing the raced body as, in Hall's terms, a schema composed of stories, anecdotes, metaphors and images, rather than as defined and determined by biology,[51] has material, physiological effects. For the protagonist of the novel, looking 'behind false names, beneath the skin we gave them', behind skin colour and appearance in the case of the marketing of race (which reveals that race cannot be biologically grounded), results in a malaise that cannot easily be cured.

Signifyin(g) science: Historicizing race as illness

The protagonist's gradual realization that he has been involved in medicalizing and commercializing race as an identity which has no clear or definitive meaning makes him physically and mentally ill. His illness is seemingly mysterious, having no obvious or given cause; 'one day he stubbed his toe. In retrospect there was some inevitability tied up in said stubbing, so he came to believe that his toe wanted to be stubbed for reasons that were unknowable. Unnameable'.[52] From the initial wound, the protagonist continues to hurt himself; 'the toe had been strangely magnetized by injury so that whenever there was something in the vicinity with stubbing polarity, his toe was immediately drawn to it',[53] in what appears as a case of self-harm, something which he acknowledges only by detaching himself from that part of his body; 'he decided his toe had developed an abuse pathology, and kept returning to the hurt as if one day it would place the pain in context'.[54] After ignoring the injury he becomes 'weak and feverish',[55] coughing, shuddering and panting until he collapses and is taken to hospital to have the toe amputated. Yet this does not cure his illness; once out of hospital 'his foot throbbed in phantom pain' and he is left with a limp and 'it had been brought to his attention that his limp was psychosomatic'.[56]

His self-inflicted toe injury partly represents an underlying desire to feel something in the emotionless, atomized life he leads – an individualized existence which is the result of his adherence to the ideals of the marketing business which instrumentalizes emotion for commercial ends. The protagonist has no real identity; not only does he have no name, but little information is given about his past or family life, other than the fact that he attended an Ivy League university called Quincy. Instead, the beginning of his story is a kind of blankness; 'he had no purpose, he had no vocation. He had a job, which he lost, and so he answered the ad in the paper'.[57] This matter-of-fact tone is the product of a personality that is emotionally detached: he cannot feel his own emotions and denies them, or only sees them through the lens of marketing; 'he hadn't met that special someone but he went out a lot, made reservations at approved restaurants. Occasionally he extended a hand across the table to spark a soulful gaze. Friends of his set him up with their sisters. He had a kind of vibe he projected. Wage earning. Self-actualizing. Nice catch'.[58] The protagonist takes his boss's description of him 'you *are* the product'[59] to heart. His concern lies more with perception than with true feeling; 'when it came to gifts, it was the appearance of thought that counts',[60] in a world where he sees everything as sellable; just before his toe becomes infected as he walks in the countryside, 'for a few minutes he allowed himself to be swayed by the sales pitch of nature'.[61] His saturation in marketing means that his whole sense of self is hollow if not non-existent, and his illness emerges as a response to the branding of self – symbolized by his use of Apex which while purportedly covering hurt (through personalized branding) ultimately causes him more pain by allowing his wound to fester.

Yet Whitehead makes clear that the illness is primarily a manifestation of a racial identity crisis brought about not only by the lack of any definitive signified for race, but by the detachment of race from racism, of identity from history and of language from context, detachments that the world of marketing has encouraged and promoted. The depersonalization that results in his toe stubbing is caused by the repression and denial of black history, a history which is present but ignored in the language that he manipulates. From the '*Hey* and *Hey, man*'[62] that he and his white colleagues greet each other with, to his blasé approach to working with them 'no skin off his back',[63] the protagonist ironically ignores the original signifieds of the language and phrases he uses. Once he arrives in Winthrop, however, the racial and racist associations of language become harder to ignore as he slowly begins to uncover the town's history. Originally founded by two freed slaves, the town's original name, Freedom, is changed soon after to that of the white, barbed-wire mogul Winthrop, who decides to settle there. Its present difficulties have arisen as Lucky Aberdeen, a millionaire software developer originally from the town, wants to change its name to New Prospera, but is opposed by the Winthrop family and the town's mayor Regina Goode, who is descended from one of the freed slave men and wants to revert to the name Freedom. The protagonist initially adopts his old way of thinking as he favours New Prospera, a name without historical or contextual significance, rejecting the name Freedom because he considers it 'so defiantly unimaginative as to approach a kind of moral weakness'.[64]

Yet a momentary loss of balance which causes him to fall over forces him to reconsider, and he begins to understand how language signifies race and racialized history in ways which continue to determine relationships in the present. The newspaper reporter who interviews him about what he intends to call the town signifies the protagonist's blackness with the headline 'CONSULTANT VOWS TO "KEEP IT REAL"',[65] while Lucky asks his advice about a name for his new business venture without any apparent irony, 'Do you think Charred and Feathered would be a good name for a chicken joint?'[66] Lucky can only ask such a question because the violence of America's history of black enslavement has been all but erased by earlier forms of marketing. The Winthrop family, having made their fortune in barbed wire, fear the loss of the town's Winthrop name to the software millionaire, as the town is flooded with corporate chain stores, the Winthrop library becoming an Outfit Outlet clothing store, and the international food franchise the Admiral competing with the bar of the Winthrop hotel. Yet Whitehead suggests that these corporate brands are simply the modern-day heirs of the likes of Winthrop, which has operated much like a corporation, the library holding the official, heavily biased history of the town commissioned by the Winthrop family, while the hotel is run by a black couple who are directly descended from the town's first inhabitants and who only have two days off a year. A name that appears to represent tradition is in fact a cover for historic racial violence; 'maybe there were some Indians or something' Albie Winthrop muses, considering the origins of the town, 'but they didn't have a road'.[67] The protagonist comes to identify with the position of the freed slaves Goode and Field who founded the town (and whose names it is clear were not freely chosen) who understood that 'to give yourself a name is power. They will try to give you a name and tell you who you are and try to make you into something else, and that is slavery'.⁶⁸ In ceding the power of naming to commerce, the protagonist has done willingly what Field and Goode were forced by Winthrop to do – give up an identity formed through self-determinism and self-naming, in favour of being named in a way which erases experience and history.

The treatment for the protagonist's illness is thus not a cheap bandage but a reckoning with language, and with the power of the naming, word-play, puns and double entendres that have characterized his sense of self. While the protagonist can only begin to recover from his illness by recovering the original significations of names and of language, by connecting his experience to that of former slaves Goode and Field, Whitehead also models an alternative mode of signification through which the linguistic and ultimately fictional forms of racialization – in particular that which is evident in contemporary racialized medicine – are brought to the fore. *Apex Hides the Hurt* Signifies in the tradition of African American writing as described by Henry Louis Gates in *The Signifying Monkey*. Gates defined Signifyin(g) as a trope and sign of the Afro-American tradition, a form of double-voiced discourse characterized by 'the open-endedness of figurative language, rather than its single-minded closure'.⁶⁹ Consisting of formal revision and intertextuality, repetition and pastiche, Signifyin(g) defers meaning by altering the meaning of signification itself; 'whereas signification depends for order and coherence on the exclusion of unconscious associations which any given word yields at any given time, Signification luxuriates in the inclusion of the free play of these associative rhetorical and semantic relations'.⁷⁰ Such free play is the opposite of what Whitehead's protagonist has attempted to achieve in his work. He has aligned himself with what Gates terms 'white meaning'⁷¹ and as Stephanie Li argues, he has a 'conception of language as based upon singularity; there is only one signifier for each signified'.⁷² Yet the novel itself Signifies in the black tradition in various ways as several critics have noted. Howard Ramsby II links the unnamed, isolated and intelligent narrator of *Apex* to a long tradition of comparable narrators in the work of African American writers including Ralph Ellison, Ishmael Reed and Charles Johnson;⁷³ Li notes that *Apex* signifies on many tropes of *Invisible Man*;⁷⁴ while Leise writes that 'Whitehead's Signifyin(g) form reverberates with the language of slavery'.⁷⁵

However, the novel not only revises and Signifies on older African American writing and the familiar tropes of the tradition but Signifies on nineteenth-century medical science. The mysterious symptoms with which the protagonist suffers bear a close resemblance to the disease of Drapetomania which was invented in 1851 by doctor and racial scientist Samuel A. Cartwright. In a report

'On the diseases and physical peculiarities of the negro race' published in the *New Orleans Medical and Surgical Journal*, Cartwright set out what he saw as the 'anatomical and physiological differences between the negro and the white man'[76] before explaining 'the diseases of the negroes' including 'pulmonary congestions, pneumonia',[77] 'fevers'[78] and 'negro consumption'[79] but also the mental illness 'Drapetomania, or the Disease Causing Slaves to Run Away'.[80] Taken from the Greek for 'runaway slave' and 'madness', Drapetomania, Cartwright hypothesized, could be diagnosed by the 'absconding from service', and was 'as much a disease of the mind as any other species of mental alienation'[81] which could be cured by a method of governance that keeps the negro in the position of the 'submissive knee-bender', a position which he claimed was set out for black people in the Bible.[82] 'They have only to be kept in that state, and treated like children, with care, kindness, attention and humanity, to prevent and cure them from running away',[83] Cartwright wrote; although it is frequently noted that the 'treatment' prescribed for runaway slaves was the removal of a toe.[84] In this way, Cartwright, who was one of the most widely known and respected physicians of the American south, laboured to defend the Southern contention that Negro slavery was morally right and socially and economically justifiable.[85]

Whitehead's protagonist's toe injury is reminiscent of the injury sustained by Kunta Kinte who in Haley's *Roots* has half his foot cut off in order to stop him trying to escape. Yet it is also a sign that he is suffering from Cartwright's fictional disease Drapetomania. Just before the peak of his illness and his collapse, he attends the Identity Awards (the award ceremony for his industry), as he has been nominated for 'Best Name – Medical'. He runs away from the ceremony because he is feverish and on the verge of delirium, as not only his body but his mind becomes overwhelmed by his realization that names can be false, misleading and obscure the truth, 'What is the word, he asked himself, for that elusive thing? It was on the tip of his tongue. What is the name for that which is always beyond our grasp? What do you call *that which escapes*?'[86] The name he imagines being given to himself in this moment of confusion is particularly significant; 'he heard them call his name as he slipped out of the room. FUGITIVE'.[87] That the protagonist's desire to escape the superficial and damaging industry he has hitherto supported is made reminiscent of earlier African American attempts to escape slavery, and that both are conceived of as a kind of illness, is curious. Whitehead's comparison suggests that the protagonist is not only trying to escape his industry but his blackness – a 'condition' that he has ignored and emptied of signification but which cannot be escaped.[88] By Signifyin(g) on the way black people's desire for self-determination and freedom was historically medicalized by racial science at this moment in the novel, Whitehead suggests that the historic pathologization of blackness continues to signify in African Americans' life experience; that the way race was made illness in the development of BiDil is merely a continuation of older attempts to medicate race, a repetition that the self-conscious Signifyin(g) technique is well placed to highlight. Gates notes that an aspect of Signifyin(g) in the nineteenth century was the parody and troping of white writing and racism by black authors – 'blacks... were quite capable of establishing the necessary distance between themselves and their condition to signify upon white racism through parody'[89] and recent scholarship by Britt Rusert has shown how nineteenth-century African American writers responded to the race sciences of their day through practices of collage, assemblage and juxtaposition.[90] Frederick Douglass, who responded to the work of racial scientists including Josiah C. Nott, George Glidden, Louis Agassiz and Samuel George Morton in *The Claims of the Negro, Ethnologically Considered* (1854), argued that there were several ways to approach the absurd assertion common among these thinkers that the negro was not a man; 'there are many ways to answer this denial. One is by ridicule; a second by denunciation; a third by argument'.[91] Whitehead chooses all three; by comically Signifyin(g) on Drapetomania, Whitehead draws attention to this tradition of satirizing race science in African American writing, and positions himself, and *Apex*, in a comparable Signifying relation to contemporary racial medicine.

Whitehead's parody of racial medicine, in the Signifyin(g) tradition, calls attention to fictive traditions in science which have sought to shape public understanding of blackness. As Rusert puts it, 'by the 1850s, science and fiction often merged through the fantastical and bizarre claims of racial science'[92] and Cartwright's Drapetomania in particular illuminates 'the site where antebellum racial science veered into the realm of fiction'.[93] *Apex Hides the Hurt* not only Signifies on earlier texts of racial science but on the relationship that these texts had to contemporaneous writing by African Americans. Rusert suggests that the 'science fictions of antebellum race science were simultaneously challenged by early black speculative fictions, which deployed science itself to imagine alternative histories of enslavement and freedom'.[94] *Apex Hides the Hurt* does something similar with the racial medicine of its day – the pharmacogenetic development of BiDil. By satirizing and Signifyin(g) on medicines like BiDil, Whitehead signals that not only are they the medical descendants of diseases such as Drapetomania and that the black body remains to a degree trapped by such biofictional creations, but that contemporary fiction itself can play a role in bringing those 'science fictions' to light, just as earlier African American fiction sought to do.

Identifying (with) blackness

While the novel reveals blackness to have been pathologized by medical science past and present, a pathologization from which the protagonist attempts to escape, the protagonist cannot escape the question of the meaning and value of blackness. How should a black person self-identify in a world where race has become a brand and been branded as illness? Is blackness a valid or useful way of (self)identifying when its biofictional shaping in medicine and beyond is ever present? These are questions with which Whitehead's protagonist must grapple during his convalescence in Winthrop, but they are also questions raised by BiDil. In basing the drug on people 'self-identified' as black, its developers set the tone for its marketing but also for its prescription; the drug encouraged black people to decide for themselves whether they needed it and in so doing made race, in Kahn's terms, 'an individual problem and a personal responsibility, and therefore of no concern to the political community at large'.[95] Operating much like personalized medicines where there is an onus on individuals to take responsibility for their own self-examination and self-improvement,[96] BiDil forced black patients to decide what their blackness meant in biological terms and to determine whether it had value in a medical context. The support that the drug received from black organizations and publics led some scientists and sociologists of science to argue that the drug's invocation of race could not be easily argued against. Francis Collins, writing in 2010 in a popular book on personalized medicine, stated that 'though we might ultimately hope to see race eliminated as a consideration in human society, an insistence on that outcome right now would cause us to ignore health disparities, and to offend many individuals for whom self-identified race is an important part of their personal identity'.[97] The belief of some black people in the identity that the drug exploited for commercial ends becomes the justification for the drug's deployment of race itself: Pollock contends that 'racialized medicine achieves its durability not from the power of racist ideology on the one hand or mechanistic understandings of bodies on the other, but because many people – in government, in social activism, in medicine, and beyond – have coalesced around it as a way to articulate their visions of what to do'.[98] She asks why scholars have focused on scientific and political critiques of race but have been 'reluctant to grapple with why prominent civil rights and black health actors have backed the drug'.[99] For Pollock the diverse positions adopted by black theorists and black organizations are complex,[100] and indeed studies have shown that black people are much more ambivalent and divided over how to position themselves in relation to racial medicine than has sometimes been acknowledged.[101]

Apex Hides the Hurt suggests a non-homogenizing way black people might begin to position themselves within the fraught and contested landscape of racial medicine. Like those at whom BiDil is aimed, the protagonist is caught between the apparently competing poles of individualism and community: racialized medicine encourages a personalized approach to sickness based on a seemingly individualized and tailored solution, as it strategically invokes racial groupings and a homogenized black community. While the protagonist's illness is to a degree caused by his isolation from black history, Whitehead suggests that the solution does not lie in the straightforward identification with 'the black community' or blackness. For what the novel's protagonist ultimately uncovers is the complex and fractured history of the founding black community of the town he is tasked with renaming. On the verge of giving up on names altogether, 'they should have kept the place nameless'[102] he thinks, he discovers a fourth possible name for the town – Struggle – which had been originally suggested by one of the town's two black founders but the existence of which has been erased. Struggle is the name suggested by Field, the suspicious and cautious man whom the town's first residents nickname 'the Dark'[103] due to the contrast between his temperament and that of his co-founder Goode, known as 'the Light'. Field 'didn't have anyone. He'd lost his family back on the plantation'[104] and advocates that the community avoid white people wherever possible, whereas religious Goode, as his name suggests, tries to see the positive and do his moral duty in every situation. The historical erasure of the suggested name Struggle in favour of Freedom (which is presented as the 'black' option for re-naming the town) simplifies the complexities and tensions within the black community, which the novel suggests has always been a site of contestation and difference.[105] The protagonist decides to name the town Struggle, and to identify with Field, not only to recover this lost history, but to signal the fact that black identity is a site of struggle; blackness is never (and has never been) unified or singular but shifts and evolves much like the signifier race itself. As Derek Maus has asserted, for the protagonist, listening to the Dark 'requires being open to more critical and less superficial interpretations of signs',[106] a way of reading blackness that Whitehead puts forward as a means of getting closer to 'the heart of the thing'.[107]

It is this way of reading and understanding blackness which might speak to debates about the uses of race in pharmacogenomics and medicine. The protagonist's eventual 'reading' of black history and community, which embraces the deferral of meaning that characterizes Gates's conception of Signification, suggests that attempts to pinpoint blackness in static terms are destined to fail. Moving beyond the limiting and circumscribed forms of identity offered up by brand consultants and by extension science, the protagonist comes to realize he will never be 'fixed' as his illness continues following his decision to name the town Struggle, 'his foot hurt more than ever'.[108] Black life is struggle, Whitehead suggests, an experience and identity characterized by ongoing suffering caused by racisms past and present as well as the struggle for self-definition and struggle against the definitions and constraints that others attempt to impose on black people:

> You call something by a name, you fix it in place. A thing or a person, it didn't matter – the name you gave it allowed you to draw a bead, take aim, shoot. But there was a flip side of calling something by the name you gave it – and that was wanting to be called by the name that you gave to yourself.[109]

An understanding of race as an intrinsically plural, diverse and disparate narrative, as a site of contestation and struggle, might give those health professionals and scientists who would diagnose on the basis of skin colour pause, while enabling black people to resist the basic options presented to them and to look beyond what appears to be right or good or anti-racist in medicines like BiDil. While it is the lack of a clear definition of 'black' which is exploited in the development of race-based medicines, the solution appears to be not to fight for a singular or fixed definition, but to redefine and re-signify the multiplicities of blackness in ways which challenge the ahistorical and apolitical presentation of race in science. The following and final chapter of this book examines how a newer, emerging strand of genetic science – epigenetics – might offer the opportunity to do just this as it brings focus to the impact of racism (past and present) on the body, as a means of accounting for racial inequalities in health.

5

Mutilation and Mutation: Epigenetics and Racist Environments in Octavia Butler's *Kindred* and Salman Rushdie's *The Satanic Verses*

A special issue of the *American Journal of Human Biology* appeared in 2009 focused on the study of 'Developmental Plasticity in a Biocultural Context'. One article in the issue, a study by Grazyna Jasienska, examined the question of why African American babies have tended to have a lower birth weight in comparison with the birth weight of European American babies, and attributed the difference not only to contemporary socio-economic inequalities, but to the conditions experienced by black Americans during slavery, the effects of which, the article claimed, have been passed on through intergenerational signals of environmental quality, or epigenetic processes.[1] Jasienska argues that while difference in socio-economic status does account for some racial differences in birth characteristics, it does not account for the significant differences in the weight of newborns between black and white women on low incomes or, within black populations, between the babies of black women born in African countries living in the United States, and those of black women who were born in the United States.[2] Jasienska suggests that the difference can be explained by the 'influence of intergenerational life conditions, especially for the female line' which for African Americans comprises the 'inadequate diet and strenuous workload' of enslaved populations who 'experienced an imbalance between energy intake and energy expenditure, and had high energetic costs of fighting infectious diseases'.[3] The low birth weight of African American children is thus partly the result of the low weight of enslaved children, the low rate of childhood growth as a result of poor nutrition and intense labour from a young age experienced by enslaved people, and the fact that enslaved mothers and grandmothers had poor nutritional development during adult life.[4] The experiences of ancestors become embodied in health disparities in the present, the genes carrying a 'memory' of these experiences, while the genes also create new memories as they are affected by the psychosocial stresses of racism in the present.

Another study in the issue focused on the environmental influences on the genes which occur during the lifetime of an individual as the cause of racial differences in health outcomes. Kuzawa and Sweet, studying US black – white disparities in cardiovascular disease, suggest that 'there is now a strong rationale to consider developmental and epigenetic mechanisms as links between early life environmental factors like maternal stress during pregnancy and adult race-based health disparities in diseases like hypertension, diabetes, stroke and coronary heart disease'.[5] According to the authors, racial differences in rates of disease can be explained by the fact that lower birth weights in African Americans are related to higher blood pressure in later life, and that lower birth weights are caused by maternal stressors and the passage of stress hormones across the placenta, which are, in turn, caused by psychosocial stress, depression, exposure to racial discrimination and residential segregation.[6] They note that 'whereas group membership and continental race are poor predictors of genetic variation, these same categories are directly related to the social and structural manifestations of inequality that impact the development of responsive biological systems'.[7] What such studies appear to demonstrate is that racial difference is a fluid, complex combination of the influence on the genes of an individual's current environment and the environment of their ancestors. Put differently, racism has biological effects which in turn create racial disparities in health; rather than biologizing social definitions of race, race is revealed as a social construct with biological consequences.

The new science upon which these studies rely is epigenetics, which, in its broadest sense, is concerned with the interaction of genes with their environment. Epigenetics is the study of the processes by which the chemicals and proteins within DNA are modified, through methylation and histone modification, in ways which affect gene expression, but not the fixed sequence of DNA. The discovery which has forced scientists to reconsider their long-held assumptions is that these epigenetic marks can be switched on or off according to the environmental conditions in which the body finds itself, and, in some cases, that such changes can be inherited by offspring and passed from generation to generation. For Tim Spector, Professor of Twin Research and Genetic Epidemiology, epigenetics challenges four fundamental assumptions that have governed genetic science: that genes singlehandedly define the essence of human beings and are the only mechanism of inheritance; that genes and heritable genetic destiny cannot be changed or modified; that an environmental event can't produce a long-lasting influence on your genes; and that you cannot inherit the effects of your ancestors' environments.[8] The more familiar linear model of development and inheritance in which genes are fixed for life and passed on unchanged has thus been fundamentally challenged by the newly revealed complexity of the gene and environment relationship. The study of epigenetic mechanisms reveals that the human body's genetic structures can change and change back, that the body is in a dynamic relationship to its environment, that culture can become embodied. In the case of race, the initial findings of epigenetic studies have the potential to work against the more traditional inscription of race as genetically real; for rather than consolidating racial categorizations, or fixing race as a deterministic essence, epigenetics reveals how the experience of being racialized influences genetic development and inheritance.

These developments have been met with a great deal of excitement in the academy, particularly among social scientists, philosophers and humanities scholars, who have viewed epigenetic science, and developments within post-genomic biology more broadly, as a sign that the entanglement of the biological and the social is finally being taken seriously within genetic science. That racialization and racism have real and profound impacts on health is not a new idea; social epidemiologists, most notably Nancy Krieger, have long argued that patterns of inequality in health and disease are fundamentally shaped by societal conditions, and that racism and discrimination can harm health by becoming embodied across the life course.[9] However epigenetics is providing scholars with a new way to frame and evidence 'the effects of white racism'[10] on the physiology of black and brown bodies, offering, as Maurizio Meloni contends, 'a key missing link to explain the molecular pathways by which transient environmental factors can leave marks or be inscribed on the biological body'.[11] Such explanatory epigenetic mechanisms have been popularized in the media where headlines such as 'Post-Traumatic Slave Syndrome and Intergenerational Trauma: Slavery Is Like a Curse Passing through the DNA of Black People'[12] and 'The Epigenetics of Being Black and Feeling Blue: Understanding African American Vulnerability to Disease'[13] have embedded a racialized understanding of epigenetics within the public imagination. Epigenetics is understood both as a mechanism which operates transgenerationally and as genetic markers which result from contemporary racial microaggressions, which can have negative health-related consequences for the mental, emotional and physical well-being of black people.[14]

Yet headlines and articles such as these have also caused a significant degree of unease among scientists and sociologists, who have increasingly criticized the media as well as their fellow academics, for making 'wild claims'[15] and creating hype around a science which is still very much in its infancy. Over the past ten years there has been, as Brigitte Nerlich has argued, 'a general shift from breathless excitement, grand claims and hype to more nuanced, modest and humble assessments of what epigenetics is and what it can achieve'.[16] Critics of epigenetic 'hype' emphasize that there is still a great deal of uncertainty around its findings and therefore that the bold and to a degree revolutionary claims being made for it simply cannot be scientifically supported. Such uncertainties and contingencies include the fact that 'there is a lack of consensus within bioscience over the meaning of epigenetic effects, mechanisms, and even the word itself', a major instability which means that, according to Martin Pickersgill, the enthusiasm for transgenerational inheritance among sociologists risks co-producing an 'alien science' that may disaffect the very communities of life scientists with which sociologists would like to collaborate.[17] The concept of transgenerational epigenetic inheritance has proved particularly controversial, with some suggesting that what appears transgenerational could in fact be the result of the experience of similar environments in the present.[18] Ruth Müller et al. have expressed concern about 'over-simplified translations from social structures to biological processes and vice versa' which may ironically lead to a new kind of determinism, arguing:

> if we hope to translate the findings of epigenetic research on the developmental mechanisms linking nutrition with disease risk into effective health policy, it is imperative that we view nutrition not as a simple exposure in isolation, or a function of individual choice, but as a resource that is constrained in complex ways by social and structural factors that distribute resources, and chances of health, unevenly across society.[19]

The rush to embrace an epigenetic view of inheritance and development risks a failure to recognize the complexities encompassed by the environment and risks 'individuals, their health and their behaviour' becoming 'bound and ruled by the epigenetic marks they have acquired in early life'.[20] This risk is only magnified when it comes to race because, as Lundy Braun et al. argue, 'once race is presumed, the ways in which multiple genetic inheritances interact with the environment within that individual seem to disappear',[21] as racial difference is assumed to be the primary factor affecting a person's life experience.

A significant element of the misunderstandings, simplifications and hype around public and lay understandings of epigenetics has been attributed to the metaphors, language and allusions through which this new science has been communicated by both scientists and the press. The ideas of the nineteenth-century biologist Jean-Baptiste Lamarck are frequently invoked in popular and academic writing on epigenetics.[22] Lamarck's thesis, set out in his 1809 *Philosophie Zoologique*, was that it was possible for organisms to acquire physical characteristics during their lifetimes, which were then inherited by their offspring.[23] It was a controversial theory which was invoked throughout the nineteenth century but which enjoyed a significant resurgence during the debates that followed Darwin's *Origin of Species* in 1859.[24] The idea that environmentally acquired characteristics might be passed on genetically was, after dominating debates for several decades, ultimately laid to rest with the Modern Evolutionary Synthesis in the 1940s when Darwinian natural selection became the basis of modern genetic science. However, the transgenerational responses identified by recent epigenetic studies have led some to conclude that Lamarck was, in fact, partially right.[25] Such invocations situate epigenetics as a kind of neo-Lamarckism and, in so doing, according to critics such as Ute Deichmann, create a misleading picture of what epigenetics actually means because, unlike Lamarckism, 'phenomena of inherited variation related to epigenetic marks... are not actively acquired... they are not adaptive (except by chance), and in many cases are detrimental for the organisms'.[26] Nevertheless the similarities between epigenetic mechanisms of inheritance and Lamarck's theories (as they were understood in opposition to Darwinism at the end of the nineteenth century) have proved irresistible to popularizers of epigenetics. Tim Spector references Rudyard Kipling's *Just So Stories* (1902), fantastic tales of how various animals came to obtain their physical characteristics through human or environmental intervention – stories which were influenced by Lamarckian ideas[27] – in the leopard-print design of his book's dust jacket. Kipling's Lamarckian-influenced stories *How the Camel Got His Hump*, *How the Leopard Got His Spots* and *How the Rhinoceros Got His Skin* are also recalled in one of the major metaphors used to communicate epigenetic processes – the idea that epigenetics 'gets under the skin'. This is a metaphor that, Nerlich notes, operates on several levels in epigenetic discourse, as it means 'to affect someone very strongly in a way that is difficult to forget' but it is also a phrase which

> like many metaphors for emotion, has a physiological basis. Think about expressions like 'to be a pain in the neck', 'to stick in one's throat', 'to step on somebody's toes', 'to get hot under the collar', etc. This intimate link between talking, meaning, thinking and physiology makes the 'getting under the skin' metaphor quite potent and probably contributed to popularising epigenetics in particular contexts.[28]

As is the case with genetics more broadly, literary references and metaphor have been frequently employed as a communicative tool to explain the meaning and mechanisms of epigenetics to a public audience, but often in ways that are then also blamed for the public misunderstanding of that science.[29]

This chapter explores whether literature might be considered differently in relation to epigenetic science; not as a source of either misleading or distorting images and metaphors, but as a means of thinking through the implications of this science, a means of amplifying and expanding both scientific and lay understandings of emerging issues in epigenetics. For while leading epigeneticist Edith Heard has claimed that 'there's a gap between the fact and the fantasy' of epigenetics and 'Now the facts are having to catch up',[30] I want to argue, as I have throughout this book, that contemporary fiction offers ways of comprehending the relationship between fact and fantasy, reality and fiction, which suggest that there might be something to be gained from taking a relational, rather than oppositional, approach to the imagined and the real as epigenetic science develops. This is nowhere more important than for the concept of race. The novels examined as case studies in this chapter, Octavia Butler's *Kindred* (1979) and Salman Rushdie's *The Satanic Verses* (1988), each explore how race is created at the intersection of the imagined and the real, through a focus on the impact of racist environments on the body; US plantation slavery in the case of the former, and late-twentieth-century hostile immigration environments in the UK in the case of the latter. While both novels were published years before epigenetics came to prominence, each imagines processes of bodily change and transformation which are comparable to the mechanisms which epigenetic science is beginning to uncover: Butler and Rushdie employ fantastical modes to represent the way experiences of racism become biologically embodied, imagining how black and brown bodies acquire certain characteristics through exposure to racist environments in the UK and United States. Their representations of the porous boundary between the body and its wider environment offer a mode of comprehending the epigenetic effects of racism as the imagined or fictional (the racist belief in the inferiority of other races) made real (in apparently 'racial' biological characteristics). These fantastic literary interrogations of the dynamic relationship between the imaginary and reality not only shed light on the entanglement of the biological with specific, historical, cultural and social environments through which epigenetic changes are formed, but reveal how fiction itself is, and might productively be, intertwined with the 'facts' of epigenetic science.

Heard sounds a note of caution about the nascent state of epigenetics, claiming that 'it's our duty as scientists to pass on the right messages',[31] something which is indisputable. Yet it is also the case that epigenetic science is currently in a state of flux and uncertainty, a state which Pickersgill contends is productive and necessary for driving science forward.[32] This state, while carrying the danger of public misunderstanding, also offers an opportunity to recognize and to explore what Mary Midgley calls the 'imaginative visions'[33] upon which science is based, and it is my contention that contemporary fiction might contribute to, and illuminate, those visions, actively and productively informing the inevitable biofictional formation of race in an equally biofictional epigenetic science. Indeed, Meloni has suggested that it might be possible to move beyond 'debates about determinism and anti-determinism in epigenetics' by looking at the long histories of theories of plasticity, histories in which literary studies has played a significant part.[34] Meloni's contention, which he develops by drawing on canonical works of European philosophy and literature, is that such histories reveal plasticity to be an ambiguous concept, a concept that while 'capable of undermining atomistic and insulated models of the body' is also historically 'deeply racialised and gendered' and therefore not necessarily emancipatory.[35] This chapter focuses instead on the import of writing concerned with the mechanisms, experience and effects of racism, and in so doing uncovers an alternative literary approach to plasticity which, while acknowledging the ways in which it may be racialized, understands that it is also something that people subject to racialization have had to learn to live with. *Kindred* and *The Satanic Verses* each interrogates how and why, as Achille Mbembe puts it, 'racism consists, most of all, in substituting what *is* with something else, with another reality', and how those who live in racist environments might not only adapt and survive, but gain new knowledge from racism's 'power to distort the real and to fix affect'.[36] These fictional portrayals offer alternative pathways for conceiving of an epigenetics of race, moving beyond debates about determinism and anti-determinism and towards an understanding of race as biofiction.

Kindred as post-genomic novel

Kindred is the tale of Dana, a twenty-six-year-old African American woman living in Los Angeles, who, on 9 June 1976, is 'called' back in time by her ancestor, Rufus Weylin. Rufus's family owns a plantation in antebellum Maryland, and among the enslaved people who work on the plantation is another of Dana's ancestors, Alice. Dana is called back in time to save her white ancestor, Rufus, from harm and illness at various points across the course of his life. Early on in the novel Dana realizes that her own survival is dependent on her ability to save Rufus; she must endeavour to keep him alive until he has raped Alice, whose subsequent child, Hagar, Dana knows to be her several times great-grandmother. As Dana ambivalently tends to Rufus, becoming a part of the plantation's black population, she is subject to the horrific violence and trauma of being enslaved. While Rufus heals from each accident or illness, Dana is by turns beaten and whipped, forcing her to experience life as a slave first-hand; only when she truly fears that she might be killed does Dana return to the 1970s, and to her new husband Kevin, who joins her on some of her trips back in time to the Weylin plantation, a place that she comes to call 'home'.[37] While Dana's visits to Rufus in the past are often years apart, and she can be stuck in Maryland for months, time works differently in the 1970s present, where only minutes, hours or days have passed, giving Dana very little time to recover from her wounds and to prepare for Rufus's next 'call'. She is only freed from moving back and forth in time when, knowing that Hagar has been born, she finally kills Rufus as he tries to rape her. However, she returns to the 1970s permanently mutilated through the loss of an arm, a loss which she is unable to explain to anyone other than Kevin, and which she must learn to live with permanently.

Butler described her novel as 'a grim fantasy',[38] a departure from the science fiction writing for which she was (and would be) predominantly known, because despite the fact that the novel involves the protagonist travelling through time, as Butler asserts, 'with *Kindred* there's absolutely no science involved. Not even the time travel'.[39] Instead, for Butler the novel is 'the kind of fantasy that nobody had really thought of as fantasy',[40] a consciously fantastical representation of enslavement which contrasts sharply with the emphasis on truth and authenticity to be found in the nineteenth-century slave narratives upon which Butler drew.[41] Yet while the novel is clearly not science fiction in that, much like Ishiguro's approach to cloning in *Never Let Me Go*, there is no discussion of or interest in the scientific ideas which may have enabled Dana to travel through time, *Kindred* does, I want to suggest, bear the imprint of Butler's wider interest in bioscience, evident in her science fiction published both before and after *Kindred*. Butler's oeuvre is full of engagements with genetics, from the selectively bred and mutated humans of her first novel *Patternmaster* (1976) to her Xenogenesis series (1987–1989), which depicts an alien race called the Oankali, who have the ability to genetically engineer themselves and the DNA of others. The latter series in particular has been read as in part a response to sociobiology, a field (considered pseudoscientific by some) concerned with the way social behaviour is determined by biology.[42] Butler's approach to the biological is, however, not deterministic, but evinces the kind of approach that is now emerging in humanities' scholarship on post-genomic biology, as encapsulated in the following exchange with an interviewer:

> ALK: So you're saying that knowledge of the body can be used to empower and not necessarily to determine? OB: Yes. Sure! ALK: Well, the determinism is what scares me about sociobiology. OB: Don't worry about it. ALK: How can you not worry about that? OB: Don't worry about the real biological determinism. Worry about what people make of it. Worry about the social Darwinism. After all, if sociobiology, or anything like it (people don't really use that term much any more for obvious reasons), is true, then denying it is certainly not going to help. What we have to do is learn to work with it and to work against people who see it as a good reason to let the poor be poor, that kind of thing-the social Darwinism: 'They must be poor because of their genes,' that kind of foolishness.[43]

Butler embraces the biological body, but not biological determinism, situating the biological as integral to knowledge of the self and of society because 'the body is all we really know that we have. We can say that there're always other things that are wonderful. And some are. But all we really know that we have is the flesh'.[44] This is a position which, as her interviewer notes, is at odds with 'postmodern thinking and writing which calculates the human body as primarily a discursive entity-perhaps in defensive response to the ways genetics studies have often allocated political power and influence according to hierarchies of raced and gendered bodies'.[45] However it is also a position which prefigures the more recent new materialist turn towards biology which Sarah Ahmed argues has been built on the erasure of earlier feminist engagements with biology,[46] engagements of the kind Butler demonstrates here and has developed in her wider fictional writing. Butler's insistence on the significance of embodied knowledge, on 'body-knowledge' as 'what's made of genetics',[47] instead offers a proto-epigenetic understanding of how the dynamic relationship between genes and their environment shapes what and how we know ourselves to be, a vision which, rather than shying away from the biological, examines what it might mean to understand ourselves in these terms, while moving beyond biological determinism. It is this form of embodied knowledge and what we might now understand as epigenetic embodiment which Butler explores in the context of the racism and racialization of US slavery in *Kindred*.

The environment of the Weylin plantation to which Dana is transported in *Kindred* is the kind of past environment identified in epigenetic studies of the intergenerational effects of slavery as the cause of disparities in health in the present. The novel depicts how this environment shapes the bodies of those who live within it, but also the bodies of their ancestors, as Dana's trips back to the past come to be defined by the pain and injuries which she permanently sustains as a result. Dana's first meeting with Rufus occurs when she rescues him from drowning, but is overwhelmingly defined by her experience of being beaten by his mother Margaret, as Dana tries to resuscitate him, before returning – at the threat of being shot – wet and muddy to the present with 'an ache in my back and shoulders where Rufus's mother had pounded with her fists'.[48] Such injuries only increase as Dana first witnesses the flogging of an enslaved person; 'I could literally smell his sweat, hear every ragged breath, every cry, every cut of the whip. I could see his body jerking, convulsing, straining against the rope as his screaming went on and on. My stomach heaved ...',[49] before experiencing something similar herself shortly afterwards, 'the man tackled me and brought me down hard ... he began hitting me, punching me with his fists'.[50] As she becomes accustomed to life on the plantation on one visit, she begins to live like other enslaved people, eating 'corn meal mush' alongside other slaves, waiting to 'get better food later on after the white folks eat'.[51] When sent to work in the fields she relates how 'I didn't think my shoulders could have hurt much worse if they'd been broken. Sweat ran down into my eyes and my hands were beginning to blister'.[52] Even when she is stationed in the house, tending to Rufus, she cannot escape the violence of the Weylins, whether it be from Margaret who 'threw scalding hot coffee at me'[53] or her husband Tom Weylin who attacks Dana after he discovers that she has been teaching Nigel, an enslaved boy, how to read, 'I never saw where the whip came from, never even saw the first blow coming. But it came – like a hot iron across my back, burning into me through my light shirt, searing my skin ... I screamed, convulsed. Weylin struck again and again, until I couldn't have gotten up at gunpoint'.[54] On each visit, Dana is forced to withstand the harsh and violent conditions of the plantation, and on each occasion is left in the present exhausted and in pain, her injuries getting worse and worse until she finally loses her left arm.

Dana comes to understand that there is a marked difference in the impact of the racist environment of the Weylin plantation on its black inhabitants and the white people whom they live alongside. Dana and Kevin each try to account for, and sometimes excuse, Rufus's behaviour, by thinking of it in environmental terms; reflecting on Rufus as a child, Dana thinks that 'his environment had left its unlikeable marks on him'[55] and Kevin counsels her that she will ultimately be unable to change Rufus's behaviour because 'his environment will be influencing him every day you're gone'.[56] The environmental effect of the plantation on white people is a psychological one, the 'marks' it leaves are on attitudes and behaviour, rather than the body, an effect which Dana worries might impact upon Kevin when he is also brought back to the past; 'if he was stranded here for years, some part of this place would rub off on him. No large part, I knew. But if he survived here, it would be because he managed to tolerate the life here'.[57] Kevin's ability to survive depends upon his ability to adjust psychologically, neither his nor any white bodies are under real threat. However for Dana and the other slaves the psychological cannot be separated from the physical; it is the terror of violence and pain which shapes their behaviour, something which Dana has to experience in order to understand. Prior to being called back, Dana's understanding of slavery is little different to Kevin's; she 'has seen people beaten on television and in the movies'[58] and waiting to be called back again she manages to find 'a compact paperback history of slavery in America'[59] which she thinks might be useful. She uses her time at home in the 1970s to 'read books about slavery, fiction and nonfiction ... I read everything I had in the house that was even distantly related to the subject',[60] yet none of it can prepare her for the reality. As Sherryl Vint contends, for Dana, 'being black and knowing "the facts" is not enough', and instead she must come to know what slavery was like through her own body, for 'as long as Dana envisions herself as a disembodied subject, she deludes herself that the experience of slavery is safely contained in the past'.[61] For Butler, the trauma of enslavement is something which African Americans must learn to live with; it is an embodied intergenerational history which black people carry with them, biologically.

Dana has little choice in the matter; she is powerless to prevent herself going back in time and returning home without her left arm, and is left to live with a significant physical disability that marks her body in the manner comparable to the inheritance of health-damaging epigenetic marks. Her life becomes in some sense determined by her ancestry in a way which critics of epigenetic science have identified as problematic. Meloni writes that 'the inheritance of acquired characters is a double-edged sword ... bad habits can become bad biology, and the scars of past exposures and traumas can give rise to ideas of specific groups being "too damaged" to be rescued'.[62] When these purportedly damaged groups correspond to racial groupings, there are concerns that a different form of biological determinism might ensue; 'claims of degeneration of specific populations for their too long exposure to pathogenic environments have been a significant part of the eugenic experience',[63] Meloni contends, so that rather than extinguishing racialization, epigenetic understandings of race risk a kind of re-racialization of social debates and are in danger of replicating oppressive biologistical projects that have drawn on the science of unfixed characteristics.[64] In this view, Dana's biological inheritance – represented by her bodily scars and mutilation – is determining and limiting, an affirmation, rather than disavowal, of the racial forms of categorization which led her ancestors to be treated as slaves and created the racist environment which marked their, and Dana's, bodies.

Yet the novel suggests that, on the contrary, a kind of freedom is in fact achieved for Dana through her acquired, intergenerational body knowledge, an inheritance which, while physiologically limiting, is also on some level empowering and healing when it is fully known and understood. For, before she is called back in time, Dana's life is already bound and ruled by an environment saturated with subtle forms of racism and sexism, to which she only becomes attuned once she experiences a bodily connection to her ancestors. The past in the novel is not only that of the early nineteenth century, but also the much more recent past of Dana's life: as the narrative moves back and forth in time, it often returns not to the present but to Dana's descriptions of her life with Kevin in the months before she began to time travel. It is in these descriptions of the more recent past that Butler draws parallels between Dana's life in the present and the experience she will have on the Weylin plantation. Dana's relationship with Kevin, around which her immediate past centres, is largely unextraordinary. They meet while they are both 'working out of a casual labor agency',[65] drawn together by the fact that they are both writers (and using agency work to supplement their income). While Dana narrates her burgeoning love for Kevin, it is punctuated by small, subtle, uncomfortable insights into his character: when they first meet, Kevin assumes that Dana flunked out of high school, then when they start thinking of living together Dana recalls how 'Kevin did suggest once that I get rid of some of my books so that I'd fit into his place'[66] and encourages her to quit her job. While Dana pushes back, Kevin gets annoyed then angry when Dana refuses to type his manuscripts; 'he said if I couldn't do him a little favour when he asked, I could leave'.[67] Kevin's microaggressions, both racial and patriarchal, demonstrate that beneath his relaxed, liberal exterior, he holds little regard for Dana's needs, independence or intellectual life.

Dana has been conditioned to put up with his attitude, but as she begins to travel back and forth in time, she begins to relate to his behaviour differently. Dana's first trip to the past occurs when she and Kevin have just moved and begins while 'we were still unpacking – or rather, I was still unpacking. Kevin had stopped when he got his office in order'.⁶⁸ As she spends more time in the nineteenth century, she begins to see small parallels between her petulant, needy and narcissistic ancestors Rufus and his father Tom, and Kevin, who while maintaining an abhorrence for slavery and defending Dana, cannot quite comprehend her experiences. His initial reactions to her inexplicable disappearance and reappearance are clumsy; in pain after being beaten by Margaret, 'Kevin hadn't helped'⁶⁹ by squeezing Dana's shoulders, and he declares 'that's a lot better' when she has cleaned herself up, when for Dana, 'it wasn't'.⁷⁰ When Dana says 'I don't feel secure here',⁷¹ it isn't only being pulled back to the past which is making her uneasy. Fighting off a patroller trying to rape her, Dana returns to the present with Kevin on top of her, who before allowing her to rest and recover wants to know 'Did he rape you?',⁷² a question he asks her again at the end of the novel about Rufus, 'What's he done to you?'.⁷³ While Dana explains that she hasn't been raped, Kevin doesn't quite believe her and his attitude betrays the sense of ownership he feels he has over her body; 'he looked at me uncertainly. "Look, if anything did happen, I could understand it. I know how it was back then." To which Dana replies, 'You mean you could forgive me for having been raped?'.⁷⁴ While Dana tries to be as clear as possible, 'I'm not property, Kevin', he 'only half understood'.⁷⁵ The sexual possessiveness Kevin feels towards Dana mirrors Rufus's proprietorship of Alice. Alice has no choice but to succumb to Rufus, who threatens to whip her if she resists, and while Dana's relationship with Kevin is chosen, it follows a more subtle patterning that Dana can only see clearly once she has been to the past; as she tries to comfort Kevin, 'he pulled away from me and walked out of the room. The expression on his face was like something I'd seen, something I was used to seeing on Tom Weylin. Something closed and ugly'.⁷⁶

Thus when Dana narrates at the start of the novel that 'the trouble began long before 9 June 1976, when I became aware of it',⁷⁷ she signals her narrative as being written with a newly acquired understanding of her (recent) past of which she has only become aware through her visits to the nineteenth century and her subsequent injuries. Her embodiment of 'the trouble' which is the history of enslavement and its unacknowledged legacies in the present is necessary for her survival as a black woman in the 1970s; for, as Butler suggests, 'sometimes we can work around our programming if we understand it'.⁷⁸ Dana's biological inheritance – the trauma of racialization and its consequences – cannot be ignored but must instead be understood in order to both live with and move beyond it, and Dana's multiple trips back in time offer some suggestion of how this might be done. For it is in adopting an altered relation to time and space that Butler suggests that Dana, and by extension African Americans, might begin to understand the nature of race and racism differently, to understand that the novel's 'grim fantasy' is not the fantastical ability to live in and with two moments in time and two different environments at once, but the white supremacy and patriarchy which distort and warp the real. Unlike the temporally linear, teleological narrative of enslavement presented by Haley in *Roots*, the narrative structure of *Kindred* moves back and forth in time, until what initially feels to Dana like a temporal disjunction becomes familiar and homely; on one of her later trips to rescue Rufus, Dana narrates how 'finally, after more woods and fields, the plain square house was before me, its downstairs windows full of yellow light. I was startled to catch myself saying wearily, "Home at last"'.[79] From the first line of the novel, 'I lost an arm on my last trip home', Dana signals that the plantation is for her as much her home as her new house with Kevin. At the Weylins' 'Kevin and I became more a part of the household, familiar, accepted, accepting'[80] and while this acclimatization disturbs Dana she is also aware that 'I had begun to feel – feel, not think – that a great deal of time had passed for me too ... Some part of me had apparently given up on time-distorted reality and smoothed things out'.[81] As the novel progresses, Dana's experience becomes less and less fantastical and more real.

On one level, the apparent ease with which Dana can exist across time is another way in which she is forced to confront the uncomfortable parallels between the past lives of her ancestors and her existence in the present. Yet her inability to remain an observer and to 'maintain the distance'[82] between past and present, however uncomfortable, is also how she learns to feel 'at home' with the truth of her family history. Her ancestry is one which, as Philip Miletic contends, problematizes 'the cultural wholeness of an African black identity' that was being promoted by the Black Power movement in the 1970s.[83] Dana's discovery that she has a white ancestor, whom she must repeatedly save, undermines an idea of race premised on genetic difference by emphasizing the entangled genealogies of white and black Americans. Instead, race is made through an embodied knowledge in and of the black body, the locus of multiple temporal and environmental junctures which coexist; Dana's body is a site where binary distinctions between the fantastic and the real are dissolved, as being black becomes – as in Whitehead's *Apex Hides the Hurt* – about how, through embodiment, to live with, but not be determined by, the (very real) pain and trauma of the past. If epigenetics, as Becky Mansfield and Julie Guthman contend, 'moves toward a notion of biological difference as part of the warp and weave of space and time',[84] then we might consider Butler's time travelling tale as a form of post-genomic writing, a novel which models, in its narrative structure, a way of living with 'a new form of racialization based on processes of becoming rather than on pre-given nature'.[85] Mansfield and Guthman caution that research into these processes of racialization, while appearing anti-racist, is in danger of pathologizing epigenetic plasticity by seeking to improve and 'normalize' epigenetic variation, which is increasingly conceived of as 'abnormal' and categorized as disease.[86] *Kindred*, however, attempts no such correction: Dana never attempts to alter history and there is no attempt to change her body from being marked and scarred. Instead, Butler presents Dana's new-found body knowledge as a form of empowerment, a means of understanding what it means to be African American – which is to live with racialization across space and time and with the fantasy of racial categorization.

Acquiring race in *The Satanic Verses*

Where *Kindred* is primarily interested in the inheritance of acquired characteristics, *The Satanic Verses* is more concerned with how biological markers might be acquired from certain environmental exposures during an individual's lifetime. A dense and complex novel, *The Satanic Verses* is about the experiences of immigrants in Britain in the 1980s under Margaret Thatcher's conservative government. The novel follows the lives of two Indian immigrants, actors Saladin Chamcha and Gibreel Farishta, as they struggle to make their way in London following their abrupt arrival in England; in one of many fantastical moments, the narrative opens with Saladin and Gibreel falling to earth from an exploded jumbo jet which has been hijacked by terrorists. In London, Gibreel struggles with mental illness, while Saladin becomes part of the multicultural community of Brickhall (an amalgam of Brick Lane and Southall) before they eventually both return to Bombay. The novel became famous for the controversy which surrounded Rushdie's depictions of Gibreel's visions, and the resulting fatwa calling for Rushdie's death which was issued on 14 February 1989. Yet this focus obscured Rushdie's detailed portrayal of experiences of racism in late-twentieth-century England, a portrayal which, I want to suggest, like *Kindred*, offers a proto-epigenetic understanding of the impact of racism upon the body.

Rushdie is a writer who has become increasingly interested in biological science and its relationship to fiction. In 2009, the twentieth anniversary of the fatwa against his life, Rushdie became a member of the advisory board of Project Reason, a not-for-profit organization (now no longer in existence) set up with the purpose of spreading secular values and scientific knowledge in society. The project, whose board members included writers Ian McEwan and Ayann Hirsi Ali, as well as several prominent contemporary biologists and geneticists including Richard Dawkins, Steven Pinker and Craig Venter, brought together thinkers from the literary and scientific worlds who share in the belief that rational thinking, science and secularism need to be asserted in the face of the irrationality and fundamentalism of religious belief, particularly as it is manifested in Islam and the strands of American Christianity which promote creationism. Rushdie's involvement is perhaps not surprising given his increasing participation in public debates about Islam following the terrorist attacks of 9/11 and 7 July 2005, debates which have often sought to construct Islamic belief as a pre-modern dogma irreconcilable with the West which, in contrast, is heralded as the embodiment of rational, progressive thought.[87] Yet what Project Reason added to the debate, and made explicit, was the specifically scientific character of the reason it promoted; the project placed biological science and evolutionary theory at the centre of its response to religious belief, as the ultimate answer to it. Rushdie has increasingly adopted the logic of evolutionary biology as a means of explaining – and defending – storytelling, as a way of foreclosing objections to literary expression, such as those put forward at the publication of *The Satanic Verses*. In recent interviews Rushdie claims that the 'story instinct is hardwired in our DNA'[88] and that 'any external limitations on our ability to speak, or on the content of our speech, therefore, interferes with something essential to us all, whether we are writers or not'.[89] Stressing the innateness and universality of storytelling through a neo-Darwinian framework in which we are all 'story-telling animals',[90] Rushdie appears to align himself with the evolutionary explanations of literature to be found in sociobiology and the Literary Darwinist movement.

In this context it might seem unlikely that Rushdie's writing could engage with the fluidity, plasticity and non-deterministic character of epigenetics – the opposite of the deterministic worldview which characterizes neo-Darwinian approaches to biology and literature. Yet as several critics have noted, Rushdie's non-fictional writing and journalism are consistently more polemical than his fiction, the ideological clarity of the former at odds with the more ambivalent, contradictory character of the latter.[91] Moreover there has been a 'profound ideological shift'[92] in Rushdie's thinking, which began with the fatwa against him in 1989, but was cemented by the events of 9/11.[93] Indeed, Rushdie's engagement with evolutionary biology prior to this 'shift', in *The Satanic Verses* itself, is of a more complex kind than the neo-Darwinian view he would later come to adopt. The novel does reflect Rushdie's scepticism towards the kinds of religious fundamentalism which deny Darwinian evolution: waking from a nap during his flight to the UK, Saladin finds himself sitting next to Eugene Dumsday, an American creationist who introduces himself as 'a man of science' and explains that he has been in India

> warning your fellow men … against Mr Darwin and his works. With the assistance of my personal fifty-seven slide presentation. I spoke of my own country, of its young people … I see them in despair, turning to narcotics … If I believed that my great-granddaddy was a chimpanzee, why, I'd be pretty depressed myself.[94]

As his name suggests, Dumsday is dumb, his blinkered religious fundamentalism can only be laughed at – Saladin's response is to 'giggle'[95] – and Dumsday's sermonizing is comically undermined when later in the novel Saladin hears him on the radio and he now embodies the things which he abhors; the devil (having 'lost the half of his tongue'[96] in the hijacking incident) and modern biomedical science, which has enabled his tongue to be rebuilt 'with flesh taken from his posterior'.[97]

Yet the novel resists taking its own fundamentalist stance towards biology and instead draws upon a pre-Darwinian theory of evolution, Lamarckism, as a means of addressing one of its foremost themes – the condition of migrancy. As Saladin and Gibreel fall through the sky they encounter 'the debris of the soul, broken memories, sloughed-off selves, severed mother-tongues, violated privacies, untranslatable jokes, extinguished futures, lost loves, the forgotten meaning of hollow, booming words, *land, belonging, home*'.[98] These are the changes wrought on the individual by migration, Rushdie suggests, and to emphasize their force, such change is depicted as being manifested in a physical change in the body of the migrant. Saladin and Gibreel metamorphose as they fall, the 'processes of their transmutation'[99] playfully explained by the narrator through reference to the early-nineteenth-century botanist Jean-Baptiste Lamarck:

Mutation?

> Yes sir, but not random. Up there in air-space, in that soft, imperceptible field which had been made possible by the century and which, thereafter, made the century possible, becoming one of its defining locations, the place of movement and of war, the planet- shrinker and power-vacuum, most insecure and transitory of zones, illusory, discontinuous, metamorphic, -because when you throw everything up in the air anything becomes possible – wayupthere, at any rate, changes took place in delirious actors that would have gladdened the heart of old Mr Lamarck: under extreme environmental pressure, characteristics were acquired.[100]

Rushdie comically invokes Lamarckian evolution as the magical science which explains the immigrants' equally magical transmutation by migration: just as Lamarck 'draws on mythic concepts of metamorphosis and transformation and explains them causally',[101] Rushdie's narrator and his characters offer Lamarck as the explanation for the migrants' newly acquired characteristics. Later in the novel, when Muhammad Sufyan, a landlord of the rooming house above the Shaandaar Café, tries to account for Saladin's mutation to the Shaandaar residents, it is Lamarck to whom he turns:

> The theories of Lamarck, I am pleased to report, were quoted by the exiled schoolteacher, who spoke in his best didactic voice. When Jumpy had recounted the unlikely story of Chamcha's fall from the sky... Sufyan, sucking teeth, made reference to the last edition of The Origin of Species. 'In which even great Charles accepted the notion of mutation in extremis, to ensure survival of species; so what if his followers – always more Darwinian than the man himself! – repudiated, posthumously, such Lamarckian heresy, insisting on natural selection and nothing but, – however, I am bound to admit, such a theory is not extended to survival of individual specimen but only to species as a whole;- in addition, regarding nature of mutation, problem is to comprehend actual utility of the change.'[102]

Here, Sufyan recognizes – in the manner of some contemporary commentators on epigenetics – that Lamarckism is limited in its ability to explain the acquisition of characteristics which aren't adaptive but are instead damaging. For it is apparent to the migrants that it is the socially and culturally hostile environment of England which dictates the nature of the characteristics they go on to acquire.

Picked up by the police and immigration officers, who abuse him in the back of their van, dragging off his clothes, beating him and making him eat his own excrement, Saladin becomes the 'animal'[103] they call him, growing horns, hairy thighs and hoofs, 'squealing like a pig'[104] before being beaten unconscious. Saladin's literal dehumanization is a direct result of the racism to which he is subject, and he is taken to a medical facility at the detention centre where he is surrounded by other immigrants who, the manticore in the bed next to him explains, have undergone similar transformations; '"there's a woman over that way," it said, "who is now mostly water-buffalo. There are businessmen from Nigeria who have grown sturdy tails. There is a group of holidaymakers from Senegal who were doing no more than changing planes when they were turned into slippery snakes"'.[105] The experience of racism manifests itself in physical, bodily changes which the immigrants themselves can hardly believe are true: in the face of the impossible, Saladin is forced to remind himself that 'he was a member of the real world',[106] that 'I am a real man',[107] and is particularly confounded by the fact that the police officers who abuse him are not alarmed by his mutation; 'what puzzled Chamcha was that a circumstance which struck him as utterly bewildering and unprecedented – that is, his metamorphosis into this supernatural imp – was being treated by the others as if it were the most banal and familiar matter they could imagine'.[108] Yet the police officers are not surprised by Saladin's appearance because for them it is not unreal or impossible; they see immigrants as animals and as less than human, and that becomes their reality. The enduring effect of racism is to make the imaginary real, as Saladin finally discovers in hospital; '"they describe us," the other whispered solemnly. "That's all. They have the power of description, and we succumb to the pictures they construct."'[109]

Rushdie's insistence that it is racism which creates race, that the immigrants' difference is constructed and made rather than biologically fixed or inherited, has clear parallels with epigenetic studies which locate seemingly racial characteristics as the biological embodiment of cultural and environmental circumstances. Rushdie's (like Butler's) representation of these processes, however, is of course 'unrealistic': changes to genetic structures are not the same as physical human–animal metamorphosis. This raises the question of what value such a magical–realist fictional representation can have for how we think about epigenetics; can Rushdie's fantastic depictions of humanity shed any light on a scientific (epigenetic) understanding of life and of race? A similar question is posed by Ian McEwan in his 2005 novel *Saturday*, in which the novel's neuroscientist protagonist, Henry Perowne, questions the efficacy of the magical–realist style of contemporary writers, including Rushdie:

> What were these authors of reputation doing – grown men and women of the twentieth century – granting supernatural powers to their characters? He never made it all the way through a single one of those irksome confections. And written for adults, not children. In more than one, heroes and heroines were born with or sprouted wings ... Others were granted a magical sense of smell, or tumbled unharmed out of high-flying aircraft.[110]

Perowne objects to fictions such as *The Satanic Verses* because they are not grounded in a 'recognizable physical reality'; their magical or supernatural forms evidence, in Perowne's view, of an 'insufficient imagination' because 'the actual, not the magical, should be the challenge'.[111] However what *The Satanic Verses* works to show is precisely that the actual and the magical are not as easily separable as Perowne imagines them to be. The value of Rushdie's magical representation of the formation of race lies in its very ability to reveal the dynamic relationship between the imaginary and the real; the immigrants' unprecedented animalistic transformations work to show the arbitrariness, absurdity, but also the ultimate power of the racist belief which shapes their reality. When Jumpy Joshi offers racism as an explanation of Saladin's transmutation – an alternative to Sufyan's invocation of Lamarck – this is a truth which the immigrants can accept: "'what has happened here? A: wrongful arrest, intimidation, violence. Two: Illegal detention, unknown medical experimentation in hospital," – murmurs of assent here, as memories of intra-vaginal inspections, Depo-Provera scandals, unauthorized post-partum sterilizations, and further back, the knowledge of Third World drug-dumping arose in every person present to give substance to the speaker's insinuations'.[112] Saladin's physical transformation can be accepted because 'what you believe depends on what you've seen, – not only what is visible, but what you are prepared to look in the face'.[113] In a manner comparable to Dana's gradual understanding of the realities of slavery in *Kindred*, once the migrants of *The Satanic Verses* acknowledge the force of their racist environment upon them, their bodies' physiological responses are no longer inexplicable or strange. In the context of an emerging epigenetic science, Rushdie's magical representation of processes of racial formation highlights what is latent in emerging epigenetic studies; namely that race is no more than a powerful biofiction made real by racism.

Towards a literary epigenetics

Writing in 2005, five years after the mapping of the human genome, geneticist Johnjoe McFadden noted that the idea that there are 'genes for' certain diseases and conditions was already beginning to crumble. Systems biology, he argued, has revealed that 'rather than having a single major function, most genes... probably play a small part in lots of tasks within the cell'.[114] Genes can no longer be considered 'discrete nuggets of genetic information' but are 'diffuse entities whose functional reality may be spread across hundreds of interacting DNA segments'.[115] The complexity of the system, in contrast to the reductionism of the gene-centric biology that dominated the latter half of the twentieth century, is comparable, in McFadden's view, to the 'holistic approaches' which have 'always dominated the humanities and social sciences'.[116] He ends his article with the following example: 'The first eight chapters of Salman Rushdie's *Midnight's*

Children describes the lives of the narrator's grandparents, parents, aunts, uncles and friends against the backdrop of the tumultuous politics of 20th-century India and Pakistan. The reason, according to the narrator, is that "to understand just one life, you have to swallow the world". Perhaps biologists ought to have read more'.[117] McFadden's suggestion, that fiction has already imagined the kinds of complexity that post-genomic biology is only now beginning to uncover, and that biologists might learn from literary ways of knowing the world, is a provocative one. Few scholars, whether literary or scientific in background, have suggested that literature might offer models or approaches which science might look towards, undoubtedly wary of reviving the clashes of the culture wars of the 1990s. Although McFadden's call for biologists to read more is perhaps made somewhat flippantly, in inviting the literary into the realm of the biological, positioning it as a discipline of comparable epistemological weight with the capacity (even when not addressing science directly) to influence how genetics is conceptualized and understood, McFadden's article raises interesting questions about the role that fiction might play in post-genomic biology as it moves towards a complex, non-deterministic conception of the gene. If new genetic understandings of the body have been in some way previously conceived of in fiction, then how can fiction guide understanding of these emerging scientific insights?

In the case of both *Kindred* and *The Satanic Verses*, fiction highlights what might be necessary for the creation of an anti-racist epigenetics; that is, an understanding of the inextricability of the body and its environment in which 'the environment' is understood to encompass both historical and contemporary racist practices. Evelyn Fox Keller, writing on the 'cellular complex' around the gene which 'not only reads, translates, and interprets that sequence, but also defines it',[118] claims that 'when scientists attempt to score the effects of nurture, that concept has already been substantially trivialized, focusing almost exclusively on physical resources. Heritability studies, for example, rarely if ever include such factors as maternal love, community values, or racist expectations in their measures. The same must be said of the new sociogenomics'.[119] The potential danger of epigenetics, and the sociological discourses taking shape around it, is that a limited understanding of the environment might in turn limit the scope of investigation and possibility. Biologists need, according to Keller, 'a language capable of expressing how the beliefs, expectations, and behaviour of others constitutes an individual's environment and, in turn, work to shape both the body and the behaviour of that individual'.[120] While Keller looks towards cultural anthropology for this language, the language of literature can also offer a point of entry for comprehending this process. *Kindred* and *The Satanic Verses* offer visions of a body–environment dynamic which foregrounds racism as a central factor in biological inheritance and development, offering fantastical representations of bodily transformation which underscore how cultural fantasies and fictions determine real, environmental conditions. The dissolution of the boundaries between reality and fiction in these texts not only parallels but also pushes further the collapse of nature/nurture and biology/culture distinctions in post-genomic biology. They create space for the possibility that fiction itself might be taken seriously as a significant shaper of human environments, for if racist fantasies can have such power, then why not anti-racist literary fictions? While these novels represent the problematic marks left on bodies by racist environments, they also express the potential that there might be in knowing the body in this way – a potential for an altered understanding of reality and truth based on an acknowledgement of the fact that 'absent environmental factors, genes have no more power to shape the development of an individual than do environmental factors in the absence of genes'.[121]

As the initial 'hype' around epigenetics dies down, more and more concerns are being raised about the potential of this science to do harm. For Mansfield and Guthman, 'epigenetics produces an intensified racialization because it redefines difference as epigenetic *damage*'[122] and 'if epigenetics is about how racism and disadvantage get under the skin, it normalizes white bodies and behaviors and reinforces the idea that people of color need to emulate the environments and behaviors of rich white people in order to protect themselves and their offspring'.[123] These concerns should certainly be taken seriously, but in the face of continuing attempts to define race more traditionally as simply 'in the genes', epigenetics provides a radical opportunity for the re-thinking of race. It enables a much-needed reassertion of the importance of both historical and contemporary forms of racial discrimination, factors often excluded from identity-focused theorizations of race in the biosciences. There is no denying the harm that ensues from racist environments, and epigenetics does not necessarily enable us to move past racial thinking altogether, but it does call for a change in our understanding of processes of racialization, a change in our notion of the boundaries between reality and fiction. Novels such as *Kindred* and *The Satanic Verses* can help us to navigate this new understanding of the formation of race, but also offer ways of overcoming the potential pitfalls that it presents. By demonstrating that the imagined must be acknowledged, accounted for and ultimately accepted as part of 'the real' in a science which itself was not long ago considered 'magical', they create space for their own fictions to be taken seriously in a genetic culture, as sites of knowledge about how people living with the experience of racialization, while they may be harmed by their biological inheritance or development, also have to learn to live with the knowledge of how it is formed. These novels are repositories of embodied knowledge which can inform a scientific reality which is constantly changing and incorporating what was previously unreal. They evidence the 'power of description', be it in the racist thought of slave owners and immigration officials or in fictional works themselves, in shaping the environments in which we live.

Conclusion

On 2 January 2019, PBS premiered a documentary on the life of Nobel Prize-winning geneticist and co-discoverer (with Francis Crick, Rosalind Franklin and Maurice Wilkins) of the structure of DNA – James Watson. In 2007, Watson, the one-time head of the Human Genome Project, had claimed in a newspaper interview that he was 'inherently gloomy about the prospect of Africa' because 'all our social policies are based on the fact that their intelligence is the same as ours – whereas all the testing says not really'.[1] In the wake of his comments a number of his planned speaking engagements were cancelled, and his employers, the Cold Spring Harbor Laboratory in Long Island, suspended him as their Chancellor. In 2014 he auctioned off his Nobel medal, citing his ostracization from the scientific community as a result of his remarks on race as the reason. Asked by the interviewer of the 2019 PBS documentary whether his views on genetics, intelligence and race had changed, Watson replied, 'No, not at all ... There's a difference on the average between blacks and whites on IQ tests. I would say the difference is genetic'.[2] These comments led to him being stripped of the last of his honorary titles, the Cold Spring Harbor Laboratory describing his comments as 'unsubstantiated and reckless personal opinions', 'reprehensible' and 'unsupported by science'.[3]

In many ways, Watson's deterministic conception of genetics, his insistence on the separation of nature from nurture, is out-of-step with the latest scientific developments and thinking in his field, an old-fashioned view of the gene which parallels what biologist Joseph Graves claims is an old-fashioned understanding of race: writing in response to the PBS documentary, Graves argues that Watson's views are a 'product of his time', of the fact that he 'was born into a rigidly segregated society. For much of his life, most biologists and anthropologists perpetuated the notion of race science', a background which leaves Watson unable to process more recent genetic findings that 'socially-defined races do not correspond to the underlying genetic variation within our species'.[4] While

Graves acknowledges the toxicity of Watson's views, and their contribution to racism in the United States, Graves implies that such genetic views of race are confined to an older generation of scientists as he presents contemporary genetics as having moved on from such ideas. It is true that Watson's extreme and overtly racist views have been widely condemned within the scientific community, a community which is now largely anti-racist in intent.[5] However as the case studies in this book highlight, contemporary genetics cannot be characterized as a science which has entirely separated itself from racial or indeed sometimes racist ways of thinking. Not only have developments such as the Human Genome Diversity Project and BiDil continued to promote racialized forms of categorization alongside the wider scientific denial of the genetic reality of race, but the rejection and attempted disruption of genetic conceptions of race, apparent in the African Eve hypothesis and the HGP, have, as is evident in the Graves's example here, often occurred through the scientific separation of the social from the genetic. Race is framed as a social problem while current genetic science is framed as distinct from that which went before. I have argued that these separations, while not overt expressions of racism of the kind espoused by Watson, have combined with the dismissal of the genetic reality of race to enable the recurrence of racial patterns of thinking and racist outcomes in a science which otherwise declares itself to be anti-racist. The anti-racist stance of contemporary genetics has occurred in the absence of a scientific consensus on what race is, and it is what Rob DeSalle and Ian Tattersall call the 'widespread confusion' that 'still exists about the nature of the evidence on which the human species is subdivided'[6] which creates the void in which people like James Watson – a real-life Dr Sick – can promote genetic racism.

This book has argued for a new, literary intervention into these debates, premised on the fact that contemporary fictions refuse the biology/culture, science/society binaries that are still promoted by scientists and literary scholars alike. Rather than accepting one scientific stance over another, or endorsing some science as straightforwardly factually correct (as some literary scholars of race have done), the contemporary novels discussed in this book compel us never to lose sight of the ways in which all ideas about race are formed from complex entanglements across the biological and cultural realms. The novels demonstrate how literature itself is bound up, in different ways, in these racial biofictions, whether it be in the influence of Alex Haley's *Roots* on the creation of popular narratives of African ancestry in bioanthropology, or in the literary metaphors and language used by the scientific community as explored in *White Teeth* and *Apex Hides the Hurt*. In articulating how facts and fantasies of race cannot be comprehended individually, how fiction and science share forms, methodologies, language and imagery, the novels offer a new understanding of race as biofictional, regardless of whether a particular racial idea or development is presented as anti-racist in formation and effect. What the novels offer at a moment when genetic science is widely understood to be anti-racist is an understanding of how this anti-racism is narratively constructed, of how the contemporary cogeneration of ideas about race across the boundaries of biology and culture means that the genetics of race is not impermeable to racism and that older racial thinking is always latent in the new. While Whitehead demonstrates this by evoking the absurd racist theories of nineteenth-century surgeon Samuel Cartwright as a precursor to pharmacogenetics' reliance on language to make race signify, Ishiguro and Rushdie evoke Darwinian and Lamarckian theories, respectively, as they imagine how earlier theories of biological similarity and change might continue to shape race's biofictional formations in the present.

In so doing, the novels resist the break with history emphasized in much contemporary genetic discourse, and instead encourage us to imagine how the continuities between bioscience past and present might not only result in the repetition of certain racial modes of thought, but might also offer an alternative to the certainties about race that genetic science attempts to assert. For by invoking the precedents for contemporary genetic ideas of race, and in so doing demonstrating how race has always been biofictional, the novels ultimately suggest that the meaning of race will never be fixed, that the biofictional nature of race means it will always be subject to change and revision as it is formed and reformed across the cultural, social and scientific spheres. Indeed, this is the suggestion of the book's final chapter; epigenetic science, in foregrounding how bodies are in a fluid, dynamic relationship with their environments, offers us a way of understanding the fluidity of race itself, which is made and re-made at the intersections of scientific fact and fiction, of the biological body and its environment (where the environment, as Butler and Rushdie demonstrate, is often shaped by the racist imaginaries of the dominant political culture). Understanding race in this way might, I argue, offer the opportunity for a renewed anti-racism in science and literary studies based on an understanding of the permeability, rather than fixity, of racialized bodies.

The global political climate in the final years of the 2010s makes it in some ways understandable that scientists have attempted to create a narrative around race which, despite (or perhaps because of) frequent interventions of the kind made by Watson, presents contemporary genetics as largely unified in its anti-racism and in its refusal of a biological basis for race. For we are living through a moment at which scientific expertise and facts are being brought into question by conservative politicians in the United States and UK who have sought to win popularity and votes through degrading expert scientific knowledge and academic expertise.[7] Partly in response to President Donald Trump's denial of the phenomena and effects of climate change and his apparent anti-vaccination stance among other positions, a worldwide March for Science was held in April 2017, 'inspired by a growing concern about the lack of science in policy' and calling for a 'science that upholds the common good, and for political leaders and policymakers to enact evidence-based policies in the public interest'.[8] In the context of the political downplaying of the efficacy of science, and the questioning and misuse of scientific ideas by right-wing politicians and groups, it is unsurprising that scientists have sought to double down on the importance of scientific fact, and of science as an objective set of disciplinary procedures based strictly on verifiable evidence. When it comes to race, the global political climate has resulted in the increasing misuse of science for racist ends. As Andrea Morris, who worked on the film about James Watson, has pointed out, 'It's not an old story of an old guy with old views' but instead the correlation between race, genetics and intelligence which Watson postulates, 'feels very current'.[9] Many scientists are concerned by the ways in which their work is being misused and misinterpreted by white supremacists, who increasingly draw on a variety of genetic technologies such as DNA ancestry tracing, and discuss scientific papers on far-right online forums as they search for scientific backing for their racist views.[10] The situation has become of so much concern that in November 2018 the American Society of Human Genetics issued a statement denouncing attempts to link genetics and racial supremacy, affirming that 'genetics demonstrates that humans cannot be divided into biologically distinct subcategories'.[11]

In this context the definite and definitive language used by geneticists who affirm the non-genetic basis of race is comprehensible, their insistence that science offers the final word on race a defence against those within science and without who are increasingly questioning this 'fact'. Literary scholars have adopted similar positions on the scientific facts of race. Not only have scholars of race largely accepted the anti-racist outlook of contemporary genetics, but on the relatively few occasions when literature and science scholarship has addressed the question of race in science, a comparable approach to science emerges: Sabine Sielke, for example, asks why 'curiously enough, while biology encourages us to "forget about" race, literary and cultural studies keep celebrating – and selling – ethnic difference. Was C.P. Snow right, after all, when he deemed the "literary intellectual" a racist while cheering the scientist as truly liberal, envisioning a bright future?'[12] While she acknowledges that 'matters are, of course, a bit more complicated',[13] here, it is literary studies, with its insistence on classifying writers according to race, indeed even in its emphasis on debating and discussing race, which, rather than science, is framed as responsible for the continuation of racial thinking within the academy.[14] Yet it is in the very lack of attention given to black and minority ethnic writers within literature and science studies that we can discern the problems with both the avoidance of race as a subject of enquiry and with the critical belief that science has once and for all solved the problem of race, tempting as it might be to accept this as fact.

In interrogating the 'facts' of anti-racist science in this book, there is a danger that my own critical stance could be aligned with those who seek to undermine science, that in questioning the objectivity and neutrality of the anti-racist discourses of contemporary genetics and the literary critical acceptance of these discourses, my approach could be interpreted (although it certainly is not) as an endorsement of their opposite – a conception of race as grounded in the genes. This is a bind which Bruno Latour addresses in relation to climate change denial, one of the things which he argues has been made possible by postmodern forms of critique in the humanities, which in the 1990s could be characterized, he contends, by the argument that 'facts are made up, that there is no such thing as natural, unmediated, unbiased access to truth, that we are always prisoners of language'.[15] For Latour, and those he has inspired in literary studies, emphasizing a lack of scientific certainty has deleterious effects: the critical questioning of scientific truth becomes just another form of the kind of popularism from which conspiracy theories arise, no matter how much the latter deforms the former.[16] The solution he proposes is to flip critique so that rather than questioning objectivity, the task is to reveal 'the real objective and incontrovertible facts hidden behind the *illusion* of prejudices'.[17] When it comes to race, this would mean the upholding of the incontrovertible fact that race is not genetic, in order to counter racist prejudice. In focusing on analysing science and scientists, humanities scholars may have chosen 'the wrong enemies' according to Latour, and the problem with critique is that 'when we try to reconnect scientific objects with their aura, their crown, their web of associations, when we accompany them back to their gathering, we always appear to *weaken* them, not to *strengthen* their claim to reality'.[18] The solution he proposes is for the critic to reposition herself as one who assembles and one who gathers together (rather than rips apart).[19]

The aim of this book has been not to destroy or break apart the scientific finding that race has no biological basis. I believe that racial categorizations, divisions between 'black' and 'white', do not correlate to specific genetic markers and that there is more genetic diversity within populations demarcated by race than there is between them. This book is also driven by the desire for an antiracist science and literary culture equipped with the tools to fight the falsehoods and stories about race being increasingly promoted by racist white supremacists. But it is precisely because of this anti-racist aim that I have been concerned to explore the political, cultural and scientific conditions which have made the apparent anti-racist stance of contemporary genetics possible. While such an analysis of the threads that make up this scientific position may appear to 'weaken' the reality that race is not genetic by uncovering the biofictional assemblages of which it is made, the consequence of not investigating the formation and effects of the anti-racist tenor of genetics is the reproduction of the very racism which this scientific stance seeks to avoid. From the apparently raceless clones of *Never Let Me Go*, to Marcus Chalfen's insistence that his genetic experimentation is post-racial in *White Teeth*, to the stereotypes of African and black people which emerge in *Roots* and which informed bioanthropological narratives on the unity of humankind, the contemporary novels in this book demonstrate how racial configurations emerge at moments when science appears to move beyond race. They show how the political post-racialism and colourblind ideologies which would deny the very existence of racism itself have gained strength from the scientific finding that race is not genetic, and explore what the consequences of this might be. Understanding how the anti-racist import of science has in fact been enabled and driven at times by a lack of concern about racism is essential if we are to move towards the alternative, anti-racist conceptions of race and racism put forward in the final chapter – an understanding of race as the biological impact of racist belief, as fiction made real through bodies' exposure to environments shaped by racist fantasies.

This book has proposed a methodology through which such configurations might be uncovered and analysed, a methodology which draws upon, rather than unthinkingly critiques, scientific ideas, in particular new post-genomic ideas about the permeability of bodies in relation to their (cultural) environments, environments which I have argued might be expanded in conception to include the fictional, the imaginary and the made-up. Yet this interdisciplinary approach has also had at its core a desire to seek out literary engagements with science, and intersections between science and fiction, which are otherwise overlooked by a field dominated by the analysis of literature written by white, Anglophone authors. While the racial backgrounds of the authors in this study has not been an organizing principle, it is perhaps unsurprising that it is in the work of writers of colour that ideas about race and science emerge, and it is in their work that alternatives to the Latourian view of the world (steeped as it is in European philosophy) might be found. Creating an interdisciplinarity based upon exchange and openness between literary studies and bioscience is not enough; what this book calls for is a decolonized approach to literature and science, an approach that does not simply encompass the analysis of work by non-white writers, but demands that the forms of knowledge found within their works and beyond be brought to bear on the methodologies that scholars in this field employ. Calls for decolonized forms of knowledge – a knowledge which foregrounds the intellectual and critical work of non-European thinkers while acknowledging the racist roots of some canonical scholarship – currently abound in the academy, in both the sciences and the humanities. That these demands for 'alternative facts' have occurred at the same moment at which academic knowledge is being questioned and distorted by popularist politicians and fascist groups has caused some confusion, and in some cases only added to academics' sense that their work is under attack. Yet the two are quite different, and in the case of calls for a decolonized knowledge, I think that this movement might actually assist scholars interested in how the traditional boundaries of the humanities and science are being, and might be, reconfigured. For what the decolonization movement calls for—and where I believe that it might inform approaches to, and understanding of, the field of literature and science—is an analysis and acknowledgement of the critical role that classification plays in shaping knowledge: both literature and science scholars and decolonization scholars are concerned with the constitution of and relationships between disciplines, in how some knowledge is variously ordered and valued in relation to other forms of knowledge.[20] Interdisciplinarity itself emerged through ethnic studies, black studies and women's studies in the 1950s, 1960s and 1970s as a means of critiquing power in the face of disciplinary mechanisms that reproduced certain relations of power.[21]

Yet interdisciplinary research today, at least that concerned with the sciences and the humanities, has largely overlooked this fact, and as a result is still often shaped and determined by the very disciplinary structures that it is seeking to move beyond. The field of literature and science studies has arguably been built upon an approach which places canonical writers and works in conversation with science (which, conversely, is often lesser known or peripheral) and leaves the structures of English studies – including the prioritization of writers traditionally considered important or significant – intact.[22] The works of black and minority ethnic writers are, it can be assumed, thought to be the province of postcolonial scholars, as is the issue of race. Thus little attention has been given to the fact that English studies as a discipline as well as the publishing industry continue to categorize and classify literature based on modes of thought which have their origins in the biological (and therefore racial) sciences. Inspired by the organizational principles of biology, attempts were made in the nineteenth century (under the aegis of genre theory) to arrange literary texts in taxonomic order.[23] The legacy of such historical exchanges, Sielke argues, can be seen today in 'technical terms (such as origin, genus, genre, gender, reproduction and mimicry) and cultural practices (like classification and taxonomy) which both biology and literary studies employ to their own particular ends',[24] literary and cultural studies having 'evolved some of their central questions and concerns, privileged theories, methods and concepts from a dialogue with the discourses of biology'.[25] The taxonomic patterns of literary studies have their roots in nineteenth-century biology which in turn, as I argued in the introduction, formed and shaped ideas about race through processes of exchange with the humanities at the height of imperialism. Thus while as Levine notes, 'despite the fact that many – if not most – of us practicing literary criticism have a distaste for nationalist and imperialist agendas, and understand literatures as transnational formations that include multiple languages and geographies', nevertheless 'the institutional patterns of nineteenth and early twentieth century English departments persist'.[26] In this way the situation of contemporary literary studies appears much like that of anti-racist science – mine is a discipline whose practitioners profess to be anti-racist but have done too little to question the underpinning assumptions that organize scholarship. The academy, at least in the UK, remains preoccupied with how British writers of ethnic minority backgrounds can be described and classified, and it is the way that such writing and scholarship is often separated from English (read white) literature that has led scholars interested in interdisciplinarity to overlook how the work of writers of colour might inform approaches to literature and science.

This book is an attempt to re-think the boundaries between science and literary studies, but also the artificial divisions within literary studies itself, to demonstrate how engaging with the idea of race, and with writers who have examined the dimensions and afterlives of this concept, can transform understanding of the relations between science and literature. The novels examined in this book each, in different ways, offer biofictional understandings of race in the contemporary era which might begin to change and to challenge approaches to race in literature and science studies, literary studies more broadly and in genetic science. They show us how our disciplinary objects cannot be neatly contained, how the co-production of race across scientific and fictional borders dissolves the classifications and distinctions between disciplines, practices and indeed racial groups that shape academic and public discourse. At a moment when the meanings of race in genetics are as contested and as fractured as ever, when institutions, political, social and educational, refuse to speak the language of race and racism, the racial formations represented in contemporary fiction offer a mode of comprehending the biofictional nature of race that speaks both to bioscience and to literary studies; a mode in which what is fact and what is fiction cannot be aligned with traditional disciplinary distinctions between science and literature.

Notes

Introduction

1. *The First Brit: Secrets of the 10,000 Year Old Man*, directed by Steven Clarke, produced by Plimsoll Productions, aired 18 February 2018, on Channel 4, https://www.channel4.com/programmes/the-first-brit-the-10000-year-old-man.
2. Ibid.
3. Ibid.
4. Ibid.
5. Ibid.
6. Ibid.
7. David Reich, '"Race" in The Age of Modern Genetics', *The New York Times*, 25 March 2018, SR1.
8. Ibid.
9. Ibid.
10. Ibid.
11. Ibid.
12. In 2016, posters appeared on the campus of Amherst College which displayed skulls of different sizes and linked them to arguments about racial differences in intelligence. Biddy Martin, 'Racist Posters on Campus', Amherst College, accessed 29 August 2018, https://www.amherst.edu/amherst-story/president/statements/node/665033. In 2018 it was reported that US white nationalists and the far-right are increasingly appropriating research on the human genome to advance their theories of racial hierarchy. Amy Harmon, 'Why White Supremacists Are Chugging Milk (and Why Geneticists Are Alarmed)', *The New York Times*, 17 October 2018, https://www.nytimes.com/2018/10/17/us/white-supremacists-science-dna.html.
13. Donna Haraway, *Modest_Witness@Second Millenium. FemaleMan©_Meets_OncoMouse™* (New York: Routledge, 1997), 220.
14. Following the airing of *The First Brit* the *Daily Mail* published an article which queried the idea that Cheddar Man was black. Tim Collins, 'Was Cheddar man white after all? There's no way to know that the first Briton had "dark to black skin" says scientist who helped reconstruct his 10,000-year-old face', *The Mail Online*, 2 March 2018, http://www.dailymail.co.uk/sciencetech/article-5453665/Was-Cheddar-man-white-all.html.

15 Jonathan Kahn et al., 'How Not to Talk About Race and Genetics', *BuzzFeed News*, 30 March 2018, https://www.buzzfeednews.com/article/bfopinion/race-genetics-david-reich.
16 Clarke, *The First Brit*.
17 David Reich, *Who We Are and How We Got Here: Ancient DNA and the New Science of the Human Past* (Oxford: Oxford University Press, 2018), 268.
18 See Amos Morris-Reich and Dirk Rupnow, 'Introduction', in *Ideas of 'Race' in the History of the Humanities*, ed. Amos Morris-Reich and Dirk Rupnow (Switzerland: Palgrave Macmillan, 2017), 9.
19 Robert J.C. Young, *Colonial Desire: Hybridity in Theory, Culture and Race* (London: Routledge, 1995), 92.
20 Morris-Reich and Rupnow, 'Introduction', 9.
21 W.E.B. Du Bois, *Dusk of Dawn: An Essay Toward an Autobiography of a Race Concept* series ed. Henry Louis Gates Jr. (New York: Oxford University Press, 2007), 50.
22 Immanuel Kant, 'Of the Different Human Races', in *The Idea of Race*, ed. Robert Bernasconi and Tommy L. Lott (Indianapolis: Hackett, 2000), 11.
23 Johann Blumenbach, 'On the Natural Variety of Mankind', in *The Idea of Race*, ed. Robert Bernasconi and Tommy L. Lott (Indianapolis: Hackett, 2000), 27.
24 Arthur de Gobineau, 'The Inequality of Human Races', in *The Idea of Race*, ed. Robert Bernasconi and Tommy L. Lott (Indianapolis: Hackett, 2000), 45.
25 Bill Ashcroft, 'Critical Histories: Postcolonialism, Postmodernism, and Race', in *Postmodern Literature and Race*, ed. Len Platt and Sara Upstone (Cambridge: Cambridge University Press, 2015), 15–16.
26 Michel Foucault, 'Right of Death and Power over Life', in *The Will to Knowledge: The History of Sexuality Volume 1*, trans. Robert Hurley (London: Penguin, 1998; 1978), 140.
27 Michel Foucault, 'Lecture 11 17 March 1976', in *Society Must Be Defended: Lectures at the College de France*, ed. Mauro Bertani and Alessandro Fontana, trans. David Macey (New York: Picador, 2003), 254.
28 Ibid., 256–257. It is no coincidence, as Priscilla Wald has argued, that Foucault's theory of biopower emerged at a time (the 1970s) when biotechnology was growing rapidly and promising new ways to administer bodies and manage life. Priscilla Wald, 'Cells, Genes, and Stories: HeLa's Journey from Labs to Literature', in *Genetics and the Unsettled Past: The Collision of DNA, Race and History*, ed. Keith Wailoo, Alondra Nelson and Catherine Lee (New Brunswick, NJ: Rutgers University Press, 2012), 257.
29 An argument made by Jenny Reardon. Jenny Reardon, 'Decoding Race and Human Difference in a Genomic Age', *differences: A Journal of Feminist Cultural Studies* 15 (2004): 42.

30 Kwame Anthony Appiah, 'Mistaken Identities: Colour', *The Reith Lectures*, BBC Radio 4, London, 5 November 2016, https://www.bbc.co.uk/programmes/b080t63w.

31 Kwame Anthony Appiah, 'Racial Identity Is a Biological Nonsense Says Reith Lecturer', interview by Hannah Ellis-Petersen, *The Guardian*, 18 October 2016, https://www.theguardian.com/society/2016/oct/18/racial-identity-is-a-biological-nonsense-says-reith-lecturer.

32 Appiah, 'Mistaken Identities'.

33 Ibid.

34 Henry Louis Gates, Jr., 'Reading "'Race', Writing, and Difference"', *PMLA* 123, no. 5 (2008): 1536.

35 Ibid., 1538.

36 Ibid.

37 Ibid.

38 Ibid.

39 Paul Gilroy, *Against Race: Imagining Political Culture beyond the Color Line* (Cambridge, MA: Belknap Press, 2000), 41 and 46.

40 Ibid., 15.

41 Ibid., 35.

42 Helen Young, *Race and Popular Fantasy Literature: Habits of Whiteness* (New York: Routledge, 2016), 7.

43 Lesley Larkin, *Race and the Literary Encounter: Black Literature from James Weldon Johnson to Percival Everett* (Bloomington: Indiana University Press, 2015), 18.

44 Sara Upstone, *Rethinking Race and Identity in Contemporary British Fiction* (New York: Routledge, 2017), 46–47.

45 Ashcroft, 'Critical Histories', 28.

46 In addition to the Reich example from the field of ancient DNA, other examples of contrary scientific standpoints include the explicit use of racial categorization in pharmacogenomics and medicine (which I discuss in Chapter 4), and the work of many 'race realists', including geneticist and University of California Professor Neil Risch, who has argued for genetic differentiation among races. Neil Risch, Esteban Burchard, Elad Ziv and Hua Tang, 'Categorization of Humans in Biomedical Research: Genes, Race and Disease', *Genome Biology* 3, no. 7 (2002).

47 Jenny Reardon, *Race to the Finish: Identity and Governance in an Age of Genomics* (Princeton, NJ: Princeton University Press, 2005), 23.

48 Reardon, 'Decoding Race', 42.

49 Ibid., 43.

50 Donna Haraway, *Primate Visions: Gender, Race, and Nature in the World of Modern Science* (New York: Routledge, 1989), 123.

51   Ibid., 12.
52   Susan Squier, *Liminal Lives: Imagining the Human at the Frontiers of Biomedicine* (Durham, NC, and London: Duke University Press, 2004), 10.
53   Arthur Jensen, 'How Much Can We Boost IQ and Scholastic Achievement?', *Harvard Educational Review* 39 (1969): 1–123.
54   Francis Crick, letter to John Edsall, 22 February 1971, Francis Crick Papers, Wellcome Library, London.
55   Edsall writes that the response of those against Shockley was 'a political reply to a political proposal'. John Edsall, letter to Francis Crick, 5 March 1971, Francis Crick Papers, Wellcome Library, London.
56   Crick was aware of such criticism. He kept a copy of a booklet produced by the Party for Workers Power on scientific racism, which contained the statement on academic freedom that Crick had signed. The booklet states, 'We, in the Party for Workers Power, have made that choice. We intend to defeat racism in all of its forms ... Specific racist books and professors must be selected against which to build a mass campaign.' *Pamphlet on Racism by Party for Workers Power*, Francis Crick Papers, Wellcome Library, London.
57   One of the most well-known arguments for the social construction of science was Bruno Latour and Steve Woolgar, *Laboratory Life: The Construction of Scientific Facts* (Princeton, NJ: Princeton University Press, 1986).
58   Stephen Jay Gould, *The Mismeasure of Man* (London: Penguin, 1997; 1981), 368.
59   See Richard C. Lewontin, 'Race and Intelligence', *Bulletin of Atomic Scientists* 26, no. 3 (1970): 2–8. The 1951 UNESCO Statement on Race, made in the aftermath of the Second World War and the Holocaust, carried the signatures of many prominent geneticists and anthropologists and stated unequivocally that 'the likenesses among men are far greater than their differences'. Ashley Montagu, *Statement on Race: An Annotated Elaboration and Exposition of the Four Statements on Race Issued by the United Nations Educational, Scientific, and Cultural Organisation*, 3rd edn. (New York: Oxford University Press, 1972; 1951), 7. However, the statement masked significant differences of opinion among the scientific community. See Marek Kohn, *The Race Gallery: The Return of Racial Science* (London: Vintage, 1996), 45.
60   David Theo Goldberg, *The Threat of Race: Reflections on Racial Neoliberalism* (Malden, MA: Blackwell, 2009), 21.
61   A. Cambridge and S. Feuchtwang, *Anti-Racist Strategies* (Aldershot: Avebury, 1991) qtd. in Phil Cohen, 'Through a Glass Darkly: Intellectuals on Race', in *New Ethnicities, Old Racisms?*, ed. Phil Cohen (London: Zed, 1999), 4.
62   Paul Gilroy, *There Ain't No Black in the Union Jack*, Routledge Classics edn. (London: Routledge, 2002; 1987), xiv.
63   Cohen, 'Through a Glass Darkly', 6.

64 Claire Worley, '"It's Not about Race. It's about the Community": New Labour and "Community Cohesion"', *Critical Social Policy* 25, no. 4 (2005): 487.
65 The Labour MP David Lammy encapsulated this emerging doctrine in 2011: 'I think we have to acknowledge today that whilst discrimination and racism remain issues, they are not the profound issues that they once were, and that there are a whole host of other social concerns that concern what happened to second and third generation black communities and broader issues that largely pertain to class.' David Lammy, 'A New Black Politics?' interview by David Goodhart, *Analysis*, BBC Radio 4, 31 October 2011, audio, https://www.bbc.co.uk/programmes/b016lbtp.
66 Michael K. Brown et al., *Whitewashing Race: The Myth of a Color-Blind Society* (Berkeley: University of California Press, 2003), vii.
67 Dorothy Roberts, *Fatal Invention: How Science, Politics and Big Business Re-Create Race in the Twenty-First Century* (New York: The New Press, 2011), 289–291.
68 See Francis S. Collins, 'What We Do and Don't Know about "Race," "Ethnicity," Genetics and Health at the Dawn of the Genome Era', *Genetics for the Human Race*, spec. issue of *Nature Genetics* 36, no. 11 (2004): S13–S15.
69 Johnny E. Williams, 'Talking About Race without Talking About Race: Color Blindness in Genomics', *American Behavioral Scientist* 59, no. 11 (2015): 1498 and 1502.
70 Catherine Bliss, *Race Decoded: The Genomic Fight for Social Justice* (Stanford, CA: Stanford University Press, 2012), 4.
71 Roberts, *Fatal Invention*, 47.
72 Such criticism comes from Troy Duster, 'Race and Reification in Science', *Science* 307, no. 5712 (2005): 1050–1051; Troy Duster, *Backdoor to Eugenics*, 2nd edn. (New York: Routledge, 2003); Richard S. Cooper, Jay S. Kaufman and Ryk Ward, 'Race and Genomics', *The New England Journal of Medicine* 348, no. 12 (2003): 1166–1170; Morris W. Foster, 'Looking for Race in All the Wrong Places: Analyzing the Lack of Productivity in the Ongoing Debate about Race and Genetics', *Human Genetics* 126 (2009): 355–362.
73 Dorothy E. Roberts, 'The Politics of Race and Science: Conservative Colorblindness and the Limits of Liberal Critique', *Du Bois Review: Social Science Research on Race* 12, no. 1 (2015): 205.
74 Roberts, *Fatal Invention*, 297.
75 Goldberg, *The Threat of Race*, 23.
76 Trevor Philips, 'Stephen Lawrence Speech: Institutions Must Catch Up with Public on Race Issues', *Race in Britain: Ten Years since the Stephen Lawrence Inquiry*, Equality and Human Rights Commission, London, 19 January 2009, http://www.equalityhumanrights.com/key-projects/race-in-britain/event-ten-years-on-from-the-macpherson-inquiry/stephen-lawrence-speech-institutions-must-catch-up-with-public-on-race-issues/.

77 Dave Gunning, *Race and Anti-Racism in Black British and British Asian Literature* (Liverpool: Liverpool University Press, 2010), 3.
78 David Smith and Kevin Rawlinson, 'Trump Insists: "I Am the Least Racist Person" Amid Outrage over Remarks', *The Guardian*, 15 January 2018, https://www.theguardian.com/us-news/2018/jan/15/i-am-not-a-racist-trump-says-after-backlash-over-shithole-nations-remark.
79 From his 2017 ban on travel to the United States for those from seven majority Muslim countries, to his separation of migrant children from their parents at the Mexican border, and his defence of white supremacists, Trump's overt racisms are too numerous to name.
80 Catherine Nash, *Genetic Geographies: The Trouble with Ancestry* (Minneapolis: University of Minnesota Press, 2015), 7.
81 Alondra Nelson, 'Bio Science: Genetic Genealogy Testing and the Pursuit of African Ancestry', *Social Studies of Science* 38, no. 5 (2008): 761–762.
82 Alondra Nelson, *The Social Life of DNA: Race, Reparations and Reconciliation after the Genome* (Boston, MA: Beacon Press, 2016), 15–17.
83 Nikolas Rose, *The Politics of Life Itself: Biomedicine, Power and Subjectivity in the Twenty-First Century* (Princeton, NJ: Princeton University Press, 2007), 160.
84 Ibid., 161.
85 Bliss, *Race Decoded*, 11.
86 Ibid., 15.
87 Rose, *The Politics of Life Itself*, 37.
88 Bliss, *Race Decoded*, 9.
89 Bruno Latour, *We Have Never Been Modern*, trans. Catherine Porter (Cambridge, MA: Harvard University Press, 1993), 2–3.
90 Ibid., 3.
91 Homi K. Bhabha, 'Culture's In-Between', in *Questions of Cultural Identity*, ed. Stuart Hall and Paul du Gay (London: Sage, 1996), 54 and 58.
92 Pnina Werbner, 'Introduction: The Dialectics of Cultural Hybridity', in *Debating Cultural Hybridity: Multi-Cultural Identities and the Politics of Anti-Racism*, ed. Pnina Werbner and Tariq Modood (London: Zed, 2000), 20.
93 Young, *Colonial Desire*, 7–8.
94 See Lola Young, 'Hybridity's Discontents: Rereading Science and "Race"', in *Hybridity and Its Discontents: Politics, Science Culture*, ed. Avtar Brah and Annie E. Coombes (London: Routledge, 2000), 158; Tobias A. Wachinger, *Posing In-Between: Postcolonial Englishness and the Commodification of Hybridity* (Frankfurt: Peter Lang, 2003), 181; Young, *Colonial Desire*, 27.
95 Young, *Colonial Desire*, 27–28.
96 Bliss, *Race Decoded*, 9.
97 Rose, *The Politics of Life Itself*, 161.

98 See Sarah Winter, 'Darwin's Saussure: Biosemiotics and Race in *Expression*', *Representations*, 107 (2009): 136 and 154.
99 Waltraud Ernst, 'Introduction: Historical and Contemporary Perspectives on Race, Science and Medicine', in *Race, Science and Medicine, 1700–1960*, ed. Waltraud Ernst and Bernard Harris (London: Routledge, 1999), 7.
100 Ibid.
101 Dorothy Roberts, 'Race and the New Biocitizen', *What's the Use of Race?: Modern Governance and the Biology of Difference*, ed. Ian Whitmarsh and David S. Jones (Cambridge, MA: MIT Press, 2010), 261.
102 Haraway, *Primate Visions*, 3.
103 Amade M'Charek, 'Beyond Fact or Fiction: On the Materiality of Race in Practice', *Cultural Anthropology* 28, no. 3 (2013): 420.
104 Ibid., 423 and 435.
105 Caroline Levine, *Forms: Whole, Rhythm, Hierarchy, Network* (Princeton, NJ: Princeton University Press, 2017), 13, 16–17.
106 Gillian Beer, *Open Fields: Science in Cultural Encounter* (Oxford: Oxford University Press, 1996), 194.
107 Evelyn Fox Keller, 'From Gene Action to Reactive Genomes', *The Journal of Physiology* 592, no. 11 (2014): 2425 and 2427.
108 Evelyn Fox Keller, 'Thinking about Biology and Culture: Can the Natural and Human Sciences Be Integrated?', *The Sociological Review Monographs* 64, no. 1 (2016): 35.
109 Evelyn Fox Keller, *The Mirage of a Space between Nature and Nurture* (Durham, NC, and London: Duke University Press, 2010), 5.
110 Ibid., 6.
111 Haraway, *Primate Visions*, 15.
112 Karola Stotz and Paul E. Griffiths, 'Biohumanities: Rethinking the Relationship between Biosciences, Philosophy and History of Science, and Society', *The Quarterly Review of Biology* 83, no. 1 (2008): 37–45.
113 Maurizio Meloni et al., 'The Biosocial: Sociological Themes and Issues', *Sociological Review Monographs* 64, no. 1 (2016): 7–25.
114 Keller, 'Thinking about Biology and Culture', 37.
115 Stotz and Griffiths, 'Biohumanities', 37.
116 Keller 'Thinking about Biology and Culture', 36–37.
117 Beer, *Open Fields*, 149.
118 Levine, *Forms*, 9.
119 Squier, *Liminal Lives*, 10.
120 Ibid., 16.
121 Gillian Beer, *Darwin's Plots: Evolutionary Narrative in Darwin, George Eliot and Nineteenth-Century Fiction* (Cambridge: Cambridge University Press, 2000; 1983), 5.

122 Levine, *Forms*, 13.
123 Venla Oikkonen, *Population Genetics and Belonging: A Cultural Analysis of Genetic Ancestry* (Basingstoke: Palgrave Macmillan, 2018), 10.
124 Deborah Lynn Steinberg, *Genes and the Bioimaginary: Science, Spectacle, Culture* (Abingdon: Routledge, 2016), 2–3.
125 Stefan Timmermans and Sara Shostack, 'Gene Worlds', *Health: An Interdisciplinary Journal for the Social Study of Health, Illness and Medicine* 20, no. 1 (2016): 33.
126 See Priscilla Wald, *Contagious: Cultures, Carriers, and the Outbreak Narrative* (Durham, NC, and London: Duke University Press, 2008); Everett Hamner, *Editing the Soul: Science and Fiction in the Genome Age* (University Park, PA: The Pennsylvania State University Press, 2017); Judith Roof, *The Poetics of DNA* (Minneapolis: University of Minnesota Press, 2007); Jackie Stacey, *The Cinematic Life of the Gene* (Durham, NC, and London: Duke University Press, 2010); Deborah Lynn Steinberg, *Genes and the Bioimaginary*; Venla Oikkonen, *Population Genetics and Belonging*; Susan Squier, *Liminal Lives*.
127 Sandra Harding, 'Science, Race, Culture, Empire', in *A Companion to Racial and Ethnic Studies*, ed. David Theo Goldberg and John Solomos (Oxford: Blackwell, 2002), 220.
128 Rita Felski, 'Introduction: Recomposing the Humanities – with Bruno Latour', *New Literary History* 47, nos. 2&3 (2016): 215.
129 Felski, 'Introduction: Recomposing the Humanities', 228.
130 Steven Connor, 'Decomposing the Humanities', *New Literary History* 47, nos. 2&3 (2016): 281.
131 Ibid.
132 Ibid., 287 and 284.
133 Bruno Latour, 'Why Has Critique Run out of Steam? From Matters of Fact to Matters of Concern', *Critical Inquiry* 30, no. 2 (2004): 232.
134 Rita Felski, 'Context Stinks!', *New Literary History* 42, no. 4 (2011): 587.
135 Mario Biagioli, 'Postdisciplinary Liaisons: Science Studies and the Humanities', *Critical Inquiry* 35 (2009): 828.
136 Felski, 'Introduction: Recomposing the Humanities', 222.
137 Huehls, Mitchum. *After Critique: Twenty-First-Century Fiction in a Neoliberal Age* (New York: Oxford University Press, 2016), 98.
138 Harding, 'Science, Race, Culture, Empire', 226.
139 Sara Ahmed, 'Open Forum, Imaginary Prohibitions: Some Preliminary Remarks on the Founding Gestures of the "New Materialism"', *European Journal of Women's Studies* 15, no. 1 (2008): 35.
140 Patricia J. Williams, 'The Elusive Variability of Race', in *Race and the Genetic Revolution: Science, Myth and Culture*, ed. Sheldon Krimsky and Kathleen Sloan (New York: Colombia University Press, 2011), 243.

141 Levine, *Forms*, 22.
142 Bill Clinton, 'Remarks Made by the President, Prime Minister Tony Blair of England (via satellite), Dr. Francis Collins, Director of the National Human Genome Research Institute, and Dr. Craig Venter, President and Chief Scientific Officer, Celera Genomics Corporation, on the Completion of the First Survey of the Entire Human Genome Project', The East Room, The White House, 26 June 2000, National Human Genome Research Institute, http://www.genome.gov/10001356.
143 Lionel Trilling, *E.M. Forster*, 3rd edn. (New York: New Directions, 1964), 65.
144 Latour, 'Why Has Critique Run out of Steam?', 227.

Chapter 1

1 Rebecca L. Cann, Mark Stoneking and Allan C. Wilson, 'Mitochondrial DNA and Human Evolution', *Nature* 325 (1987): 33.
2 Ibid., 34.
3 Richard Leakey, *The Origin of Humankind* (New York: HarperCollins, 1994), 88.
4 Neanderthal fossils were discovered to be not as old as previously thought and modern–human looking fossils had been discovered in Southern Africa and Ethiopia. See Bernard Wood, *Human Evolution: A Very Short Introduction* (Oxford: Oxford University Press, 2005), 104.
5 Roger Lewin, *Bones of Contention: Controversies in the Search for Human Origins*, 2nd edn. (Chicago: University of Chicago Press, 1997), 330.
6 Robert N. Proctor, 'Three Roots of Human Recency: Molecular Anthropology, the Refigured Archeulean, and the UNESCO Response to Auschwitz', *Current Anthropology* 44, no. 2 (2003): 224–225.
7 Venla Oikkonen, 'Mitochondrial Eve and the Affective Politics of Human Ancestry', *Signs* 40, no. 3 (2015): 753.
8 'We Are All Children of Africa', review of *African Exodus: The Origins of Modern Humanity* by Chris Stringer and Robin McKie, *The Journal of Blacks in Higher Education* 17 (1997): 134.
9 Jane Gitschier, 'All About Mitochondrial Eve: An Interview with Rebecca Cann', *PLoS Genetics* 6, no. 5 (2010): 4.
10 Jason Antrosio, 'More Mothers than Mitochondrial Eve', *Living Anthropologically*, 2013, accessed 4 March 2019, http://www.livinganthropologically.com/anthropology/mitochondrial-eve/. Quoting Proctor, 'Three Roots of Human Recency', 225.
11 Itabari Njeri, 'Colorism: In American Society, Are Lighter-Skinned Blacks Better Off?', *Los Angeles Times*, 24 April 1988, http://articles.latimes.com/1988-04-24/news/vw-2472_1_skin-color.

12 Roger Lewin contends that 'as soon as Mitochondrial Eve made her appearance, the underlying genetic data were vigorously criticized, on several fronts. The rate of accumulation of mutations used by Wilson and others – the ticking of the molecular clock – was said to be too fast. And the interpretation of the "common ancestor" at the root of the tree has also been attacked'. Roger Lewin, *The Origin of Modern Humans* (New York: Scientific American Library, 1993), 96. See also Francisco J Ayala, 'The Myth of Eve: Molecular Biology and Human Origins', *Science* 270, no. 5244 (December 1995): 1930–1936.
13 Ann Gibbons, 'A New View of the Birth of *Homo sapiens*', *Science* 331, no. 6016 (January 2011): 392–394.
14 Carl Zimmer, 'Interbreeding with Neanderthals', *Discover Magazine*, 4 March 2013, http://discovermagazine.com/2013/march/14-interbreeding-neanderthals.
15 In 2014 a male skeleton found in South Africa was named as Eve's 'closest relative' after its DNA was sequenced. Michael Slezak, 'Found: Closest Link to Eve, Our Universal Ancestor', *New Scientist*, 9 October 2014, https://www.newscientist.com/article/mg22429904-500-found-closest-link-to-eve-our-universal-ancestor/.
16 Alexandra Hofmänner, 'The African Eve Effect in Science', *Archaeologies: Journal of the World Archaeological Congress* 7, no. 1 (2011): 256.
17 Ibid., 259.
18 Ibid., 279.
19 Kathleen Fuller, 'Pathological Science and MtEve', *Anthrohealth Blog*, accessed 29 April 2016, http://anthrohealth.net/blog/pathological-science-and-mteve.
20 Michael H. Brown, *The Search for Eve* (New York: Harper and Row, 1990), 107.
21 Fuller, 'Pathological Science'.
22 Lewin, *The Origin*, 8 and 97.
23 Lewin, *Bones of Contention*, 327.
24 Richard Dawkins, *River Out of Eden: A Darwinian View of Life* (London: Phoenix, 1994), xiv.
25 Helen Taylor, '"The Griot from Tennessee": The Saga of Alex Haley's Roots', *Critical Quarterly* 37, no. 2 (1995): 48.
26 Ibid.
27 Keith Wailoo, 'Who Am I?: Genes and the Problem of Historical Identity', in *Genetics and the Unsettled Past: The Collision of DNA, Race and History*, ed. Keith Wailoo, Alondra Nelson and Catherine Lee (New Brunswick, NJ: Rutgers University Press, 2012), 14.
28 Antrosio, 'More Mothers than Mitochondrial Eve'.
29 Chris Stringer and Robin McKie, *African Exodus: The Origins of Modern Humanity* (London: Pimlico, 1996), 234.
30 John H. Relethford, *Reflections of Our Past: How Human History Is Revealed in Our Genes* (Boulder, CO: Westview Press, 2003), 4.

31 Norman A. Johnson, *Darwinian Detectives: Revealing the Natural History of Genes and Genomes* (New York: Oxford University Press, 2007), 89.
32 Steve Jones, *The Language of the Genes* (London: Flamingo, 2000), 29.
33 Ibid., 32.
34 Deborah Lynn Steinberg, 'Reading Genes/Writing Nation: Reith, "Race" and the Writings of Geneticist Steve Jones', in *Hybridity and Its Discontents: Politics, Science, Culture*, ed. Avtar Brah and Annie E. Coombes (London: Routledge, 2000), 142.
35 Ibid., 141.
36 Relethford, *Reflections*, 8, Marianne Sommer also makes this point in '"It's a living History, told by the real survivors of the Times-DNA": Anthropological genetics in the tradition of biology as applied history', in *Genetics and the unsettled past: The collision of DNA, Race, and History*, eds. Keith Wailoo, Alondra Nelson and Catherine Lee (New Brunswick, NJ: Rutgers University Press, 2012), 230–231.
37 Alex Haley, *Roots* (London: Vintage, 1991), vii–viii.
38 Taylor, 'The Griot', 56.
39 Haley, *Roots*, 681.
40 Jerome de Groot, *Consuming History: Historians and Heritage in Contemporary Popular Culture* (Oxon: Routledge, 2009), 84.
41 Stephanie Athey, 'Poisonous Roots and the New World Blues: Rereading Seventies Narration and Nation in Alex Haley and Gayl Jones', *Narrative* 7, no. 2 (1999): 174.
42 Relethford, *Reflections*, 1.
43 Ibid., 4–5.
44 Ibid., x.
45 Sommer, 'It's a Living History', 231.
46 According to Stringer and McKie, one of the reasons biologists so upset palaeoanthropologists was 'the idea that the living can teach us anything about the past is a reversal of their cherished view that we can best learn about ourselves from studying our pre-history'. See Stringer and McKie, *African Exodus*, 114–115.
47 Stephen Oppenheimer, *Out of Eden: The Peopling of the World* (London: Constable and Robinson, 2003), xxi.
48 Johnson, *Darwinian Detectives*, 94.
49 Robert J. Norrell, *Alex Haley and the Books That Changed a Nation* (New York: St Martin's Press, 2015), 127.
50 Athey, 'Poisonous Roots', 173–174.
51 A point made by David Chioni Moore, 'the farther back one can trace a single ancestor, the less and less that ancestor represents you, except – and this is a significant point – by a process of retroactive and selective affiliation … Alex Haley could have identified any of these non-African ancestors as his root, but as a matter of practice and American social mandate, that is hard to imagine'. David Chioni Moore, 'Routes: Alex Haley's Roots and the Rhetoric of Genealogy', *Transition: An International Review* 64 (1994): 15.

52 Brown, *The Search for Eve*, 99.
53 Ibid., 98.
54 Daniel Dennett, *Darwin's Dangerous Idea* (London: Penguin Science, 1995), 96.
55 Haley, *Roots*, 688.
56 Stringer and McKie, *African Exodus*, preface.
57 Ibid., 234.
58 'The Journey of Mankind,' Bradshaw Foundation, accessed 9 January 2018, http://www.bradshawfoundation.com/stephenoppenheimer/index.php.
59 There are many examples of black intellectuals crediting *Roots* with bringing about a wider change in black people's understanding of their ancestry. Linton Kwesi Johnson, for example, wrote that 'for black people in Britain, *Roots* has given us a new sense of identity and belonging, a new feeling of racial pride. It provides a basis for the answering of the question: how can I as a black person place myself in the modern world, in the twentieth century?'. Linton Kwesi Johnson, 'Responses to Roots', *Race & Class* 19, no. 1 (1977): 84.
60 Stringer and McKie, *African Exodus*, 230.
61 Ibid., 231.
62 Sykes, *The Seven Daughters*, 15–16.
63 Ibid., 356–357.
64 Norrell, *Alex Haley*, 119.
65 Correspondence from Ina Corinne Brown to Alex Haley, 12 September 1972, Sc MG 472, Box 10, Folder 2, Alex Haley papers, Schomburg Center for Research in Black Culture, The New York Public Library, New York, United States of America.
66 Daniel T. Rodgers, *Age of Fracture* (Cambridge, MA: The Belknap Press of Harvard University Press, 2011), 117.
67 Norrell, *Alex Haley*, 195.
68 Harold Courlander, 'Kunta Kinte's Struggle to Be African', *Phylon: A Review of Race and Culture* 47, no. 4 (1986): 295.
69 Ibid., 295.
70 Ibid., 297.
71 Ibid., 301.
72 Haley, *Roots*, 22.
73 Ibid., 56, 162 and 183.
74 Ibid., 192.
75 Ibid., 295.
76 Norrell, *Alex Haley*, 91.
77 Alex Haley, *The Autobiography of Malcolm X* (New York: Ballantine, 1999), 164.
78 Haley, *Roots*, 306–307.
79 Haley, *The Autobiography*, 165.
80 Ibid., 168.

81 Ibid., 184.
82 Critic Leslie Fielder described Kunta Kinte as 'less a portrait of Haley's first American ancestor, legendary or real, than of Malcolm X as Haley perceived him', Kunta and Malcolm both being 'inverted Racist[s], convinced that all Whites not only invariably do evil to all Blacks, but that they have an offensive odor, and are properly classified not as human but as *toubob*, "devils," who must be resisted unto death'. Quoted in Norrell, *Alex Haley*, 157.
83 Alex Haley, interview by Murray Fisher, *Playboy*, January 1977, 57–79.
84 Alex Haley, 'My Furthest-Back Person, the African', *The New York Times*, 16 July 1972, SM12.
85 Philip Curtin, 'Recent Trends in African Historiography and Their Contribution to History in General', in *General History of Africa Vol. 1 Methodology and African Prehistory*, ed. Josephe Ki-Zebro (Paris: UNESCO and London: Heinemann, 1981), 58.
86 Arnold Temu and Bonaventure Surai, *Historians and Africanist History: A Critique* (Holland: Zed Press, 1981), 6–7.
87 Haley, *Roots*, 49, 114, 135, 322.
88 Ibid., 294.
89 Ibid., 281.
90 Ibid., 292–293.
91 As Ambalavaner Sivanandan notes, 'there is no hint in the book, which continues where the film leaves off and takes us right up to Haley's day, of the Civil Rights struggle, the Black Power Movement or the nascent revolution of the Panthers. All the resistance and rebellion of Haley's ancestors seem suddenly to stop short of revolution'. Ambalavaner Sivanandan, 'Responses to Roots', *Race & Class* 19, no. 1 (1977): 105.
92 Haley, *Roots*, 102.
93 Taylor, 'The Griot', 51.
94 Ibid.
95 As Randy Laist suggests, '*Roots* destabilizes conventional categories of fiction and reality in a way that mirrors the sense in which slavery itself is a tragic historical reality supported by an elaborate fiction of racial superiority. By challenging the Western separation of history and fiction, *Roots* has been enormously successful in provoking dialogue and deepening our understanding of the "factions" that constitute our social environment'. Randy Laist, 'Alex Haley's Roots and Hyperreal Historiography', *Mediascape* (2013), http://www.tft.ucla.edu/mediascape/Winter2013_Roots.html.
96 Taylor, 'The Griot', 53.
97 *The Cambridge Companion to Africa American Slave Narratives*, for example, mentions Haley in its chronological timeline of publications at the start but he is not mentioned again. Audrey Fisch, *The Cambridge Companion to Africa American*

Slave Narratives (Cambridge: Cambridge University Press, 2007). For further discussion on this see David Chioni Moore, 'Routes'. See also John Dugdale, 'Roots of the Problem: The Controversial History of Alex Haley's Book', *The Guardian*, 9 February 2017, https://www.theguardian.com/books/booksblog/2017/feb/09/alex-haley-roots-reputation-authenticity.

98   Taylor, 'The Griot', 48.
99   Norrell, *Alex Haley*, 161.
100 Ibid.
101 Ibid., 164.
102 *The Real Eve* dir. Andrew Piddington (2002 USA).
103 Spencer Wells, *The Journey of Man: A Genetic Odyssey* (London: Allen Lane, 2002), 39.
104 Priscilla Wald, 'Blood and Stories: How Genomics Is Rewriting Race, Medicine and Human History', *Patterns of Prejudice* 40, nos. 4–5 (2006): 324.
105 Brown, *The Search for Eve*, 317.
106 J.S. Jones, 'A Thousand and One Eves', *Nature* 345, no. 31 (1990): 395.
107 Roger Lewin, 'On the Ancestrail Trail', review of *The Search for Eve*, by Michael H. Brown, *New Scientist*, 5 January 1991, https://www.newscientist.com/article/mg12917504-000-review-on-the-ancestrail-trail/.
108 Natalie Angier, 'On the Trail of Everybody's Mother', *New York Times*, 8 April 1990, http://www.nytimes.com/1990/04/08/books/on-the-trail-of-everybody-s-mother.html.
109 Josiah Clark, *Types of Mankind, Or, Ethnological Researches Based upon the Ancient Monuments, Paintings, Sculptures and Crania of Races and upon Their Natural, Geographical, Philological, and Biblical History*, 4th edn. (Philadelphia, PA: Lippincott, Grambo & Co., 1860), 182.
110 Ibid., 184 and 189.
111 Wald, 'Blood and Stories', 331–332.
112 Priscilla Wald, 'Future Perfect: Grammar, Genes, and Geography', *New Literary History* 31, no. 4 (2000): 704.
113 Stringer and McKie, *African Exodus*, 8.
114 Rebecca Cann, 'The Scientists behind Mitochondrial Eve Tell Us about the "Lucky Mother" Who Changed Human Evolution Forever'. Interview by Alasdair Wilkins, *Gizmodo*, 27 January 2012, https://io9.gizmodo.com/5879991/the-scientists-behind-mitochondrial-eve-tell-us-about-the-lucky-mother-who-changed-human-evolution-forever?tag=evolution.
115 Steven Blevins, *Living Cargo: How Black Britain Performs Its Past* (Minneapolis: University of Minnesota Press, 2016), 154–161.
116 Du Bois, *Dusk of Dawn*, 59.
117 Wald, 'Future Perfect', 705.

118 Louis Kushnuck, 'Responses to Roots', *Race & Class* 19, no. 1 (1977): 81.
119 Ibid.
120 Gairdner Moment, 'Roots and the Biologist', *BioScience* 29, no. 6 (1978): 364.
121 Alondra Nelson, 'Roots and Genes', *Aeon*, 4 January 2016, https://aeon.co/essays/from-roots-to-dna-kits-the-quest-for-african-american-identity. See also Alondra Nelson, 'Bio Science: Genetic Genealogy Testing', 763. Jerome de Groot also notes that 'much popular genealogy, particularly in the USA, is influenced by the writings of Alex Haley'. Jerome de Groot, *Consuming History*, 84.
122 Sykes, *The Seven*, 15.
123 Ibid., 16.
124 Dawkins, *River Out of Eden*, 47.
125 Wells, *The Journey of Man*, xv.
126 Haley, *Roots*, 674 and 675.

Chapter 2

1 Eugene A. Foster et al., 'Jefferson Fathered Slave's Last Child', *Nature* 396 (1998): 27.
2 Ibid.
3 See Sloan R. Williams, 'Genetic Genealogy: The Woodson Family's Experience', *Culture, Medicine and Psychiatry* 29, no. 2 (2005): 225–252.
4 Roberta Bivins, 'Hybrid Vigour? Genes, Genomics, and History', *Genomics, Society and Policy* 4, no. 1 (2008): 17.
5 Marianne Sommer, *History Within: The Science, Culture and Politics of Bones, Organisms, and Molecules* (Chicago: Chicago University Press, 2016), 315.
6 Luca Cavalli-Sforza, 'The Human Genome Diversity Project', Address delivered to a Special Meeting of UNESCO, Paris, 12 September 1994, https://digital.library.unt.edu/ark:/67531/metadc697236/m2/1/high_res_d/505327.pdf.
7 Ibid., 2–3.
8 Ibid., 3, 7.
9 Sommer, *History Within*, 315.
10 Mark A. Jobling and Chris Tyler-Smith, 'The Human Y Chromosome: An Evolutionary Marker Comes of Age', *Nature Reviews Genetics* 4 (2003): 598.
11 L. Luca Cavalli-Sforza, 'The Human Genome Diversity Project: Past, Present and Future', *Nature Reviews Genetics* 6 (2005): 335.
12 Cavalli-Sforza, 'The Human Genome Diversity Project', Address, 9.
13 Reardon, 'Decoding Race', 52.
14 Ibid., 56, 58.
15 Cavalli-Sforza, 'The Human Genome Diversity Project: Past, Present and Future', 340.

16 Reardon, 'Decoding Race', 52.
17 Amade M'Charek, *The Human Genome Diversity Project: An Ethnography of Scientific Practice* (Cambridge: Cambridge University Press, 2010), 2, 13.
18 L. Luca Cavalli-Sforza et al., 'Call for a Worldwide Survey of Human Genetic Diversity: A Vanishing Opportunity for the Human Genome Project', *Genomics* 11 (1991): 490.
19 Sommer, *History Within*, 311.
20 Karen Young Kreeger, 'Proposed Human Genome Diversity Project Still Plagued by Controversy and Questions', *The Scientist* 1 (1996), accessed 16 January 2018, https://www.the-scientist.com/?articles.view/articleNo/18100/title/Proposed-Human-Genome-Diversity-Project-Still-Plagued-By-Controversy-And-Questions/.
21 Troy Duster, 'A Post-Genomic Surprise. The Molecular Reinscription of Race in Science, Law and Medicine', *The British Journal of Sociology* 66, no. 1 (2015): 1–27.
22 Sommer, *History Within*, 314, 323.
23 Luca Cavalli-Sforza, Paolo Menozzi and Alberto Piazza, *The History and Geography of Human Genes* (Princeton, NJ: Princeton University Press, 1994), 136. For critical discussions of this see Jennifer L. Hochschild, 'To Test or Not? Singular or Multiple Heritage? Genomic Ancestry Testing and Americans' Racial Identity', *Du Bois Review* 12, no. 2 (2015): 324; Roberts, *Fatal Invention*, 67. Jonathan Marks, 'Systematics in Anthropology: Where Science Confronts the Humanities (and Consistently Loses)', in *Conceptual Issues in Modern Human Origins Research*, ed. Geoffrey A. Clark and Catherine M. Willermet (New York: Aldine de Gruyter, 1997), 56.
24 Cavalli-Sforza, 'The Human Genome Diversity Project: Past, Present and Future', 337.
25 Reardon, 'Decoding Race', 43.
26 Cavalli-Sforza, 'The Human Genome Diversity Project', Address, 10.
27 Although the HGDP struggled to gain approval to collect genetic data, it gathered data from other research workers who had collected cell lines from indigenous populations and added it to a central collection. See Cavalli-Sforza, 'The Human Genome Diversity Project: Past, Present and Future', 333.
28 23andMe, 'Discover More about Your DNA Story', accessed 16 January 2018, https://www.23andme.com/en-gb/dna-ancestry/.
29 African Ancestry, 'Trace Your DNA. Find Your Roots', accessed 16 January 2018, http://www.africanancestry.com/home/.
30 Roots for Real, 'Your Ancestry Discovered', accessed 16 January 2018, http://www.rootsforreal.com/service_en.php#mtdna.
31 Ibid.
32 African Ancestry, 'Trace Your DNA'.

33 As Nash has argued, 'Though "ethnicity" is often used to refer to groups sharing a cultural heritage and is often used to avoid the biological associations of race, it is not a neat and tidy alternative, since along with ideas of the nation, both "ethnicity" and "race" encompass ideas of shared ancestry. Nation, ethnicity, and race share this imaginative familial foundation'. Nash, *Genetic Geographies*, 17.

34 23andMe, accessed 16 January 2018, https://www.23andme.com/en-gb/dna-ancestry/.

35 Hochschild, 'To Test or Not?' 331.

36 Nelson, 'Bio Science: Genetic Genealogy Testing', 776.

37 A. Nordgren and E.T. Juengst, 'Can Genomics Tell Me Who I Am? Essentialistic Rhetoric in Direct-to-Consumer DNA Testing', *New Genetics and Society* 28, no. 2 (2009): 169.

38 Kazuo Ishiguro, interview by Karen Grigsby Bates, *Day to Day on NPR Radio*, 4 May 2005, in *Conversations with Kazuo Ishiguro*, ed. Brian W. Shaffer and Cynthia F. Wong (Jackson: University Press of Mississippi, 2008), 202.

39 Lisa Fluet, 'Immaterial Labors: Ishiguro, Class, Affect', *Novel* 40, no. 3 (2007): 267.

40 Ann Whitehead, 'Writing with Care: Kazuo Ishiguro's *Never Let Me Go*', *Contemporary Literature* 52, no. 1 (2011): 76.

41 Eluned Summers-Bremner, '"Poor Creatures": Ishiguro's and Coetzee's Imaginary Animals', *Mosaic: A Journal for the Interdisciplinary Study of Literature* 39, no. 4 (2006): 145.

42 Sarah Brouillette, *Literature and the Creative Economy* (Stanford, CA: Stanford University Press, 2014), 204.

43 Shameem Black, 'Ishiguro's Inhuman Aesthetics', *Modern Fiction Studies* 55, no. 4 (2009): 785.

44 Margaret Atwood, 'Brave New World', *Slate*, 1 April 2005, http://www.slate.com/articles/arts/books/2005/04/brave_new_world.html. Further disavowals of the novel's biotechnological premise include Andrew Barrow's observation that the novel 'has as little to do with genetic engineering and the cloning controversy as *The Remains of the Day* has to do with butlering' in Andrew Barrow 'Artist of a Floating World', review of *Never Let Me Go*, by Kazuo Ishiguro, *The Independent*, 25 February 2005; Patricia Waugh's claim that 'a comment on the laboratory routines of genetic engineering is precisely what the novel is not', in Patricia Waugh, 'Contemporary British Fiction', in *The Cambridge Companion to Modern British Culture*, ed. Michael Higgins, Clarissa Smith and John Storey (Cambridge: Cambridge University Press, 2010), 132; and M. John Harrison's comment that 'Ishiguro's contribution to the cloning debate turns out to be sleight of hand, eye candy, cover for his pathological need to be subtle'. M John Harrison, 'Clone Alone', review of *Never Let Me Go*, by Kazuo Ishiguro, *The Guardian*, 26 February 2005. Gabriele Griffin is the exception: her article sets out

to address 'how science figures both in this particular novel and in contemporary culture more widely'. Gabriele Griffin, 'Science and the Cultural Imaginary: The Case of Kazuo Ishiguro's *Never Let Me Go*', *Textual Practice* 23, no. 4 (2009): 645.

45 In 1997 scientists at the Roslin Institute in Edinburgh announced the birth of Dolly the sheep, the first mammal to be born whose embryo was created from a cloned cell, sparking huge debate about whether this represented a step closer to the possibility of cloning a human being. As Ishiguro himself acknowledges, 'Around that time, in 2001, there was a lot of stuff about cloning, about stem-cell research, about Dolly the Sheep. It was very much in the air'. Kazuo Ishiguro, 'A Conversation about Life and Art with Kazuo Ishiguro', interview with Cynthia F. Wong and Grace Crommett, 2006, *Conversations with Kazuo Ishiguro*, ed. Brian W. Shaffer and Cynthia F. Wong (Jackson: University Press of Mississippi, 2008), 213.

46 One of the most recent terms used to replace race is 'biogeographical ancestry', a term which Lisa Gannett contends serves the needs of the commercial arms of genetics while continuing to build on older racial concepts. Lisa Gannett, 'Biogeographical Ancestry and Race', *Studies in History and Philosophy of Biological and Biomedical Sciences* 47 (2014): 174.

47 Judith Roof, *The Poetics of DNA* (Minneapolis: Minnesota University Press, 2007), 146.

48 Kazuo Ishiguro, *Never Let Me Go* (London: Faber and Faber, 2005), 138.

49 Alys Weinbaum, 'Racial Aura: Walter Benjamin and the Work of Art in a Biotechnological Age', *Literature and Medicine* 26, no. 1 (2007): 217.

50 Ibid.

51 Ibid.

52 Ibid., 226.

53 Ibid., 233.

54 Gilroy, *Against Race*, 47.

55 Black, 'Ishiguro's Inhuman', 797. Black has also noted the peripheral references to racial inequality in the novel, arguing that it 'speaks to the fate of postcolonial and migrant laborers who sustain the privileges of First World economies' and that 'Ishiguro's characteristic style, renders these resemblances to the current globalizing world conspicuous through their near-invisibility'. Black, 'Ishiguro's Inhuman', 796–797.

56 Catherine Waldby and Robert Mitchell, *Tissue Economies: Blood, Organs, and Cell Lines in Late Capitalism* (Durham, NC: Duke University Press, 2006),161. Whereas Gilroy cites organ transplantation as one of the technologies through which race might be erased, because organs can be transplanted transracially (Gilroy, *Against Race*, 20), the current globalized trade in organs for transplant in fact reinforces the unequal racial relationships upon which it is based.

57 Ishiguro, *Never*, 114, 115, 140.

58 Ibid., 114.
59 Ibid., 80.
60 Ibid., 108.
61 Ibid., 259.
62 Ibid., 244, 245.
63 Philomena Essed and David Theo Goldberg, 'Cloning Cultures: The Social Injustices of Sameness', *Ethnic and Racial Studies* 25, no. 6 (2002): 1068.
64 Ishiguro, *Never*, 245, 261.
65 Whitehead, 'Writing with Care', 62.
66 Ishiguro, *Never*, 244, 245, 253.
67 David Theo Goldberg, 'Call and Response', *Patterns of Prejudice* 44, no. 1 (2010): 92.
68 Albert Memmi, *The Colonizer and the Colonized* (1965; Boston, MA: Beacon Press, 1991), 105.
69 Ishiguro, *Never*, 64–65.
70 Ibid., 113.
71 Ibid., 16.
72 Ibid., 16, 31.
73 Ibid., 16.
74 Ibid., 173.
75 Ibid., 255.
76 Henry Louis Gates Jr., 'Editor's Introduction: Writing, Race and the Difference It Makes', *Critical Inquiry* 12, no. 1 (1985): 8.
77 Ibid., 9.
78 Ibid.
79 Martin Puchner puts it slightly differently: 'the teachers encourage students to produce art works, "to prove you had souls at all" a belief that may echo W.E.B. Du Bois's declaration that "until the art of the black folk compels recognition they will not be rated as human"'. Martin Puchner, 'When We Were Clones', *Raritan* 27, no. 4 (2008): 37.
80 Weinbaum, 'Racial Aura', 219.
81 Ibid., 217.
82 Black has argued that 'Ishiguro's inhuman style' is an ethical move that suggests that 'only by recognizing what in ourselves is mechanical, manufactured, and replicated – in a traditional sense, not fully human – will we escape the barbarities committed in the name of preserving purely human life'. Black, 'Ishiguro's Inhuman', 786. Similarly, Rebecca Walkowitz has claimed that Kathy's narration underscores the 'value of unoriginal expression' and that Ishiguro's point is that 'it is inadequate, and even unethical, to treat uniqueness as the defining quality of art, culture, and human life'. Rebecca Walkowitz, 'Unimaginable Largeness: Kazuo Ishiguro, Translation, and the New World Literature', *Novel* 40, no. 3 (2007): 224, 235.

83 Charles Darwin, *The Expression of the Emotions in Man and Animals* (1872; Chicago: Chicago University Press, 1965), 359, 351.
84 For some of the most influential work on this subject, see Paul Ekman and Wallace V. Friesen, 'Constants across Cultures in the Face and Emotion', *Journal of Personality and Social Psychology* 17 (1971): 124–129; and Martha C. Nussbaum, *Upheavals of Thought: The Intelligence of Emotions* (Cambridge: Cambridge University Press, 2001).
85 Winter, 'Darwin's Saussure', 130.
86 Ishiguro, *Never*, 113–114.
87 John Mullan, 'Afterword: On First Reading *Never Let Me Go*', in *Kazuo Ishiguro, Contemporary Critical Perspectives Ser*, ed. Sean Matthews and Sebastian Groes (London: Continuum, 2010), 106.
88 Ishiguro, *Never*, 3.
89 Ibid., 282.
90 Ibid., 113, 120.
91 See Nicholas Dames, '"The Withering of the Individual": Psychology in the Victorian Novel', in *A Concise Companion to the Victorian Novel*, ed. Francis O'Gorman (Oxford: Blackwell, 2005), 101.
92 Ishiguro, *Never*, 32, 39, 139.
93 Ibid., 95–96.
94 Ibid., 113.
95 Ibid., 87.
96 Ibid., 77.
97 Ibid., 143.
98 Ibid., 225.
99 Darwin, *The Expression*, 364.
100 Ishiguro, *Never*, 232.
101 Ibid., 266.
102 Ibid., 265, 267.
103 Ibid., 36.
104 Puchner, 'When We Were Clones', 38.
105 Ishiguro, *Never*, 132.
106 Ibid., 137–138.
107 Ibid., 251.
108 John Mullan makes a similar point: 'The novel imagines the speculative attachments that might grow in place of all natural connection to others. It is a telling fictional enquiry in a culture that is preoccupied, in any number of popular forms, with the "re-discovery" of genealogy'. Mullan, 'Afterword', 113.
109 *Motherland: A Genetic Journey*, Dir. Archie Baron, BBC2, 14 February, 2003.
110 'Genetic Journey to the Motherland', *Science Museum Antenna*, accessed 14 May 2012, http://www.sciencemuseum.org.uk/antenna/motherland/131.asp.

111 'Sense about Genetic Ancestry Testing', *Sense About Science*, accessed 22 January 2018, https://archive.senseaboutscience.org/data/files/resources/119/Sense-About-Genetic-Ancestry-Testing.pdf.
112 Troy Duster, 'Ancestry Testing and DNA: Uses, Limits and *Caveat Emptor*', in *Race and the Genetic Revolution: Science, Myth and Culture*, ed. Sheldon Krimsky and Kathleen Sloan (New York: Columbia University Press, 2011), 102.
113 Richard Dawkins, *The Ancestor's Tale: A Pilgrimage to the Dawn of Life* (London: Phoenix, 2004), 59.
114 Ibid., 59.
115 Dawkins, *River Out of Eden*, 65.
116 Fatimah L. Jackson, 'Genomics: DNA and Diasporas', review of *The Social Life of DNA: Race, Reparations, and Reconciliation after the Genome*, by Alondra Nelson, *Nature* 529 (2016): 280.
117 Stuart Murray, 'Care and the Self: Biotechnology, Reproduction, and the Good Life', *Philosophy, Ethics and Humanities in Medicine* 2, no. 6 (2007), BioMed Central, http://www.peh-med.com/content/2/1/6.
118 Ibid.
119 Donna Haraway, *Simians, Cyborgs and Women: The Reinvention of Nature* (London: Free Association, 1991) 156.
120 Black, 'Ishiguro's Inhuman', 797.
121 Ishiguro, *Never*, 89.
122 Ibid., 89–90.
123 Ibid., 121.
124 George Eliot, *Daniel Deronda* Wordsworth Classics (1876; Hertfordshire: Wordsworth Editions, 2003), 154.
125 Derek Attridge, *The Singularity of Literature* (London: Routledge, 2004), 123.
126 Ibid., 4.
127 Darwin, *The Expression*, 358–359.
128 Eliot, *Daniel Deronda*, 153.

Chapter 3

1 Francis Collins, 'Remarks Made by the President'.
2 Bill Clinton, 'Remarks Made by the President'.
3 Craig Venter, 'Remarks Made by the President'.
4 Brigitte Nerlich, Robert Dingwall and David D. Clarke, 'The Book of Life: How the Completion of the Human Genome Project Was Revealed to the Public', *Health: An Interdisciplinary Journal for the Social Study of Health, Illness and Medicine* 6, no. 4 (2002): 458.
5 Ibid., 460.

6   Ibid., 465.
7   Collins, 'Remarks Made by the President'.
8   Venter, 'Remarks Made by the President'.
9   Jackie Stacey, *The Cinematic Life of the Gene* (Durham, NC, and London: Duke University Press, 2010), 71.
10 Patricia Waugh, 'Science and Fiction in the 1990s', in *British Fiction of the 1990s*, ed. Nick Bentley (Oxon: Routledge, 2005), 58.
11 Steinberg, *Genes and the Bioimaginary*, 52, 55.
12 Ibid., 56.
13 Lily E. Kay, *Who Wrote the Book of Life?: A History of the Genetic Code* (Stanford, CA: Stanford University Press, 2000), 2.
14 Roof, *The Poetics of DNA*, 48–50.
15 Clinton, 'Remarks Made by the President'.
16 Venter, 'Remarks Made by the President'.
17 Collins, 'Remarks Made by the President'.
18 Steinberg, *Genes and the Bioimaginary*, 59.
19 Waugh, 'Science and Fiction in the 1990s', 69.
20 Goldberg, *The Threat of Race*, 15.
21 John A. Powell, 'The Colorblind Multiracial Dilemma: Racial Categories Reconsidered', *U.S.F.L. Rev.* 31 (1996): 790.
22 Goldberg, *The Threat of Race*, 192–193.
23 Waugh, 'Science and Fiction in the 1990s', 69.
24 Goldberg, *The Threat of Race*, 1.
25 For Dominic Head, the novel demonstrates that 'we are all hybrid post-colonials, biologically as well as culturally, and the pursuit of ethnic origins is a pointless objective'. Dominic Head, 'Zadie Smith's *White Teeth*: Multiculturalism for the Millennium', in *Contemporary British Fiction*, ed. Richard J. Lane, Rod Mengham and Philip Tew (Malden: Polity Press, 2003), 114. Molly Thompson argues that *White Teeth* reveals 'an inevitable consequence of multiculturalism is a fusion of culturally and biologically derived-roots'. Molly Thompson, '"Happy Multicultural Land"? The Implications of an "excess of belonging" in Zadie Smith's *White Teeth*', in *Write Black, Write British: From Post Colonial to Black British Literature*, ed. Kadija Sesay (Hertford: Hansib, 2005), 135. An anonymous reviewer in *The Economist* called the novel 'post-post-colonial' – 'Pulling Teeth', *The Economist*, 17 February 2000, http://www.economist.com/node/283204. For Tracey L. Walters, 'Smith's point is that racial homogeneity is on the verge of extinction' and she 'persuades us to accept that racial categories in Britain have transformed into alternative modes of representation and therefore a new discourse is required to discuss identity'. Tracey L. Walters, '"We're All English Now Mate Like It or Lump It": The Black/Britishness of Zadie Smith's *White Teeth*', in *Write Black, Write British: From Post Colonial to Black British Literature*, ed. Kadija Sesay (Hertford: Hansib, 2005), 316.

26 Lionel Trilling, *E.M. Forster*, 3rd edn. (New York: New Directions, 1964), 65.
27 Zadie Smith, 'Love, Actually', *The Guardian*, 1 November 2003, https://www.theguardian.com/books/2003/nov/01/classics.zadiesmith.
28 Waugh, 'Science and Fiction in the 1990s', 70.
29 Steinberg, *Genes and the Bioimaginary*, 66.
30 Trilling, *E.M. Forster*, 65.
31 Zadie Smith, 'Dreaming Up Finch', interview by Ben Greenman, *The New Yorker*, 16 December 2002.
32 Zadie Smith, 'Acknowledgements', *On Beauty* (London: Penguin, 2006).
33 Smith, 'Dreaming Up Finch'.
34 James Wood, 'Human, All Too Inhuman', *The New Republic*, 24 July 2000, https://newrepublic.com/article/61361/human-inhuman.
35 Ibid.
36 Zadie Smith, 'A Interview with Zadie Smith', Book Browse, accessed 4 March 2019, https://www.bookbrowse.com/author_interviews/full/index.cfm/author_number/344/zadie-smith.
37 Smith, 'Love, Actually'.
38 Ibid.
39 Smith, *White Teeth*, 190.
40 Ibid.
41 See for example Molly Thompson, '"Happy Multicultural Land"? The Implications of an "excess of belonging" in Zadie Smith's *White Teeth*'; Head, 'Zadie Smith's *White Teeth*'; Tracey L. Walters, 'We're All English Now Mate Like It or Lump It'.
42 Claire Squires, *Zadie Smith's White Teeth: A Reader's Guide* (New York: Continuum Contemporaries, 2002), 38.
43 Susie Thomas, 'Zadie Smith's False Teeth: The Marketing of Multiculturalism', *Literary London: Interdisciplinary Studies in the Representation of London* 4, no. 1 (2006), http://www.literarylondon.org/london-journal/march2006/thomas.html.
44 Ashley Dawson, *Mongrel Nation: Diasporic Culture and the Making of Postcolonial Britain* (Ann Arbor: University of Michigan Press, 2007), 152.
45 Smith, *White Teeth*, 327.
46 Roof, *The Poetics of DNA*, 149.
47 Smith, *White Teeth*, 525.
48 Roof, *The Poetics of DNA*, 201.
49 Smith, *White Teeth*, 161.
50 Ibid., 314.
51 Roof, *The Poetics of DNA*, 17.
52 Smith, *White Teeth*, 340.
53 Ibid., 418–419.
54 Ibid., 518.
55 Ibid., 531.

56 Ibid., 518.
57 Ibid., 308.
58 Ibid., 358.
59 Ibid., 314.
60 Ibid., 309.
61 Ibid., 326.
62 Ibid., 320.
63 Ibid., 319.
64 Ibid., 324.
65 Ibid., 375.
66 Ibid., 329, 368.
67 Ibid., 129.
68 Ibid., 126.
69 Ibid., 136.
70 Goldberg, *The Threat of Race*, 189.
71 Williams, 'Talking About Race', 1501.
72 Ibid., 1498.
73 Ibid., 1509.
74 Goldberg, *The Threat of Race*, 1.
75 Patricia Waugh, 'Revising the Two Cultures Debate: Science, Literature and Value', in *The Arts and Sciences of Criticism*, ed. David Fuller and Patricia Waugh (Oxford: Oxford University Press, 1999), 40.
76 Smith, *White Teeth*, 312.
77 Ibid., 417.
78 Ibid., 416.
79 Ibid., 417–418.
80 Christina Patterson, 'A Willesden Ring of Confidence', *The Independent*, 22 January 2000, 9.
81 Smith, *White Teeth*, 366.
82 Zadie Smith, 'Speaking in Tongues', in *Changing My Mind: Occasional Essays* (London: Hamish Hamilton, 2009), 145. In this case the writer Smith has in mind is Shakespeare.
83 Zadie Smith, 'A Writer's Truth', interview with Camille Dodero, *The Boston Phoenix*, 18–24 July 2003.
84 Smith, *White Teeth*, 379.
85 Ibid., 400.
86 Ibid., 303.
87 Ibid., 255.
88 Ibid., 339.
89 Ibid., 431.
90 Ibid., 531.

91 Ibid., 431.
92 Roof, *The Poetics of DNA*, 23.
93 Smith, 'Love, Actually'.
94 Ibid.
95 Trilling, *E.M. Forster*, 65.
96 Ibid.
97 James Wood, 'Human, All Too Inhuman'.
98 Ibid.
99 Trilling, *E.M. Forster*, 65.
100 Smith, *White Teeth*, 365.
101 Ibid., 541.
102 Ibid., 489.
103 Smith, 'Dreaming Up Finch'.
104 Smith, *White Teeth*, 312.
105 Ibid., 339.
106 Ibid., 341.
107 Trilling, *E.M. Forster*, 65, 66.
108 Smith, 'Love, Actually'.
109 Smith, *White Teeth*, 360, 532.
110 Ibid., 341.
111 Ibid., 289.
112 Trilling, *E.M. Forster*, 64.
113 Smith, *White Teeth*, 416.
114 Dominic Head, *The Cambridge Introduction to Modern British Fiction 1950–2000* (Cambridge: Cambridge University Press, 2002), 233–234.
115 Roof, *The Poetics of DNA*, 145.

Chapter 4

1 Rachel Dolezal, interview by Matt Lauer, *Today*, NBC 16 June 2015, https://www.youtube.com/watch?v=lG9Q2_Hv83k.
2 Editorial, 'Illuminating BiDil', *Nature Biotechnology* 23, no. 8 (2005): 903.
3 Anne L. Taylor et al., 'Combination of Isosorbide Dinitrate and Hydralazine in Blacks with Heart Failure', *The New England Journal of Medicine* 351, no. 20 (2004): 2050.
4 Joseph A. Franciosa et al., 'African-American Heart Failure Trial (A-HeFT): Rationale, Design, and Methodology', *Journal of Cardiac Failure* l8, no. 3 (2002): 133.
5 Ibid.
6 Taylor, 'Combination of Isosorbide Dinitrate and Hydralazine in Blacks', 2055.

7   Jay Cohn, *Saving Sam: Drugs, Race, and Discovering the Secrets of Heart Disease* (Minneapolis, MN: Wisdom Editions, 2014), 9, Kindle.
8   Celeste Condit et al., 'Attitudinal Barriers to Delivery of Race-Targeted Pharmacogenomics among Informed Lay Persons', *Genetics in Medicine* 5, no. 5 (2003): 388.
9   Jonathan Kahn, *Race in a Bottle: The Story of BiDil and Racialized Medicine in a Post-Genomic Age* (New York: Columbia University Press, 2013), 42–43.
10 Kahn, *Race in a Bottle*, 89.
11 Sarah Blacker, 'Epistemic Trafficking: On the Concept of Race-Specific Medicine', *English Studies in Canada* 36, no. 1 (2010): 136.
12 Blacker, 'Epistemic Trafficking', 130.
13 Kahn, *Race in a Bottle*, 21, 22.
14 Britt M. Rusert and Charmaine D.M. Royal, 'Grassroots Marketing in a Global Era: More Lessons from BiDil', *Journal of Law and Medical Ethics* 39, no. 1 (2011): 80.
15 Rusert and Royal, 'Grassroots Marketing', 85.
16 Susan M. Reverby, '"Special Treatment": BiDil, Tuskegee, and the Logic of Race', *The Journal of Law Medicine & Ethics* 36, no. 3 (2008): 479.
17 Editorial, 'Illuminating BiDil', 903.
18 Cohn, *Saving Sam*, 9, Kindle.
19 Kahn, *Race in a Bottle*, 117, 120.
20 Anne Pollock, *Medicating Race: Heart Disease and Durable Preoccupations with Difference* (Durham, NC: Duke University Press, 2012), 169.
21 Pollock, *Medicating Race*, 23.
22 Lundy Braun, *Breathing Race into the Machine: The Surprising Career of the Spirometer from Plantation to Genetics* (Minneapolis: University of Minnesota Press, 2014).
23 Kahn, *Race in a Bottle*, 106.
24 Colson Whitehead, *Apex Hides the Hurt* (New York: Doubleday, 2006), 108.
25 Colson Whitehead, 'What's in a Name: Colson Whitehead on *Apex Hides the Hurt*'. Interview by Tom Nolan, *American Booksellers Association*, 2 March 2006, http://www.bookweb.org/news/whats-name-colson-whitehead-apex-hides-hurt.
26 Colson Whitehead, 'The New Eclecticism: An Interview with Colson Whitehead'. Interview by Linda Selzer, *Callaloo* 31, no. 2 (2008): 399.
27 Whitehead, *Apex*, 130.
28 Ibid., 109.
29 Ibid., 89.
30 Ibid., 109.
31 Ibid., 89.
32 Ibid., 90.
33 Ibid., 3.

34 Ibid., 176.
35 Ibid., 21.
36 Ibid., 130.
37 Ibid., 34–35.
38 Ibid., 89–90.
39 *Oxford English Dictionary Online*, s.v. 'Semiotics', accessed 18 December 2018, http://www.oed.com/view/Entry/175724?rskey=BRtNVF&result=2&isAdvanced=false#eid.
40 As Derek C. Maus also argues, '*Apex Hides the Hurt* is an extended deliberation about the semiotic relationship between things (called "signifiers" in semiotic discourse) and their meanings "signifieds"' and 'From a semiotic perspective, [the protagonist] recognizes that his industry makes its money by obscuring denotive meanings behind illusory connotative ones; his names help construct codes that ensure that his clients' signs (their products and services) communicate only their desirability and nothing else'. Derek C. Maus, *Understanding Colson Whitehead* (Columbia: University of South Carolina Press, 2014), 76.
41 Whitehead, *Apex*, 44.
42 Ibid., 52.
43 Ibid., 5.
44 Stuart Hall, 'Race, The Floating Signifier (Transcript)', *Media Education Foundation*, 1997, 8, accessed 18 December 2018, http://www.mediaed.org/transcripts/Stuart-Hall-Race-the-Floating-Signifier-Transcript.pdf.
45 Ibid., 6.
46 Whitehead, *Apex*, 130.
47 Ibid., 183.
48 Ibid., 192.
49 Rusert and Royal, 'Grassroots Marketing', 83. Christen Rachul et al. also note that 'terminology shifts in frequency as the genetic research that is presented in peer-reviewed literature is reinterpreted in press releases and newspaper articles. For example, the term "population" appears most frequently in the peer-reviewed literature. However, "population" is the second most frequent term in the press releases and is only the fourth most frequent term in the newspaper articles. There seems to be a greater focus on terms such as "African" and "black" in the newspaper articles, especially in comparison with the peer-reviewed articles. The term "African" is the second most frequent term in the journal articles, and the term "black" is the eighth most frequent term; however, in the newspaper articles, these terms are first and second most frequent terms, respectively'. Christen Rachul, Colin Ouellette and Timothy Caulfield, 'Tracing the Use and Source of Racial Terminology in Representations of Genetic Research', *Genetics in Medicine* 13, no. 4 (2011): 315.
50 Kahn, *Race in a Bottle*, 16.

51 Hall, 'Race, The Floating Signifier', 16.
52 Whitehead, *Apex*, 129.
53 Ibid., 139.
54 Ibid., 139.
55 Ibid., 180.
56 Ibid., 23 and 20.
57 Ibid., 21.
58 Ibid., 58.
59 Ibid., 146.
60 Ibid., 130.
61 Ibid., 152.
62 Ibid., 3.
63 Ibid., 34.
64 Ibid., 83.
65 Ibid., 155.
66 Ibid., 167.
67 Ibid., 80.
68 Ibid., 206.
69 Henry Louis Gates, Jr., *The Signifying Monkey: A Theory of African American Literary Criticism* (1988; New York: Oxford University Press, 2014), 47.
70 Ibid., 55.
71 Ibid., 52.
72 Stephanie Li, *Signifying without Specifying: Racial Discourse in the Age of Obama* (New Brunswick, NJ: Rutgers University Press, 2012), 88.
73 Howard Rambsy II, 'The Rise of Colson Whitehead: Hi-Tech Narratives of Literary Ascent', in *New Essays on the African American Novel from Hurston and Ellison to Morrison and Whitehead*, ed. Lovalerie King and Linda F. Selzer (New York: Palgrave Macmillan, 2008), 226.
74 Li, *Signifying without Specifying*, 70.
75 Christopher Leise, 'With Names, No Coincidence: Colson Whitehead's Postracial Puritan Allegory', *African American Review* 47, nos. 2–3 (2014): 291.
76 Samuel A. Cartwright, 'Report on the Diseases and Physical Peculiarities of the Negro Race', *The New Orleans Medical and Surgical Journal* 7, May (1851): 692.
77 Ibid., 699.
78 Ibid., 700.
79 Ibid., 704.
80 Ibid., 707.
81 Ibid., 707.
82 Ibid., 708.
83 Ibid., 709.

84 See for example Kevin White, *An Introduction to the Sociology of Health and Illness* (London: Sage, 2002), 41–42.
85 James Denny Guillory, 'The Pro-Slavery Arguments of Dr. Samuel A. Cartwright', *Louisiana History: The Journal of the Louisiana Historical Association* 9, no. 3 (1968): 210.
86 Whitehead, *Apex*, 183.
87 Ibid., 171.
88 Put differently by Li, the protagonist is 'a fugitive from racial identity or at least from the language conventionally used to describe race'. Li, *Signifying without Specifying*, 77.
89 Gates, *The Signifying Monkey*, 102.
90 Britt Rusert, *Fugitive Science: Empiricism and Freedom in Early African American Culture* (New York: NYU Press, 2017), 21.
91 Frederick Douglass, *The Claims of the Negro, Ethnologically Considered* (Rochester, NY: Lee, Mann and Co., 1854), 7, Frederick Douglass Papers at the Library of Congress, http://hdl.loc.gov/loc.mss/mfd.21036.
92 Rusert, *Fugitive Science*, 177.
93 Ibid., 179.
94 Ibid.
95 Kahn, *Race in a Bottle*, 3.
96 Richard Tutton, *Genomics and the Reimagining of Personalized Medicine* (Surrey: Ashgate, 2014), 9.
97 Francis Collins, *The Language of Life: DNA and the Revolution in Personalised Medicine* (London: Profile Books, 2010), 163.
98 Anne Pollock, *Medicating Race*, 11.
99 Ibid., 179.
100 Ibid., 122–126.
101 For example, a study of self-identified African Americans with coronary heart disease found that black people understood their illness to be linked to 'racial, cultural, social, and economic disadvantage that accumulate over their life course, as well as to a more distant history of stratification and violence inflicted on the generations who preceded them'. Leslie Dubbin, Monica McLemore and Janet K. Shim, 'Illness Narratives of African Americans Living with Coronary Heart Disease: A Critical Interactionist Analysis', *Qualitative Health Research* 27, no. 4 (2017): 505.
102 Whitehead, *Apex*, 199.
103 Ibid.
104 Ibid., 205.
105 Leise makes a similar point: 'Teasing out the tension between Goode and Field into the twenty-first century, Whitehead's novel explodes the notion of a singular

"black America" or "African American" community.' Leise, 'With Names, No Coincidence', 286.
106 Maus, *Understanding Colson Whitehead*, 85.
107 Whitehead, *Apex*, 183.
108 Ibid., 212.
109 Ibid., 192.

Chapter 5

1 Grazyna Jasienska, 'Low Birth Weight of Contemporary African Americans: An Intergenerational Effect of Slavery?', *American Journal of Human Biology* 21, no. 1 (2009): 16.
2 Ibid., 17 and 21.
3 Ibid., 22.
4 Ibid.
5 Christopher W. Kuzawa and Elizabeth Sweet, 'Epigenetics and the Embodiment of Race: Developmental Origins of US Racial Disparities in Cardiovascular Health', *American Journal of Human Biology* 21, no. 1 (2009): 2.
6 Ibid., 8.
7 Ibid., 10.
8 Tim Spector, *Identically Different: Why You Can Change Your Genes* (London: Orion, 2012), 24.
9 See Nancy Krieger, 'Living and Dying at the Crossroads: Racism, Embodiment, and Why Theory Is Essential for a Public Health of Consequence', *American Journal of Public Health* 106, no. 5 (2016): 832–833. Also, Nancy Krieger, 'If "Race" Is the Answer, What Is the Question? – on "Race," Racism, and Health: A Social Epidemiologist's Perspective', *Is 'Race' Real? A Web Forum organized by the Social Science Research Council*, 7 June 2006, http://raceandgenomics.ssrc.org/Krieger/.
10 Shannon Sullivan, 'Inheriting Racist Disparities in Health: Epigenetics and the Transgenerational Effects of White Racism', *Critical Philosophy of Race* 1, no. 2 (2013): 193.
11 Maurizio Meloni, 'Epigenetics for the Social Sciences: Justice, Embodiment, and Inheritance in the Postgenomic Age', *New Genetics and Society* 34, no. 2 (2015): 138.
12 Dave Love, 'Post-Traumatic Slave Syndrome and Intergenerational Trauma: Slavery is Like a Curse Passing Through the DNA of Black People', *Atlanta Black Star*, 5 June 2016, https://atlantablackstar.com/2016/06/05/post-traumatic-slave-syndrome-and-intergenerational-trauma-slavery-is-like-a-curse-passing-through-the-dna-of-black-people/.

13. Darron T. Smith, 'The Epigenetics of Being Black and Feeling Blue: Understanding African American Vulnerability to Disease' *Huffington Post*, 14 June 2013, https://www.huffingtonpost.com/darron-t-smith-phd/the-epigenetics-of-being-_b_4094226.html?guccounter=1.
14. Ibid.
15. George Davy Smith, 'Essay Review: Epigenetics for the Masses: More Than Audrey Hepburn and Yellow Mice?', *International Journal of Epidemiology* 41 (2012): 307.
16. Brigitte Nerlich, 'The Epigenetic Muddle and the Trouble with Science', *Making Science Public* (blog), 5 August 2016, http://blogs.nottingham.ac.uk/makingsciencepublic/2016/08/05/epigenetic-muddle/.
17. Martyn Pickersgill, 'Epistemic Modesty, Ostentatiousness and the Uncertainties of Epigenetics: On the Knowledge Machinery of (Social) Science', *The Sociological Review Monographs* 64, no. 1 (2016): 197, 199.
18. See Ueli Grossniklaus et al., 'Transgenerational Epigenetic Inheritance: How Important Is It?', *Nature Reviews Genetics* 14 (2013): 228–235.
19. Ruth Müller et al., 'The Biosocial Genome? Interdisciplinary Perspectives on Environmental Epigenetics, Health and Society', *EMBO Reports* (2017): 1 and 3, https://doi.org/10.15252/embr.201744953.
20. Ibid.
21. Lundy Braun, Anne Fausto-Sterling, Duana Fullwiley, Evelynn M. Hammonds, Alondra Nelson, William Quivers, Susan M. Reverby, Alexandra E. Shields, 'Racial Categories in Medical Practice: How Useful Are They?', *PLoS Medicine* 4, no. 9 (2007): 1426.
22. For a further discussion of this see Fern Elsdon-Baker, 'Contested Inheritance: Debates on the Role of "Inheritance of Acquired Characteristics" in Late Nineteenth Century Darwinian and Weismannian Thought', *Textual Practice* 29, no. 3 (2015): 547–571.
23. Jean Baptiste Lamarck, *Philosophie Zoologique*, 1809, trans. Hugh Elliot as *Zoological Philosophy: An Exposition with Regard to the Natural History of Animals with Introductory Essays by David L. Hull and Richard W. Burkhardt Jr* (New York: Cambridge University Press, 2011; 1914).
24. L.J. Jordanova, *Lamarck* (Oxford: Oxford University Press, 1984), 100.
25. See for example Kevin V. Morris, 'Lamarck and the Missing Lnc', *The Scientist*, 1 October 2012, http://www.the-scientist.com/?articles.view/articleNo/32637/title/Lamarck-and-the-Missing-Lnc/.
26. Ute Deichmann, 'Why Epigenetics Is Not a Vindication of Lamarckism – and Why That Matters', *Studies in History and Philosophy of Biological and Biomedical Sciences* 57 (2016): 81.
27. Lamarck famously wrote of the giraffe – 'It is interesting to observe the result of habit in the peculiar shape and size of the giraffe … obliged to browse on the leaves of trees and to make constant efforts to reach them. From this habit

long maintained in all its race ... its neck is lengthened'. Lamarck, *Philosophie Zoologique*, 122.

28   Brigitte Nerlich, 'When Epigenetics Gets under the Skin', *Making Science Public* (blog), 15 August 2016, http://blogs.nottingham.ac.uk/makingsciencepublic/2016/08/15/epigenetics-gets-skin/.

29   An example of such usage is the introduction to Nessa Carey's popular science book *The Epigenetics Revolution* in which she compares DNA to a script, asking her readers to think of the way cells read genetic code as like different film versions of *Romeo and Juliet*. She states that 'the same script can result in different productions'. Nessa Carey, *The Epigenetics Revolution* (London: Icon, 2012), 3. Siddhartha Mukherjee compares the way genes are turned on and off in response to events, and epigenetic marks gradually layered above genes, to 'Prospero, raging against the deformed Caliban in "The Tempest"', as 'Caliban is destined to remain a genetic automaton, a windup ghoul – vastly more pathetic than anything human. He experiences the world, but he has no capacity to be changed by it; he has a genome that lacks an epigenome'. Siddhartha Mukherjee, 'Same but Different: How Epigenetics Can Blur the Line between Nature and Nurture', *The New Yorker*, 2 May 2016, https://www.newyorker.com/magazine/2016/05/02/breakthroughs-in-epigenetics.

30   Edith Heard, 'We Can't Undo What Our Parents Have Given Us in Terms of Our Genes', interview by Catherine de Lange, *The Guardian*, 23 June 2013, https://www.theguardian.com/science/2013/jun/23/rational-heroes-edith-heard-epigenetics.

31   Ibid.

32   Pickersgill, 'Epistemic modesty', 198.

33   Mary Midgley, *Science and Poetry* (London: Routledge, 2001), 25.

34   Maurizio Meloni, 'A Postgenomic Body: Histories, Genealogies, Politics', *Body and Society* 24, no. 3 (2018): 5.

35   Ibid., 25–26.

36   Achille Mbembe, *Critique of Black Reason* (Durham, NC: Duke University Press, 2017), 32.

37   Octavia E. Butler, *Kindred* (Boston, MA: Beacon Press, 1989), 9.

38   Robert Crossley, 'Introduction', in *Kindred*, ed. Octavia E. Butler (Boston, MA: Beacon Press, 1989), xii.

39   Octavia Butler, 'An Interview with Octavia E. Butler', interview by Randall Kenan, *Callaloo* 14, no. 2 (1991): 496.

40   Octavia Butler, 'Black Women and the Science Fiction Genre', interview by Frances M. Beal, *Black Scholar* 17, no. 2, March–April (1986): 14.

41   See Sherryl Vint, '"Only by Experience": Embodiment and the Limitations of Realism in Neo-Slave Narratives', *Science Fiction Studies* 34, no. 2 (2007): 243.

42   J. Adam Johns, 'Becoming Medusa: Octavia Butler's "Lilith's Brood" and Sociobiology', *Science Fiction Studies* 37, no. 3 (2010): 382.

43 Octavia Butler, '"Radio Imagination": Octavia Butler on the Poetics of Narrative Embodiment', interview by Marilyn Mehaffy and AnaLouise Keating, *MELUS* 26, no. 1 (2001): 57.
44 Ibid., 59.
45 Ibid.
46 Ahmed, 'Open Forum, Imaginary Prohibitions', 24.
47 Butler, 'Radio Imagination', 58.
48 Butler, *Kindred*, 15.
49 Ibid., 36.
50 Ibid., 42.
51 Ibid., 73.
52 Ibid., 213.
53 Ibid., 81.
54 Ibid., 107.
55 Ibid., 32.
56 Ibid., 77.
57 Ibid.
58 Ibid., 36.
59 Ibid., 115.
60 Ibid.,116.
61 Sherryl Vint, 'Only by Experience', 248.
62 Maurizio Meloni, 'Epigenetics for the Social Sciences: Justice, Embodiment, and Inheritance in the Postgenomic Age', *New Genetics and Society* 34, no. 2 (2015): 136.
63 Maurizio Meloni, 'Race in an Epigenetic Time: Thinking Biology in the Plural', *The British Journal of Sociology* 68, no. 3 (2017): 390, 389.
64 Ibid., 402.
65 Butler, *Kindred*, 52.
66 Ibid., 108.
67 Ibid., 109.
68 Ibid., 12.
69 Ibid., 15.
70 Ibid., 18.
71 Ibid., 17.
72 Ibid., 45.
73 Ibid., 245.
74 Ibid.
75 Ibid., 246.
76 Ibid., 194.
77 Ibid., 11.
78 Octavia E. Butler, 'We Keep Playing the Same Record: A Conversation with Octavia E. Butler', interview by Stephen W. Potts, *Science Fiction Studies* 23, no. 3 (1996): 333.

79 Butler, *Kindred*, 127.
80 Ibid., 97.
81 Ibid., 127.
82 Ibid., 101.
83 Philip Miletic, 'Octavia E. Butler's Response to Black Arts/Black Power Literature and Rhetoric in Kindred', *African American Review* 49, no. 3 (2016): 267.
84 Becky Mansfield and Julie Guthman, 'Epigenetic Life: Biological Plasticity, Abnormality, and New Configurations of Race and Reproduction', *Cultural Geographies* 21, no. 1 (2015): 4.
85 Ibid., 6.
86 Ibid., 5.
87 In 2001 Rushdie stated that 'if terrorism is to be defeated, the world of Islam must take on board the secularist-humanist principles on which the modern is based, and without which their countries' freedom will remain a distant dream'. Salman Rushdie, 'November 2001: Not About Islam?' in *Step across This Line: Collected Non-Fiction 1992–2002* (London: Jonathan Cape, 2002), 397.
88 Salman Rushdie, 'Salman Rushdie and His Mythic Legacy', interview by Vibhuti Patel, *Wall Street Journal*, 27 November 2010, http://online.wsj.com/article/SB10001424052748704638304575636763279031150.html.
89 Salman Rushdie, 'A Response by Salman Rushdie', in *Midnight's Diaspora: Critical Encounters with Salman Rushdie*, ed. Daniel Herwitz and Ashutosh Varshney (Ann Arbor: University of Michigan Press, 2008), 140.
90 Salman Rushdie, 'Step Across This Line', in *Step across This Line: Collected Non-Fiction 1992–2002* (London: Jonathan Cape, 2002), 408.
91 Sabina Sawhney and Simona Sawhney argue that Rushdie's 'political writings are incongruent with the general trajectory of his work'. Sabina Sawhney and Simona Sawhney, 'Introduction: Reading Rushdie after 11 September 2001', *Twentieth-Century Literature* 47, no. 4 (2001): 437; Robert Spencer claims that 'critics ought to attend more to Rushdie's literary than his political output' because 'it is the non-didactic quality of the former that makes them superior forms of critical intervention'. Robert Spencer, 'Salman Rushdie and the "War on Terror"', *Journal of Postcolonial Writing* 46, nos. 3–4 (2010): 262.
92 Anshuman A. Mondal, '*The Ground beneath Her Feet* and *Fury*: The Reinvention of Location', in *The Cambridge Companion to Salman Rushdie*, ed. Abdulrazak Gurnah (Cambridge: Cambridge University Press, 2007), 169.
93 Timothy Brennan, 'The Cultural Politics of Rushdie Criticism: All or Nothing', in *Critical Essays on Salman Rushdie*, ed. Keith Booker (New York: G.K. Hall, 1999), 120.
94 Salman Rushdie, *The Satanic Verses* (1988; London: Vintage, 1998), 76.
95 Ibid., 77.
96 Ibid., 418.

97   Ibid.
98   Ibid., 4.
99   Ibid., 5.
100 Ibid.
101 Beer, *Darwin's Plots*, 19.
102 Rushdie, *The Satanic Verses*, 251.
103 Ibid., 159.
104 Ibid., 161.
105 Ibid., 168.
106 Ibid., 74.
107 Ibid., 135.
108 Ibid., 158.
109 Ibid., 168.
110 Ian McEwan, *Saturday* (London: Vintage, 2006), 67.
111 Ibid., 67.
112 Ibid., 252.
113 Ibid.
114 Johnjoe McFadden, 'The Unselfish Gene', *The Guardian*, 6 May 2005, http://www.guardian.co.uk/education/2005/may/06/science.highereducation.
115 Ibid.
116 Ibid.
117 Ibid.
118 Keller, *The Mirage of a Space*, 6.
119 Keller, 'Thinking about Biology and Culture', 38.
120 Ibid.
121 Evelyn Fox Keller, *The Mirage of a Space*, 6.
122 Mansfield and Guthman, 'Epigenetic Life', 12.
123 Ibid., 13.

Conclusion

1   James Watson, 'The Elementary DNA of Dr Watson,' interview by Charlotte Hunt-Grubbe, *The Sunday Times*, 14 October 2007, https://www.thetimes.co.uk/article/the-elementary-dna-of-dr-watson-gllb6w2vpdr.
2   James Watson, quoted in Josh Gabbatiss, 'James Watson: The Most Controversial Statements Made by the Father of DNA', *The Independent*, 13 January 2009, https://www.independent.co.uk/news/science/james-watson-racism-sexism-dna-race-intelligence-genetics-double-helix-a8725556.html.

3   Josh Gabbatiss, 'DNA Pioneer James Watson Has Final Honours Stripped amid Racism Row', *The Independent*, 12 January 2019, https://www.independent.co.uk/news/science/james-watson-racism-honours-dna-double-helix-cold-spring-harbor-laboratory-a8724896.html, https://www.cshl.edu/statement-by-cold-spring-harbor-laboratory-addressing-remarks-by-dr-james-d-watson-in-american-masters-decoding-watson/.
4   Joseph Graves, 'James Watson's Racism Is a Product of His Time – but That Doesn't Excuse It', *CNN*, 16 January 2019, https://edition.cnn.com/2019/01/15/opinions/james-watson-not-alone-in-racist-thinking-graves/index.html.
5   See Bliss, *Race Decoded*.
6   Rob DeSalle and Ian Tattersall, *Troublesome Science: The Misuse of Genetics and Genomics in Understanding Race* (New York: Columbia University Press, 2018), x.
7   Josie Gill, 'Decolonizing Literature and Science', *Configurations* 26, no. 3 (2018): 284.
8   'Our Mission', March for Science, accessed 5 March 2019, https://www.marchforscience.com/our-mission.
9   Andrea Morris, quoted in Amy Harmon, 'James Watson Had a Chance to Salvage His Reputation on Race. He Made Things Worse', *The New York Times*, 1 January 2019, https://www.nytimes.com/2018/10/17/us/white-supremacists-science-dna.html.
10 Ibid.
11 Editorial, 'ASHG Denounces Attempts to Link Genetics and Racial Supremacy', *The American Journal of Human Genetics* 103 (2018): 636.
12 Sabine Sielke, 'Biology', in *The Routledge Companion to Literature and Science*, ed. Bruce Clarke with Manuela Rossini (Oxon: Routledge, 2011), 36.
13 Ibid., 36.
14 In fact, C.P. Snow claims in his *Two Cultures* lecture of 1959 that scientists are 'freer than most people from racial feeling; their own culture is in its human relations a democratic one' while it is the humanities which are responsible for slavery and racism, rather than science. C.P. Snow, *The Two Cultures* 1959 (Cambridge: Cambridge University Press, 1998), 48.
15 Bruno Latour, 'Why Has Critique Run out of Steam?', 227
16 Ibid., 228.
17 Ibid., 227.
18 Ibid., 237.
19 Ibid., 246.
20 Gill, 'Decolonizing Literature and Science', 286.
21 Kandice Chuh, '"America" Is Not the Object: An Interview with Kandice Chuh, President of the American Studies Association', interview by Sarah Mesle, *Los Angeles Review of Books*, 9 November 2017, https://lareviewofbooks.org/article/america-is-not-the-object-an-interview-with-kandice-chuh-president-of-the-american-studies-association/#!.

22 As Kanta Dihal contends, literature and science studies has not been as adept at confronting its past and present Western bias and racial prejudices as other related fields such as science fiction studies. Kanta Dihal, 'On Science Fiction as a Separate Field', in 'State of the Unions', ed. Melissa M. Littlefield and Martin Willis, special issue, *Journal of Literature and Science* 10, no. 1 (2017): 34.
23 Sielke, 35.
24 Ibid., 31.
25 Ibid., 34.
26 Levine, *Forms*, 59.

Bibliography

23andMe. 'Discover More about Your DNA Story'. Accessed 16 January 2018. https://www.23andme.com/en-gb/dna-ancestry/.

African Ancestry, 'Trace Your DNA. Find Your Roots'. Accessed 16 January 2018. http://www.africanancestry.com/home/.

Ahmed, Sara. 'Open Forum, Imaginary Prohibitions: Some Preliminary Remarks on the Founding Gestures of the "New Materialism"'. *European Journal of Women's Studies* 15, no. 1 (2008): 23–39.

Angier, Natalie. 'On the Trail of Everybody's Mother'. *The New York Times*, 8 April 1990. http://www.nytimes.com/1990/04/08/books/on-the-trail-of-everybody-s-mother.html.

Antrosio, Jason. 'More Mothers than Mitochondrial Eve'. *Living Anthropologically,* 2013. http://www.livinganthropologically.com/anthropology/mitochondrial-eve/.

Appiah, Kwame Anthony. 'Mistaken Identities: Colour'. *The Reith Lectures*, BBC Radio 4, London, 5 November 2016. https://www.bbc.co.uk/programmes/b080t63w.

Appiah, Kwame Anthony. 'Racial Identity Is a Biological Nonsense Says Reith Lecturer'. Interview by Hannah Ellis-Petersen, *The Guardian*, 18 October 2016. https://www.theguardian.com/society/2016/oct/18/racial-identity-is-a-biological-nonsense-says-reith-lecturer.

Ashcroft, Bill. 'Critical Histories: Postcolonialism, Postmodernism, and Race'. In *Postmodern Literature and Race*, edited by Len Platt and Sara Upstone, 13–30. Cambridge: Cambridge University Press, 2015.

Athey, Stephanie. 'Poisonous Roots and the New World Blues: Rereading Seventies Narration and Nation in Alex Haley and Gayl Jones'. *Narrative* 7, no. 2 (1999): 169–193.

Attridge, Derek. *The Singularity of Literature*. London: Routledge, 2004.

Atwood, Margaret. 'Brave New World'. *Slate*, 1 April 2005. http://www.slate.com/articles/arts/books/2005/04/brave_new_world.html.

Ayala, Francisco J. 'The Myth of Eve: Molecular Biology and Human Origins'. *Science* 270, no. 5244 (1995): 1930–1936.

Baron, Archie. Director. *Motherland: A Genetic Journey*, BBC2, 14 February 2003.

Barrow, Andrew. 'Artist of a Floating World'. Review of *Never Let Me Go*, by Kazuo Ishiguro. *The Independent*. 25 February 2005.

Beer, Gillian. *Darwin's Plots: Evolutionary Narrative in Darwin, George Eliot and Nineteenth-Century Fiction*. 1983. Cambridge: Cambridge University Press, 2000.

Beer, Gillian. *Open Fields: Science in Cultural Encounter*. Oxford: Oxford University Press, 1996.

Bhabha, Homi K. 'Culture's In-Between'. In *Questions of Cultural Identity*, edited by Stuart Hall and Paul du Gay, 53–60. London: Sage, 1996.

Biagioli, Mario. 'Postdisciplinary Liaisons: Science Studies and the Humanities'. *Critical Inquiry* 35 (2009): 816–833.

Bivins, Roberta. 'Hybrid Vigour? Genes, Genomics, and History'. *Genomics, Society and Policy* 4, no. 1 (2008): 12–22.

Black, Shameem. 'Ishiguro's Inhuman Aesthetics'. *Modern Fiction Studies* 55, no. 4 (2009): 785–807.

Blacker, Sarah. 'Epistemic Trafficking: On the Concept of Race-Specific Medicine'. *English Studies in Canada* 36, no. 1 (2010): 127–148.

Blevins, Steven. *Living Cargo: How Black Britain Performs Its Past*. Minneapolis: University of Minnesota Press, 2016.

Bliss, Catherine. *Race Decoded: The Genomic Fight for Social Justice*. Stanford, CA: Stanford University Press, 2012.

Blumenbach, Johann. 'On the Natural Variety of Mankind'. In *The Idea of Race*, edited by Robert Bernasconi and Tommy L. Lott, 27–37. Indianapolis: Hackett, 2000.

Bradshaw Foundation. 'The Journey of Mankind'. Accessed 9 January 2018. http://www.bradshawfoundation.com/stephenoppenheimer/index.php.

Braun, Lundy. *Breathing Race into the Machine: The Surprising Career of the Spirometer from Plantation to Genetics*. Minneapolis: University of Minnesota Press, 2014.

Braun Lundy, Anne Fausto-Sterling, Duana Fullwiley, Evelynn M. Hammonds, Alondra Nelson, William Quivers, Susan M. Reverby and Alexandra E. Shields. 'Racial Categories in Medical Practice: How Useful Are They?'. *PLoS Medicine* 9, vol. 4 (2007): 1423–1428.

Brennan, Timothy. 'The Cultural Politics of Rushdie Criticism: All or Nothing'. In *Critical Essays on Salman Rushdie*, edited by Keith Booker, 129–153. New York: G.K. Hall, 1999.

Brouillette, Sarah. *Literature and the Creative Economy*. Stanford, CA: Stanford University Press, 2014.

Brown, Ina Corinne. Correspondence with Alex Haley, 12 September 1972. Sc MG 472, Box 10, Folder 2, Alex Haley papers, Schomburg Center for Research in Black Culture, The New York Public Library, New York, United States of America.

Brown, Michael H. *The Search for Eve*. New York: Harper and Row, 1990.

Brown, Michael K., Martin Carnoy, Elliott Currie, Troy Duster, David B. Oppenheimer, Marjorie M. Shultz and David Wellman. *Whitewashing Race: The Myth of a Color-Blind Society*. Berkeley: University of California Press, 2003.

Butler, Octavia E. 'Black Women and the Science Fiction Genre'. Interview by Frances M. Beal. *Black Scholar*, March–April (1986): 14–18.

Butler, Octavia E. 'An Interview with Octavia E. Butler'. Interview by Randall Kenan. *Callaloo* 14, no. 2 (1991): 495–504.

Butler, Octavia E. *Kindred*. Boston, MA: Beacon Press, 1989.

Butler, Octavia E. '"Radio Imagination": Octavia Butler on the Poetics of Narrative Embodiment'. Interview by Marilyn Mehaffy and AnaLouise Keating. *MELUS* 26, no. 1 (2001): 45–76.

Butler, Octavia E. 'We Keep Playing the Same Record: A Conversation with Octavia E. Butler'. Interview by Stephen W. Potts, *Science Fiction Studies* 23, no. 3 (1996): 331–338.

Cambridge, A., and S. Feuchtwang. *Anti-Racist Strategies*. Aldershot: Avebury, 1991.

Cann, Rebecca. 'All About Mitochondrial Eve: An Interview with Rebecca Cann'. Interview by Jane Gitschier, *PLoS Genetics* 6, no. 5 (2010): 1–4.

Cann, Rebecca. 'The Scientists behind Mitochondrial Eve Tell Us about the "Lucky Mother" Who Changed Human Evolution Forever'. Interview by Alasdair Wilkins, *Gizmodo*, 27 January 2012. https://io9.gizmodo.com/5879991/the-scientists-behind-mitochondrial-eve-tell-us-about-the-lucky-mother-who-changed-human-evolution-forever?tag=evolution.

Cann, Rebecca L., Mark Stoneking, and Allan C. Wilson. 'Mitochondrial DNA and Human Evolution'. *Nature* 325 (1987): 31–36.

Carey, Nessa. *The Epigenetics Revolution*. London: Icon, 2012.

Cartwright, Samuel A. 'Report on the Diseases and Physical Peculiarities of the Negro Race'. *The New Orleans Medical and Surgical Journal* 7, May (1851): 691–715.

Cavalli-Sforza, Luca. 'The Human Genome Diversity Project'. Address delivered to a Special Meeting of UNESCO, Paris, 12 September 1994. https://digital.library.unt.edu/ark:/67531/metadc697236/m2/1/high_res_d/505327.pdf.

Cavalli-Sforza, L. Luca. 'The Human Genome Diversity Project: Past, Present and Future'. *Nature Reviews Genetics* 6 (2005): 333–340.

Cavalli-Sforza, Luca, Paolo Menozzi, and Alberto Piazza. *The History and Geography of Human Genes*. Princeton, NJ: Princeton University Press, 1994.

Cavalli-Sforza, L. Luca, Allan C. Wilson, C.R. Cantor, R.M. Cook-Deccan, and M.C. King. 'Call for a Worldwide Survey of Human Genetic Diversity: A Vanishing Opportunity for the Human Genome Project'. *Genomics* 11 (1991): 490–491.

Chioni Moore, David. 'Routes: Alex Haley's Roots and the Rhetoric of Genealogy'. *Transition: An International Review* 64 (1994): 4–21.

Clark, Josiah. *Types of Mankind, or, Ethnological Researches Based upon the Ancient Monuments, Paintings, Sculptures and Crania of Races and upon Their Natural, Geographical, Philological, and Biblical History*. 4th edn. Philadelphia: Lippincott, Grambo & Co., 1860.

Cohen, Phil. 'Through a Glass Darkly: Intellectuals on Race'. In *New Ethnicities, Old Racisms?*, edited by Phil Cohen, 1–17. London: Zed, 1999.

Cohn, Jay. *Saving Sam: Drugs, Race, and Discovering the Secrets of Heart Disease*. Minneapolis, MN: Wisdom Editions, 2014.

Collins, Francis. *The Language of Life: DNA and the Revolution in Personalised Medicine*. London: Profile Books, 2010.

Collins, Francis. 'What We Do and Don't Know about "Race," "Ethnicity," Genetics and Health at the Dawn of the Genome Era'. *Genetics for the Human Race*, spec. issue of *Nature Genetics* 36, no. 11 (2004): S13–S15.

Collins, Tim. 'Was Cheddar man white after all? There's no way to know that the first Briton had "dark to black skin" says scientist who helped reconstruct his 10,000-year-old face'. *The Mail Online*, 2 March 2018. http://www.dailymail.co.uk/sciencetech/article-5453665/Was-Cheddar-man-white-all.html.

Condit, Celeste, A. Templeton, B.R. Bates, J.L. Bevan and T.M. Harris. 'Attitudinal Barriers to Delivery of Race-Targeted Pharmacogenomics among Informed Lay Persons'. *Genetics in Medicine* 5, no. 5 (2003): 385–392.

Connor, Steven. 'Decomposing the Humanities'. *New Literary History* 47, nos. 2&3 (2016): 275–288.

Cooper, Richard S., Jay S. Kaufman, and Ryk Ward. 'Race and Genomics'. *The New England Journal of Medicine* 348, no. 12 (2003): 1166–1170.

Courlander, Harold. 'Kunta Kinte's Struggle to Be African'. *Phylon: A Review of Race and Culture* 47, no. 4 (1986): 294–302.

Crick, Francis. Letter to John Edsall, 22 February 1971. Francis Crick Papers, Wellcome Library, London.

Curtin, Philip. 'Recent Trends in African Historiography and Their Contribution to History in General'. In *General History of Africa Vol. 1 Methodology and African Prehistory*, edited by Josephe Ki-Zebro, 54–71. Paris: UNESCO and London: Heinemann, 1981.

Dames, Nicholas. '"The Withering of the Individual": Psychology in the Victorian Novel'. In *A Concise Companion to the Victorian Novel*, edited by Francis O'Gorman, 91–112. Oxford: Blackwell, 2005.

Darwin, Charles. *The Expression of the Emotions in Man and Animals*. 1872. Chicago: Chicago University Press, 1965.

Davy Smith, George. 'Essay Review: Epigenetics for the Masses: More Than Audrey Hepburn and Yellow Mice?'. *International Journal of Epidemiology* 41 (2012): 303–308.

Dawkins, Richard. *River Out of Eden: A Darwinian View of Life*. London: Phoenix, 1994.

Dawkins, Richard. *The Ancestor's Tale: A Pilgrimage to the Dawn of Life*. London: Phoenix, 2004.

Dawson, Ashley. *Mongrel Nation: Diasporic Culture and the Making of Postcolonial Britain*. Ann Arbor: University of Michigan Press, 2007.

De Gobineau, Arthur. 'The Inequality of Human Races'. In *The Idea of Race*, edited by Robert Bernasconi and Tommy L. Lott, 45–53. Indianapolis, IN: Hackett, 2000.

De Groot, Jerome. *Consuming History: Historians and Heritage in Contemporary Popular Culture*. Oxon: Routledge, 2009.

Deichmann, Ute. 'Why Epigenetics Is Not a Vindication of Lamarckism – and Why That Matters'. *Studies in History and Philosophy of Biological and Biomedical Sciences* 57 (2016): 80–82.

Dennett, Daniel. *Darwin's Dangerous Idea*. London: Penguin Science, 1995.

DeSalle, Rob, and Ian Tattersall. *Troublesome Science: The Misuse of Genetics and Genomics in Understanding Race*. New York: Columbia University Press, 2018.

Dihal, Kanta. 'On Science Fiction as a Separate Field'. In 'State of the Unions'. Special Issue edited by Melissa M. Littlefield and Martin Willis, *Journal of Literature and Science* 10, no. 1 (2017): 32–36.

Dolezal, Rachel. Interview by Matt Lauer, *Today*, NBC 16 June 2015. https://www.youtube.com/watch?v=lG9Q2_Hv83k.

Douglass, Frederick. *The Claims of the Negro, Ethnologically Considered*. Rochester, NY: Lee, Mann and Co., 1854. Frederick Douglass Papers at the Library of Congress. http://hdl.loc.gov/loc.mss/mfd.21036

Du Bois, W.E.B. *Dusk of Dawn: An Essay Toward an Autobiography of a Race Concept*. 1940. Series edited by Henry Louis Gates Jr. New York: Oxford University Press, 2007.

Dubbin, Leslie, Monica McLemore and Janet K. Shim. 'Illness Narratives of African Americans Living with Coronary Heart Disease: A Critical Interactionist Analysis'. *Qualitative Health Research* 27, vol. 4 (2017): 497–508.

Dugdale, John. 'Roots of the Problem: The Controversial History of Alex Haley's Book'. *The Guardian*, 9 February 2017. https://www.theguardian.com/books/booksblog/2017/feb/09/alex-haley-roots-reputation-authenticity.

Duster, Troy. 'Ancestry Testing and DNA: Uses, Limits and *Caveat Emptor*'. In *Race and the Genetic Revolution: Science, Myth and Culture*, edited by Sheldon Krimsky and Kathleen Sloan, 99–115. New York: Columbia University Press, 2011.

Duster, Troy. *Backdoor to Eugenics*. 2nd edn. New York: Routledge, 2003.

Duster, Troy. 'A Post-Genomic Surprise. The Molecular Reinscription of Race in Science, Law and Medicine'. *The British Journal of Sociology* 66, no. 1 (2015): 1–27.

Duster, Troy. 'Race and Reification in Science'. *Science* 307, no. 5712 (2005): 1050–1051.

Editorial. 'ASHG Denounces Attempts to Link Genetics and Racial Supremacy'. *The American Journal of Human Genetics* 103 (2018): 636–636.

Editorial. 'Illuminating BiDil'. *Nature Biotechnology* 23, no. 8 (2005): 903.

Edsall, John. Letter to Francis Crick, 5 March 1971. Francis Crick Papers, Wellcome Library, London.

Ekman, Paul, and Wallace V. Friesen. 'Constants Across Cultures in the Face and Emotion'. *Journal of Personality and Social Psychology* 17 (1971): 124–129.

Eliot, George. *Daniel Deronda*. 1876. Hertfordshire: Wordsworth Editions, 2003.

Elsdon-Baker, Fern. 'Contested Inheritance: Debates on the Role of "Inheritance of Acquired Characteristics" in Late Nineteenth Century Darwinian and Weismannian Thought'. *Textual Practice* 29, no. 3 (2015): 547–571.

Ernst, Waltraud. 'Introduction: Historical and Contemporary Perspectives on Race, Science and Medicine'. In *Race, Science and Medicine, 1700–1960*, edited by Waltraud Ernst and Bernard Harris, 1–28. London: Routledge, 1999.

Essed, Philomena, and David Theo Goldberg. 'Cloning Cultures: The Social Injustices of Sameness'. *Ethnic and Racial Studies* 25, no. 6 (2002): 1066–1082.

Felski, Rita. 'Context Stinks!'. *New Literary History* 42, no. 4 (2011): 573–591.

Felski, Rita. 'Introduction: Recomposing the Humanities – with Bruno Latour'. *New Literary History* 47, nos. 2&3 (2016): 215–229.

The First Brit: Secrets of the 10,000 Year Old Man. Directed by Steven Clarke. Produced by Plimsoll Productions, aired 18 February 2018, on Channel 4. https://www.channel4.com/programmes/the-first-brit-the-10000-year-old-man.

Fisch, Audrey. *The Cambridge Companion to Africa American Slave Narratives*. Cambridge: Cambridge University Press, 2007.

Fluet, Lisa. 'Immaterial Labors: Ishiguro, Class, Affect'. *Novel* 40, no. 3 (2007): 265–288.

Foster Eugene A., M.A. Jobling, P.G. Taylor, P. Donnelly, P. de Knijff, Rene Mieremet, T. Zerjal and C. Tyler-Smith. 'Jefferson Fathered Slave's Last Child'. *Nature* 396 (1998): 27–28.

Foster, Morris W. 'Looking for Race in All the Wrong Places: Analyzing the Lack of Productivity in the Ongoing Debate about Race and Genetics'. *Human Genetics* 126 (2009): 355–362.

Foucault, Michel. 'Lecture 11 March 17, 1976'. *Society Must Be Defended: Lectures at the College de France*, edited by Mauro Bertani and Alessandro Fontana. Translated by David Macey. New York: Picador, 2003.

Foucault, Michel. *The Will to Knowledge: The History of Sexuality Volume 1*. Translated by Robert Hurley. 1978. London: Penguin, 1998.

Franciosa, Joseph A., A.L. Taylor, J.N. Cohn, C.W. Yancy, S. Ziesche, A. Olukotun, E. Ofili, K. Ferdinand, J. Loscalzo and M. Worcel. 'African-American Heart Failure Trial (A-HeFT): Rationale, Design, and Methodology'. *Journal of Cardiac Failure* 18, no. 3 (2002): 128–135.

Fuller, Kathleen. 'Pathological Science and MtEve'. *Anthrohealth Blog*. Accessed 29 April 2016. http://anthrohealth.net/blog/pathological-science-and-mteve.

Gabbatiss, Josh. 'DNA Pioneer James Watson Has Final Honours Stripped amid Racism Row'. *The Independent*, 12 January 2019. https://www.independent.co.uk/news/science/james-watson-racism-honours-dna-double-helix-cold-spring-harbor-laboratory-a8724896.html and https://www.cshl.edu/statement-by-cold-spring-harbor-laboratory-addressing-remarks-by-dr-james-d-watson-in-american-masters-decoding-watson/.

Gabbatiss, Josh. 'James Watson: The Most Controversial Statements Made by the Father of DNA'. *The Independent*, 13 January 2009. https://www.independent.co.uk/news/science/james-watson-racism-sexism-dna-race-intelligence-genetics-double-helix-a8725556.html.

Gannett, Lisa. 'Biogeographical Ancestry and Race'. *Studies in History and Philosophy of Biological and Biomedical Sciences* 47 (2014): 173–184.

Gates, Henry Louis Jr, 'Editor's Introduction: Writing, Race and the Difference It Makes'. *Critical Inquiry* 12, no. 1 (1985): 1–20.

Gates, Henry Louis Jr. 'Reading "'Race', Writing, and Difference"'. *PMLA* 123, no. 5 (2008): 1534–1539.

Gates, Henry Louis Jr, *The Signifying Monkey: A Theory of African American Literary Criticism*. 1988. New York: Oxford University Press, 2014.

Gibbons, Ann. 'A New View of the Birth of *Homo sapiens*'. *Science* 331, no. 6016 (2011): 392–394.

Gill, Josie. 'Decolonizing Literature and Science'. *Configurations* 26, no. 3 (2018): 283–288.

Gilroy, Paul. *Against Race: Imagining Political Culture beyond the Color Line*. Cambridge, MA: Belknap Press, 2000.

Gilroy, Paul. *There Ain't No Black in the Union Jack*. Routledge Classics edn. 1987. London: Routledge, 2002.

Goldberg, David Theo. 'Call and Response'. *Patterns of Prejudice* 44, no. 1 (2010): 89–106.

Goldberg, David Theo. *The Threat of Race: Reflections on Racial Neoliberalism*. Malden, MA: Blackwell, 2009.

Gould, Stephen Jay. *The Mismeasure of Man*. 1981. London: Penguin, 1997.

Graves, Joseph. 'James Watson's Racism Is a Product of His Time - but That Doesn't Excuse It'. *CNN*, 16 January 2019. https://edition.cnn.com/2019/01/15/opinions/james-watson-not-alone-in-racist-thinking-graves/index.html.

Griffin, Gabriele. 'Science and the Cultural Imaginary: The Case of Kazuo Ishiguro's *Never Let Me Go*'. *Textual Practice* 23, no. 4 (2009): 645–663.

Grossniklaus, Ueli, William G. Kelly, Anne C. Ferguson-Smith, Marcus Pembrey and Susan Lindquist. 'Transgenerational Epigenetic Inheritance: How Important Is It?'. *Nature Reviews Genetics* 14 (2013): 228–235.

Guillory, James Denny. 'The Pro-Slavery Arguments of Dr. Samuel A. Cartwright'. *Louisiana History: The Journal of the Louisiana Historical Association* 9, no. 3 (1968): 209–227.

Gunning, Dave. *Race and Anti-Racism in Black British and British Asian Literature*. Liverpool: Liverpool University Press, 2010.

Haley, Alex. *The Autobiography of Malcolm X*. New York: Ballantine, 1999.

Haley, Alex. Interview by Murray Fisher, *Playboy*, January 1977, 57–79.

Haley, Alex. 'My Furthest-Back Person, the African'. *The New York Times*, 16 July 1972. SM12.

Haley, Alex. *Roots*. 1976. London: Vintage, 1991.

Hall, Stuart. 'Race, The Floating Signifier (Transcript)'. *Media Education Foundation*, 1997, 8. Accessed 22 August 2019. http://www.mediaed.org/transcripts/Stuart-Hall-Race-the-Floating-Signifier-Transcript.pdf.

Hamner, Everett. *Editing the Soul: Science and Fiction in the Genome Age*. University Park, PA: The Pennsylvania State University Press, 2017.

Haraway, Donna. *Modest_Witness@Second Millenium. FemaleMan©_Meets_OncoMouse™*. New York: Routledge, 1997.

Haraway, Donna. *Primate Visions: Gender, Race, and Nature in the World of Modern Science*. New York: Routledge, 1989.

Haraway, Donna. *Simians, Cyborgs and Women: The Reinvention of Nature*. London: Free Association, 1991.

Harding, Sandra. 'Science, Race, Culture, Empire'. In *A Companion to Racial and Ethnic Studies*, edited by David Theo Goldberg and John Solomos, 217–228. Oxford: Blackwell, 2002.

Harmon, Amy. 'James Watson Had a Chance to Salvage His Reputation on Race. He Made Things Worse'. *The New York Times*, 1 January 2019. https://www.nytimes.com/2018/10/17/us/white-supremacists-science-dna.html.

Harmon, Amy. 'Why White Supremacists Are Chugging Milk (and Why Geneticists Are Alarmed)'. *The New York Times*, 17 October 2018. https://www.nytimes.com/2018/10/17/us/white-supremacists-science-dna.html.

Harrison, M. John. 'Clone Alone'. Review of *Never Let Me Go*, by Kazuo Ishiguro. *The Guardian*, 26 February 2005.

Head, Dominic. *The Cambridge Introduction to Modern British Fiction 1950–2000*. Cambridge: Cambridge University Press, 2002.

Head, Dominic. 'Zadie Smith's *White Teeth*: Multiculturalism for the Millennium'. In *Contemporary British Fiction*, edited by Richard J. Lane, Rod Mengham and Philip Tew, 106–119. Malden, MA: Polity Press, 2003.

Heard, Edith. 'We Can't Undo What Our Parents Have Given Us in Terms of Our Genes'. Interview by Catherine de Lange. *The Guardian*, 23 June 2013. https://www.theguardian.com/science/2013/jun/23/rational-heroes-edith-heard-epigenetics.

Herwitz, Daniel, and Ashutosh Varshney, eds. *Midnight's Diaspora: Critical Encounters with Salman Rushdie*. Ann Arbor: University of Michigan Press, 2008.

Hochschild, Jennifer L. 'To Test or Not? Singular or Multiple Heritage? Genomic Ancestry Testing and Americans' Racial Identity'. *Du Bois Review* 12, no. 2 (2015): 321–347.

Hofmänner, Alexandra. 'The African Eve Effect in Science'. *Archaeologies: Journal of the World Archaeological Congress* 7, no. 1 (2011): 251–289.

Huehls, Mitchum. *After Critique: Twenty-First-Century Fiction in a Neoliberal Age*. New York: Oxford University Press, 2016.

Hunt-Grubbe, Charlotte. 'The Elementary DNA of Dr Watson'. *The Sunday Times*, 14 October 2007. https://www.thetimes.co.uk/article/the-elementary-dna-of-dr-watson-gllb6w2vpdr.

Ishiguro, Kazuo. 'A Conversation about Life and Art with Kazuo Ishiguro'. Interview by Cynthia F. Wong and Grace Crommett, 2006. In *Conversations with Kazuo Ishiguro*, edited by Brian W. Shaffer and Cynthia F. Wong, 204–220. Jackson: University Press of Mississippi, 2008.

Ishiguro, Kazuo. Interview by Karen Grigsby Bates, *Day to Day on NPR Radio*, 4 May, 2005. In *Conversations with Kazuo Ishiguro*, edited by Brian W. Shaffer and Cynthia F. Wong, 199–203. Jackson: University Press of Mississippi, 2008.

Ishiguro, Kazuo. *Never Let Me Go*. London: Faber and Faber, 2005.

Jackson, Fatimah L. 'Genomics: DNA and Diasporas'. Review of *The Social Life of DNA: Race, Reparations, and Reconciliation after the Genome* by Alondra Nelson'. *Nature* 529 (2016): 279–280.

Jasienska, Grazyna. 'Low Birth Weight of Contemporary African Americans: An Intergenerational Effect of Slavery?'. *American Journal of Human Biology* 21, no. 1 (2009): 16–24.

Jensen, Arthur. 'How Much Can We Boost IQ and Scholastic Achievement?'. *Harvard Educational Review* 39 (1969): 1–123.

Jobling, Mark A., and Chris Tyler-Smith. 'The Human Y Chromosome: An Evolutionary Marker Comes of Age'. *Nature Reviews Genetics* 4 (2003): 598–612.

Johns, J. Adam. 'Becoming Medusa: Octavia Butler's "Lilith's Brood" and Sociobiology'. *Science Fiction Studies* 37, no. 3 (2010): 382–400.

Johnson, Linton Kwesi. 'Responses to Roots'. *Race & Class* 19, no. 1 (1977): 77–105.

Johnson, Norman A. *Darwinian Detectives: Revealing the Natural History of Genes and Genomes*. New York: Oxford University Press, 2007.

Jones, J.S. 'A Thousand and One Eves'. *Nature* 345, no. 31 (1990): 395–396.

Jones, Steve. *The Language of the Genes*. London: Flamingo, 2000.

Jordanova, L.J. *Lamarck*. Oxford: Oxford University Press, 1984.

Kahn, Jonathan. *Race in a Bottle: The Story of BiDil and Racialized Medicine in a Post-Genomic Age*. New York: Columbia University Press, 2013.

Kahn, Jonathan, Alondra Nelson, Joseph Graves, Marcy Darnovsky, Osagie Obasogie et al. 'How Not to Talk About Race and Genetics'. *BuzzFeed News*, 30 March 2018. https://www.buzzfeednews.com/article/bfopinion/race-genetics-david-reich.

Kant, Immanuel. 'Of the Different Human Races'. In *The Idea of Race*, edited by Robert Bernasconi and Tommy L. Lott, 8–22. Indianapolis, IN: Hackett, 2000.

Kay, Lily E. *Who Wrote the Book of Life?: A History of the Genetic Code*. Stanford, CA: Stanford University Press, 2000.

Keller, Evelyn Fox. 'From Gene Action to Reactive Genomes'. *The Journal of Physiology* 592, no. 11 (2014): 2423–2429.

Keller, Evelyn Fox. *The Mirage of a Space between Nature and Nurture*. Durham, NC, and London: Duke University Press, 2010.

Keller, Evelyn Fox. 'Thinking about Biology and Culture: Can the Natural and Human Sciences Be Integrated?'. *The Sociological Review Monographs* 64, no. 1 (2016): 26–41.

Kohn, Marek. *The Race Gallery: The Return of Racial Science*. London: Vintage, 1996.

Kreiger, Nancy. 'If "Race" Is the Answer, What Is the Question? - on "Race," Racism, and Health: A Social Epidemiologist's Perspective'. *Is 'Race' Real? A Web Forum organized by the Social Science Research Council*, 7 June 2006. http://raceandgenomics.ssrc.org/Krieger/.

Kreiger, Nancy. 'Living and Dying at the Crossroads: Racism, Embodiment, and Why Theory Is Essential for a Public Health of Consequence'. *American Journal of Public Health* 106, no. 5 (2016): 832–833.

Kushnuck, Louis. 'Responses to Roots'. *Race & Class* 19, no. 1 (1977): 77–105.

Kuzawa, Christopher W., and Elizabeth Sweet. 'Epigenetics and the Embodiment of Race: Developmental Origins of US Racial Disparities in Cardiovascular Health'. *American Journal of Human Biology* 21, no. 1 (2009): 2–15.

Laist, Randy. 'Alex Haley's Roots and Hyperreal Historiography'. *Mediascape* (2013). http://www.tft.ucla.edu/mediascape/Winter2013_Roots.html.

Lamarck, Jean Baptiste. *Philosophie Zoologique* 1809. Translated by Hugh Elliot as *Zoological Philosophy: An Exposition with Regard to the Natural History of Animals with Introductory Essays by David L. Hull and Richard W. Burkhardt Jr.* 1914. New York: Cambridge University Press, 2011.

Lammy, David. 'A New Black Politics?'. Interview by David Goodhart, *Analysis*, BBC Radio 4, 31 October 2011. Audio. https://www.bbc.co.uk/programmes/b016lbtp.

Larkin, Lesley. *Race and the Literary Encounter: Black Literature from James Weldon Johnson to Percival Everett*. Bloomington: Indiana University Press, 2015.

Latour, Bruno. *We Have Never Been Modern*. Translated by Catherine Porter. Cambridge, MA: Harvard University Press, 1993.

Latour, Bruno. 'Why Has Critique Run out of Steam? From Matters of Fact to Matters of Concern'. *Critical Inquiry* 30, no. 2 (2004): 225–248.

Latour, Bruno, and Steve Woolgar. *Laboratory Life: The Construction of Scientific Facts*. Princeton, NJ: Princeton University Press, 1986.

Leakey, Richard. *The Origin of Humankind*. New York: Harper Collins, 1994.

Leise, Christopher. 'With Names, No Coincidence: Colson Whitehead's Postracial Puritan Allegory'. *African American Review* 47, nos. 2–3 (2014): 285–300.

Levine, Caroline. *Forms: Whole, Rhythm, Hierarchy, Network*. Princeton, NJ: Princeton University Press, 2017.

Lewin, Roger. *Bones of Contention: Controversies in the Search for Human Origins*. 2nd edn. Chicago: University of Chicago Press, 1997.

Lewin, Roger. 'On the Ancestrail Trail'. Review of *The Search for Eve*, by Michael H. Brown, *New Scientist*, 5 January 1991. https://www.newscientist.com/article/mg12917504-000-review-on-the-ancestrail-trail/.

Lewin, Roger. *The Origin of Modern Humans*. New York: Scientific American Library, 1993.

Lewontin, Richard C. 'Race and Intelligence'. *Bulletin of Atomic Scientists* 26, no. 3 (1970): 2–8.

Li, Stephanie. *Signifying without Specifying: Racial Discourse in the Age of Obama*. New Brunswick, NJ: Rutgers University Press, 2012.

Love, Dave. 'Post-Traumatic Slave Syndrome and Intergenerational Trauma: Slavery Is Like a Curse Passing Through the DNA of Black People'. *Atlanta Black Star*, 5 June 2016. https://atlantablackstar.com/2016/06/05/post-traumatic-slave-syndrome-and-intergenerational-trauma-slavery-is-like-a-curse-passing-through-the-dna-of-black-people/.

Mansfield, Becky, and Julie Guthman. 'Epigenetic Life: Biological Plasticity, Abnormality, and New Configurations of Race and Reproduction'. *Cultural Geographies* 21, no. 1 (2015): 3–20.

Marks, Jonathan. 'Systematics in Anthropology: Where Science Confronts the Humanities (and Consistently Loses)'. In *Conceptual Issues in Modern Human Origins Research*, edited by Geoffrey A. Clark and Catherine M. Willermet, 45–59. New York: Aldine de Gruyter, 1997.

Martin, Biddy. 'Racist Posters on Campus'. Amherst College. Accessed 29 August 2018. https://www.amherst.edu/amherst-story/president/statements/node/665033.

Maus, Derek C. *Understanding Colson Whitehead*. Columbia: University of South Carolina Press, 2014.

Mbembe, Achille. *Critique of Black Reason*. Durham, NC: Duke University Press, 2017.

McEwan, Ian. *Saturday*. London: Vintage, 2006.

McFadden, Johnjoe. 'The Unselfish Gene'. *The Guardian*, 6 May 2005. http://www.guardian.co.uk/education/2005/may/06/science.highereducation.

M'Charek, Amade. 'Beyond Fact or Fiction: On the Materiality of Race in Practice'. *Cultural Anthropology* 28, no. 3 (2013): 420–442.

M'Charek, Amade. *The Human Genome Diversity Project: An Ethnography of Scientific Practice*. Cambridge: Cambridge University Press, 2010.

Meloni, Maurizio. 'Epigenetics for the Social Sciences: Justice, Embodiment, and Inheritance in the Postgenomic Age'. *New Genetics and Society* 34, no. 2 (2015): 125–151.

Meloni, Maurizio. 'A Postgenomic Body: Histories, Genealogies, Politics'. *Body and Society* 24, no. 3 (2018): 3–38.

Meloni, Maurizio. 'Race in an Epigenetic Time: Thinking Biology in the Plural'. *The British Journal of Sociology* 68, no. 3 (2017): 389–409.

Meloni, Maurizio, Simon Williams and Paul Martin. 'The Biosocial: Sociological Themes and Issues'. *Sociological Review Monographs* 64, no. 1 (2016): 7–25.

Memmi, Albert. *The Colonizer and the Colonized*. 1965. Boston, MA: Beacon Press, 1991.

Mesle, Sarah. '"America" Is Not the Object: An Interview with Kandice Chuh, President of the American Studies Association'. *Los Angeles Review of Books*, 9 November 2017. https://lareviewofbooks.org/article/america-is-not-the-object-an-interview-with-kandice-chuh-president-of-the-american-studies-association/#!.

Metzl, Jonathan M. *The Protest Psychosis: How Schizophrenia Became a Black Disease*. Boston, MA: Beacon Press, 2011.

Midgley, Mary. *Science and Poetry*. London: Routledge, 2001.

Miletic, Philip. 'Octavia E. Butler's Response to Black Arts/Black Power Literature and Rhetoric in Kindred'. *African American Review* 49, no. 3 (2016): 261–275.

Moment, Gairdner. 'Roots and the Biologist'. *BioScience* 29, no. 6 (1978): 363–364.

Mondal, Anshuman A. '*The Ground beneath Her Feet* and *Fury*: The Reinvention of Location'. In *The Cambridge Companion to Salman Rushdie*, edited by Abdulrazak Gurnah, 169–183. Cambridge: Cambridge University Press, 2007.

Montagu, Ashley. *Statement on Race: An Annotated Elaboration and Exposition of the Four Statements on Race Issued by the United Nations Educational, Scientific, and Cultural Organisation*. 3rd edn. 1951. New York: Oxford University Press, 1972.

Morris, Kevin V. 'Lamarck and the Missing Lnc'. *The Scientist*, 1 October 2012. http://www.the-scientist.com/?articles.view/articleNo/32637/title/Lamarck-and-the-Missing-Lnc/.

Morris-Reich, Amos, and Dirk Rupnow. 'Introduction'. In *Ideas of 'Race' in the History of the Humanities*, edited by Amos Morris-Reich and Dirk Rupnow, 1–31. Switzerland: Palgrave Macmillan, 2017.

Mukherjee, Siddhartha. 'Same but Different: How Epigenetics Can Blur the Line between Nature and Nurture'. *The New Yorker*, 2 May 2016. https://www.newyorker.com/magazine/2016/05/02/breakthroughs-in-epigenetics.

Mullan, John. 'Afterword: On First Reading *Never Let Me Go*'. In *Kazuo Ishiguro*, Contemporary Critical Perspectives Series, edited by Sean Matthews and Sebastian Groes, 104–113. London: Continuum, 2010.

Müller, Ruth, Clare Hanson, Mark Hanson, Michael Penkler, Georgia Samaras, Luca Chiapperino, John Dupré et al. 'The Biosocial Genome? Interdisciplinary Perspectives on Environmental Epigenetics, Health and Society'. *EMBO Reports* 18, no. 10 (2017): 1–6. https://doi.org/10.15252/embr.201744953.

Murray, Stuart. 'Care and the Self: Biotechnology, Reproduction, and the Good Life'. *Philosophy, Ethics and Humanities in Medicine* 2, no. 6 (2007), BioMed Central. http://www.peh-med.com/content/2/1/6.

Nash, Catherine. *Genetic Geographies: The Trouble with Ancestry*. Minneapolis: University of Minnesota Press, 2015.

Nelson, Alondra. 'Bio Science: Genetic Genealogy Testing and the Pursuit of African Ancestry'. *Social Studies of Science* 38, no. 5 (2008): 759–783.

Nelson, Alondra. 'Roots and Genes'. *Aeon*, 4 January 2016. https://aeon.co/essays/from-roots-to-dna-kits-the-quest-for-african-american-identity.

Nelson, Alondra. *The Social Life of DNA: Race, Reparations and Reconciliation after the Genome*. Boston, MA: Beacon Press, 2016.

Nerlich, Brigitte. 'The Epigenetic Muddle and the Trouble with Science'. *Making Science Public* (blog), 5 August 2016. http://blogs.nottingham.ac.uk/makingsciencepublic/2016/08/05/epigenetic-muddle/.

Nerlich, Brigitte. 'When Epigenetics Gets under the Skin'. *Making Science Public* (blog), 15 August 2016. http://blogs.nottingham.ac.uk/makingsciencepublic/2016/08/15/epigenetics-gets-skin/.

Nerlich, Brigitte, Robert Dingwall and David D. Clarke. 'The Book of Life: How the Completion of the Human Genome Project Was Revealed to the Public'. *Health: An Interdisciplinary Journal for the Social Study of Health, Illness and Medicine* 6, no. 4 (2002): 445–469.

Njeri, Itabari. 'Colorism: In American Society, Are Lighter-Skinned Blacks Better Off?'. *Los Angeles Times*, 24 April 1988. http://articles.latimes.com/1988-04-24/news/vw-2472_1_skin-color.

Nordgren A., and E.T. Juengst. 'Can Genomics Tell Me Who I Am? Essentialistic Rhetoric in Direct-to-Consumer DNA Testing'. *New Genetics and Society* 28, no. 2 (2009): 157–172.

Norrell, Robert J. *Alex Haley and the Books That Changed a Nation*. New York: St Martin's Press, 2015.

Nussbaum, Martha C. *Upheavals of Thought: The Intelligence of Emotions*. Cambridge: Cambridge University Press, 2001.

Oikkonen, Venla. 'Mitochondrial Eve and the Affective Politics of Human Ancestry'. *Signs* 40, no. 3 (2015): 747–772.

Oikkonen, Venla. *Population Genetics and Belonging: A Cultural Analysis of Genetic Ancestry*. Basingstoke: Palgrave Macmillan, 2018.

Oppenheimer, Stephen. *Out of Eden: The Peopling of the World*. London: Constable and Robinson, 2003.

Pamphlet on Racism by Party for Workers Power. Francis Crick Papers, Wellcome Library, London.

Patterson, Christina. 'A Willesden Ring of Confidence'. *The Independent*. 22 January 2000.

Philips, Trevor. 'Stephen Lawrence Speech: Institutions Must Catch Up with Public on Race Issues'. *Race in Britain: Ten Years since the Stephen Lawrence Inquiry*, Equality and Human Rights Commission, London, 19 January 2009. http://www.equalityhumanrights.com/key-projects/race-in-britain/event-ten-years-on-from-the-macpherson-inquiry/stephen-lawrence-speech-institutions-must-catch-up-with-public-on-race-issues/.

Pickersgill, Martyn. 'Epistemic Modesty, Ostentatiousness and the Uncertainties of Epigenetics: On the Knowledge Machinery of (Social) Science'. *The Sociological Review Monographs* 64, no. 1 (2016): 186–202.

Piddington, Andrew. Director. *The Real Eve* (2002). USA.

Pollock, Anne. *Medicating Race: Heart Disease and Durable Preoccupations with Difference*. Durham, NC: Duke University Press, 2012.

Powell, John A. 'The Colorblind Multiracial Dilemma: Racial Categories Reconsidered'. *U.S.F.L. Rev.* 31 (1996): 789–806.

Proctor, Robert N. 'Three Roots of Human Recency: Molecular Anthropology, the Refigured Archeulean, and the UNESCO Response to Auschwitz'. *Current Anthropology* 44, no. 2 (2003): 213–239.

Puchner, Martin. 'When We Were Clones'. *Raritan* 27, no. 4 (2008): 34–49.

'Pulling Teeth'. Anonymous review. *The Economist*, 17 February 2000. http://www.economist.com/node/283204.

Rachul, Christen, Colin Ouellette and Timothy Caulfield. 'Tracing the Use and Source of Racial Terminology in Representations of Genetic Research'. *Genetics in Medicine* 13, no. 4 (2011): 314–319.

Rambsy, Howard, II. 'The Rise of Colson Whitehead: Hi-Tech Narratives of Literary Ascent'. In *New Essays on the African American Novel from Hurston and Ellison to Morrison and Whitehead*, edited by Lovalerie King and Linda F. Selzer, 221–240. New York: Palgrave Macmillan, 2008.

Reardon, Jenny. 'Decoding Race and Human Difference in a Genomic Age'. *Differences: A Journal of Feminist Cultural Studies* 15 (2004): 38–65.

Reardon, Jenny. *Race to the Finish: Identity and Governance in an Age of Genomics*. Princeton, NJ: Princeton University Press, 2005.

Reich, David. '"Race" in The Age of Modern Genetics'. *The New York Times*, 25 March 2018. SR1.

Reich, David. *Who We Are and How We Got Here: Ancient DNA and the New Science of the Human Past*. Oxford: Oxford University Press, 2018.

Relethford, John H. *Reflections of Our Past: How Human History Is Revealed in Our Genes*. Boulder, CO: Westview Press, 2003.

Reverby, Susan M. '"Special Treatment": BiDil, Tuskegee, and the Logic of Race'. *The Journal of Law Medicine & Ethics* 36, no. 3 (2008): 478–484.

Risch, Neil, Esteban Burchard, Elad Ziv and Hua Tang. 'Categorization of Humans in Biomedical Research: Genes, Race and Disease'. *Genome Biology* 3, no. 7 (2002): comment2007.1–comment2007.12.

Roberts, Dorothy. *Fatal Invention: How Science, Politics and Big Business Re-Create Race in the Twenty-First Century*. New York: The New Press, 2011.

Roberts, Dorothy. 'Race and the New Biocitizen'. *What's the Use of Race?: Modern Governance and the Biology of Difference*, edited by Ian Whitmarsh and David S. Jones, 259–276. Cambridge, MA: MIT Press, 2010.

Roberts, Dorothy E. 'The Politics of Race and Science: Conservative Colorblindness and the Limits of Liberal Critique'. *Du Bois Review: Social Science Research on Race* 12, no. 1 (2015): 199–211.

Rodgers, Daniel T. *Age of Fracture*. Cambridge, MA: The Belknap Press of Harvard University Press, 2011.

Roof, Judith. *The Poetics of DNA*. Minneapolis: Minnesota University Press, 2007.

Roots for Real, 'Your Ancestry Discovered'. Accessed 16 January 2018. http://www.rootsforreal.com/service_en.php#mtdna.

Rose, Nikolas. *The Politics of Life Itself: Biomedicine, Power and Subjectivity in the Twenty-First Century*. Princeton, NJ: Princeton University Press, 2007.

Rusert, Britt. *Fugitive Science: Empiricism and Freedom in Early African American Culture*. New York: NYU Press, 2017.

Rusert, Britt M., and Charmaine D.M. Royal. 'Grassroots Marketing in a Global Era: More Lessons from BiDil'. *Journal of Law and Medical Ethics* 39, no. 1 (2011): 79–90.

Rushdie, Salman. 'Salman Rushdie and His Mythic Legacy'. Interview by Vibhuti Patel. *Wall Street Journal*, 27 November 2010. http://online.wsj.com/article/SB10001424052748704638304575636763279031150.html.

Rushdie, Salman. *The Satanic Verses*. 1988; London: Vintage, 1998.

Rushdie, Salman. *Step across This Line: Collected Non-Fiction 1992–2002*. London: Jonathan Cape, 2002.

Sawhney, Sabina, and Simona Sawhney. 'Introduction: Reading Rushdie after 11 September 2001'. *Twentieth-Century Literature* 47, no. 4 (2001): 431–443.

Science Museum. 'Genetic Journey to the Motherland'. *Science Museum Antenna*. Accessed 14 May 2012. http://www.sciencemuseum.org.uk/antenna/motherland/131.asp.

Sense About Science. 'Sense about Genetic Ancestry Testing'. Accessed 22 January 2018. https://archive.senseaboutscience.org/data/files/resources/119/Sense-About-Genetic-Ancestry-Testing.pdf.

Sielke, Sabine. 'Biology', In *The Routledge Companion to Literature and Science*, edited by Bruce Clarke with Manuela Rossini, 29–40. Oxon: Routledge, 2011.

Sivanandan, Ambalavaner. 'Responses to Roots'. *Race & Class* 19, no. 1 (1977): 77–105.

Slezak, Michael. 'Found: Closest Link to Eve, Our Universal Ancestor'. *New Scientist*, 9 October 2014. https://www.newscientist.com/article/mg22429904-500-found-closest-link-to-eve-our-universal-ancestor/.

Smith, Darron T. 'The Epigenetics of Being Black and Feeling Blue: Understanding African American Vulnerability to Disease'. *Huffington Post*, 14 June 2013. https://www.huffingtonpost.com/darron-t-smith-phd/the-epigenetics-of-being-_b_4094226.html?guccounter=1.

Smith, David, and Kevin Rawlinson. 'Trump Insists: "I Am the Least Racist Person" amid Outrage over Remarks'. *The Guardian*, 15 January 2018, https://www.theguardian.com/us-news/2018/jan/15/i-am-not-a-racist-trump-says-after-backlash-over-shithole-nations-remark.

Smith, Zadie. *Changing My Mind: Occasional Essays*. London: Hamish Hamilton, 2009.

Smith, Zadie. 'Dreaming Up Finch'. Interview by Ben Greenman, *The New Yorker*, 16 December 2002.

Smith, Zadie. 'An Interview with Zadie Smith'. Book Browse. Accessed 4 March 2019. https://www.bookbrowse.com/author_interviews/full/index.cfm/author_number/344/zadiesmith.

Smith, Zadie. 'Love, Actually'. *The Guardian*, 1 November 2003. https://www.theguardian.com/books/2003/nov/01/classics.zadiesmith.

Smith, Zadie. *On Beauty*. London: Penguin, 2006.

Smith, Zadie. 'A Writer's Truth'. Interview with Camille Dodero, *The Boston Phoenix*, 18–24 July 2003.

Snow, C.P. *The Two Cultures*. 1959. Cambridge: Cambridge University Press, 1998.

Sommer, Marianne. '"It's a living History, told by the real survivors of the Times-DNA": Anthropological genetics in the tradition of biology as applied history', in *Genetics and the unsettled past: The collision of DNA, Race, and History*, edited by Keith Wailoo, Alondra Nelson and Catherine Lee, 205–224. New Brunswick: NJ: Rutgers University Press, 2012.

Sommer, Marianne. *History Within: The Science, Culture and Politics of Bones, Organisms, and Molecules*. Chicago: Chicago University Press, 2016.

Spector, Tim. *Identically Different: Why You Can Change Your Genes*. London: Orion, 2012.

Spencer, Robert. 'Salman Rushdie and the "War on Terror"'. *Journal of Postcolonial Writing* 46, nos. 3–4 (2010): 251–265.

Squier, Susan. *Liminal Lives: Imagining the Human at the Frontiers of Biomedicine*. Durham, NC, and London: Duke University Press, 2004.

Squires, Claire. *Zadie Smith's White Teeth: A Reader's Guide*. New York: Continuum Contemporaries, 2002.

Stacey, Jackie. *The Cinematic Life of the Gene*. Durham, NC, and London: Duke University Press, 2010.

Steinberg, Deborah Lynn. *Genes and the Bioimaginary: Science, Spectacle, Culture*. Surrey: Ashgate, 2015.

Steinberg, Deborah Lynn. 'Reading Genes/Writing Nation: Reith, "Race" and the Writings of Geneticist Steve Jones'. In *Hybridity and Its Discontents: Politics, Science, Culture*, edited by Avtar Brah and Annie E. Coombes, 137–153. London: Routledge, 2000.

Stotz, Karola, and Paul E. Griffiths. 'Biohumanities: Rethinking the Relationship between Biosciences, Philosophy and History of Science, and Society'. *The Quarterly Review of Biology* 83, no. 1 (2008): 37–45.

Stringer, Chris, and Robin McKie. *African Exodus: The Origins of Modern Humanity*. London: Pimlico, 1996.

Sullivan, Shannon. 'Inheriting Racist Disparities in Health: Epigenetics and the Transgenerational Effects of White Racism'. *Critical Philosophy of Race* 1, no. 2 (2013): 190–218.

Summers-Bremner, Eluned. '"Poor Creatures": Ishiguro's and Coetzee's Imaginary Animals'. *Mosaic: A Journal for the Interdisciplinary Study of Literature* 39, no. 4 (2006): 145–160.

Taylor, Anne L., Susan Ziesche, Clyde Yancy, Peter Carson, Ralph D'Agostino, Jr., Keith Ferdinand, Malcolm Taylor et al. 'Combination of Isosorbide Dinitrate and Hydralazine in Blacks with Heart Failure'. *The New England Journal of Medicine* 351, no. 20 (2004): 2049–2057.

Taylor, Helen. '"The Griot from Tennessee": The Saga of Alex Haley's *Roots*'. *Critical Quarterly* 37, no. 2 (1995): 46–62.

Temu, Arnold, and Bonaventure Surai. *Historians and Africanist History: A Critique*. Holland: Zed Press, 1981.

Thomas, Susie. 'Zadie Smith's False Teeth: The Marketing of Multiculturalism'. *Literary London: Interdisciplinary Studies in the Representation of London* 4, no. 1 (2006). http://www.literarylondon.org/london-journal/march2006/thomas.html.

Thompson, Molly. '"Happy Multicultural Land"? The Implications of an 'Excess of Belonging' in Zadie Smith's *White Teeth*'. In *Write Black, Write British: From Post Colonial to Black British Literature*, edited by Kadija Sesay, 122–140. Hertford: Hansib, 2005.

Timmermans, Stefan, and Sara Shostack. 'Gene Worlds'. *Health: An Interdisciplinary Journal for the Social Study of Health, Illness and Medicine* 20, no. 1 (2016): 33–48.

Trilling, Lionel. *E.M. Forster*. 3rd edn. New York: New Directions, 1964.

Tutton, Richard. *Genomics and the Reimagining of Personalized Medicine*. Surrey: Ashgate, 2014.

Upstone, Sara. *Rethinking Race and Identity in Contemporary British Fiction*. New York: Routledge, 2017.

Vint, Sherryl. '"Only by Experience": Embodiment and the Limitations of Realism in Neo-Slave Narratives'. *Science Fiction Studies* 34, no. 2 (2007): 241–261.

Wachinger, Tobias A. *Posing In-Between: Postcolonial Englishness and the Commodification of Hybridity*. Frankfurt: Peter Lang, 2003.

Wailoo, Keith. 'Who Am I?: Genes and the Problem of Historical Identity'. In *Genetics and the Unsettled Past: The Collision of DNA, Race and History*, edited by Keith

Wailoo, Alondra Nelson and Catherine Lee, 13–19. New Brunswick, NJ: Rutgers University Press, 2012.

Wald, Priscilla. 'Blood and Stories: How Genomics Is Rewriting Race, Medicine and Human History'. *Patterns of Prejudice* 40, nos. 4–5 (2006): 303–333.

Wald, Priscilla. 'Cells, Genes, and Stories: HeLa's Journey from Labs to Literature'. In *Genetics and the Unsettled Past: The Collision of DNA, Race and History*, edited by Keith Wailoo, Alondra Nelson and Catherine Lee, 247–265. New Brunswick, NJ: Rutgers University Press, 2012.

Wald, Priscilla. *Contagious: Cultures, Carriers, and the Outbreak Narrative*. Durham, NC, and London: Duke University Press, 2008.

Wald, Priscilla. 'Future Perfect: Grammar, Genes, and Geography'. *New Literary History* 31, no. 4 (2000): 681–708.

Waldby, Catherine, and Robert Mitchell. *Tissue Economies: Blood, Organs, and Cell Lines in Late Capitalism*. Durham, NC: Duke University Press, 2006.

Walkowitz, Rebecca. 'Unimaginable Largeness: Kazuo Ishiguro, Translation, and the New World Literature'. *Novel* 40, no. 3 (2007): 216–239.

Walters, Tracey L. '"We're All English Now Mate Like It or Lump It": The Black/Britishness of Zadie Smith's *White Teeth*'. In *Write Black, Write British: From Post Colonial to Black British Literature*, edited by Kadija Sesay, 314–321. Hertford: Hansib, 2005.

Waugh, Patricia. 'Contemporary British Fiction'. In *The Cambridge Companion to Modern British Culture*, edited by Michael Higgins, Clarissa Smith and John Storey, 115–136. Cambridge: Cambridge University Press, 2010.

Waugh, Patricia. 'Revising the Two Cultures Debate: Science, Literature and Value'. In *The Arts and Sciences of Criticism*, edited by David Fuller and Patricia Waugh, 33–59. Oxford: Oxford University Press, 1999.

Waugh, Patricia. 'Science and Fiction in the 1990s'. In *British Fiction of the 1990s*, edited by Nick Bentley, 57–77. Oxon: Routledge, 2005.

'We Are All Children of Africa'. Review of *African Exodus: The Origins of Modern Humanity* by Chris Stringer and Robin McKie. *The Journal of Blacks in Higher Education* 17 (1997): 134–135.

Weinbaum, Alys. 'Racial Aura: Walter Benjamin and the Work of Art in a Biotechnological Age'. *Literature and Medicine* 26, no. 1 (2007): 207–239.

Wells, Spencer. *The Journey of Man: A Genetic Odyssey*. London: Allen Lane, 2002.

Werbner, Pnina. 'Introduction: The Dialectics of Cultural Hybridity'. In *Debating Cultural Hybridity: Multi-Cultural Identities and the Politics of Anti-Racism*, edited by Pnina Werbner and Tariq Modood, 1–26. London: Zed, 2000.

White House. 'Remarks Made by the President, Prime Minister Tony Blair of England (via satellite), Dr. Francis Collins, Director of the National Human Genome Research Institute, and Dr. Craig Venter, President and Chief Scientific Officer, Celera Genomics Corporation, on the Completion of the First Survey of the Entire Human Genome Project'. The East Room, The White House, 26 June 2000. National Human Genome Research Institute. http://www.genome.gov/10001356.

White, Kevin. *An Introduction to the Sociology of Health and Illness*. London: Sage, 2002.

Whitehead, Ann. 'Writing with Care: Kazuo Ishiguro's *Never Let Me Go*'. *Contemporary Literature* 52, no. 1 (2011): 54–83.

Whitehead, Colson. *Apex Hides the Hurt*. New York City: Doubleday, 2006.

Whitehead, Colson. 'The New Eclecticism: An Interview with Colson Whitehead'. Interview by Linda Selzer, *Callaloo* 31, no. 2 (2008): 393–401.

Whitehead, Colson. 'What's in a Name: Colson Whitehead on *Apex Hides the Hurt*'. Interview by Tom Nolan, *American Booksellers Association*, 2 March 2006. Accessed 8 July 2018. http://www.bookweb.org/news/whats-name-colson-whitehead-apex-hides-hurt.

Williams, Johnny E. 'Talking About Race without Talking About Race: Color Blindness in Genomics'. *American Behavioural Scientist* 59, no. 11 (2015): 1496–1517.

Williams, Patricia J. 'The Elusive Variability of Race'. In *Race and the Genetic Revolution: Science, Myth and Culture*, edited by Sheldon Krimsky and Kathleen Sloan, 241–254. New York: Colombia University Press, 2011.

Williams, Sloan R. 'Genetic Genealogy: The Woodson Family's Experience'. *Culture, Medicine and Psychiatry* 29, no. 2 (2005): 225–252.

Winter, Sarah. 'Darwin's Saussure: Biosemiotics and Race in *Expression*'. *Representations* 107 (2009): 128–161.

Wood, Bernard. *Human Evolution: A Very Short Introduction*. Oxford: Oxford University Press, 2005.

Wood, James. 'Human, All Too Inhuman'. *The New Republic*, 24 July 2000. https://newrepublic.com/article/61361/human-inhuman.

Worley, Claire. '"It's Not about Race. It's about the Community": New Labour and "Community Cohesion"'. *Critical Social Policy* 25, no. 4 (2005): 483–496.

Young, Helen. *Race and Popular Fantasy Literature: Habits of Whiteness*. New York: Routledge, 2016.

Young, Lola. 'Hybridity's Discontents: Rereading Science and "Race"'. In *Hybridity and Its Discontents: Politics, Science, Culture*, edited by Avtar Brah and Annie E. Coombes, 154–170. London: Routledge, 2000.

Young, Robert J.C. *Colonial Desire: Hybridity in Theory, Culture and Race*. London: Routledge, 1995.

Young Kreeger, Karen. 'Proposed Human Genome Diversity Project Still Plagued by Controversy and Questions'. *The Scientist*, 14 October 1996. https://www.the-scientist.com/?articles.view/articleNo/18100/title/Proposed-Human-Genome-Diversity-Project-Still-Plagued-By-Controversy-And-Questions/.

Zimmer, Carl. 'Interbreeding with Neanderthals'. *Discover Magazine*, 4 March 2013. http://discovermagazine.com/2013/march/14-interbreeding-neanderthals.

Index

Adam 32, 34
affirmative action 13–14, 82
Africa. *See also* Africans
   in anthropological writing 4–5, 35–6, 43–4, 46–7
   history 43, 47, 52
   human origins in 4, 21, 26, 31–2, 36, 42–3, 46–50, 53
African American Lives (TV series) 7, 55
African Americans 3–4, 15, 107, 111
   African lineage 38, 40–1, 49–50
   birth weight 121–2
   disease 108, 122–3
   enslavement of 131–5
   genetic ancestry tracing 7, 15, 42, 55, 60, 74 (*see also* genetic ancestry testing)
   medicine and 101, 103–5, 117, 122 (*see also* BiDil)
   popularity of *Roots* among 37–8, 40, 55
   representation of 32, 48, 52
   writing by 107, 112, 115, 117
African ancestry 4, 35–7, 40, 42–3, 53–4, 60, 146
   representation of 73–4
African Ancestry (company) 60
AfricanDNA (company) 55
African Eve or Mitochondrial Eve hypothesis 3–4, 15, 21, 26, 58, 146
   anti-racism and 26, 32, 35, 42–3, 53
   controversy 32–3
   DNA analysis 31, 33, 39, 40–1, 53
   narrative representation 34–5, 42, 50–3
   racial implications 3–4, 15, 21, 26, 32, 41, 52–3
   recent challenges 33–4
Africans. *See also* Africa
   anthropological discourses on 44–5, 52–3
   Enlightenment view of 67
   representation of 26, 44–5, 47, 50, 52, 150

Afro-American autobiography 28
Agassiz, Louis 117
Ahmed, Sara 129
Ali, Ayann Hirsi 136
Allan C. Wilson 31, 33–4, 40, 58, 162 n.1
American Journal of Human Biology 121
American Society of Human Genetics 148
anthropology 26, 33–5, 46. *See also* Roots
   Africa and 35, 43–7, 50, 52 (*see also* Africa; Africans)
anti-racialism 12, 19, 83
anti-racism
   biofiction and 24–5, 30, 147, 149–50, 152
   in contemporary fiction 30, 49–50, 99, 109, 141–2
   epigenetics and 135, 141–2, 150
   genetic anthropology and 42–3
   Human Genome Diversity Project 58
   narrative construction of 5, 83–5, 147
   1980s and 1990s 12, 82
   1970s 9, 12, 54
   policy 12, 23, 104–7
   popular science writing and 50, 53
   in science 1–6, 10–18, 26–7, 30, 32, 53, 85, 100, 120, 146, 148 (*see also* African Eve; BiDil; Human Genome Project)
Antrosio, Jason 32
Apex Hides the Hurt. 21, 23, 28, 101–20, 134, 146. *See also* Whitehead, Colson
   BiDil and 106–7, 112, 117–18
   marketing in 107–8, 112–14
   racial identity 106–8, 111–13, 119–20
   racial medicine 105–7, 111–12, 115–18, 120
   self-identification (racial) 108, 118–20
   semiotics 109–10, 115
Appiah, Kwame Anthony 6–7
Arnold, Matthew 7
Association of Black Cardiologists 28, 104

Attridge, Derek 76
Australian aboriginal populations 33, 59

Beer, Gillian 20, 22
Bell Curve study 42
Benjamin, Walter 63
Bhabha, Homi K. 17
Bible, The 34–5, 116
BiDil. *See also* racial medicine
    anti-racism and 14, 103–5, 107, 120
    drug development 3, 14, 21, 103–5, 112, 117
    FDA approval 28, 101
    marketing 28, 104–6, 107–8, 110
    public understanding of 101, 103–4
    race and 28, 102–7, 108, 112, 117, 119, 146
    racial self-identification and 28, 103, 107–8, 118
bioethics 17
biofiction
    concept 5, 9–10
    as disciplinary assemblage 22, 95, 118, 150
    fiction and 19, 21, 95, 117, 147
    literary approach 5–10, 19–20, 22–5, 30
    narrative form and 77, 83
    new racial formations and 23–5, 147
    race and 18–26, 30, 83, 107, 117, 127, 140, 146–7, 152–3
biological anthropology 3–4
biopolitics 6, 16, 19
biopower 6, 155 n.28
biosocial 16, 20
biotechnology 10, 61–3, 155 n.28
Black Britons 15, 42, 60, 73
Blacker, Sarah 104
black history 38, 47, 49, 53, 107, 113, 119, 120
blackness 6, 12, 103, 107, 114, 116–20
Black Panthers 48
Black Power Movement 134, 166 n.91
Black, Shameem 64, 75
black women 41, 45, 121
Blair, Tony 79
Bliss, Catherine 16, 18
blood 54, 58, 88, 89, 108, 122
Blumenbach, Johann 6

body 72, 112, 116, 127, 129, 130–1, 133, 137
    environment and 25, 27, 63, 122–3, 126, 130, 140–2, 147
    knowledge and 55, 70, 129, 132, 135
    raced 8, 22, 112, 117, 120, 127, 131, 134–5, 138
    as source of historical information 55, 131
    as text 28, 81–2, 84, 129
Brauer, Gunter 42
Braun, Lundy 105, 124
    Breathing Race into the Machine 105
Britain. *See* UK
Brown, Ina Corrine 44
Brown, Michael H, *The Search for Eve* 33, 52
Butler, Octavia E. 5, 21, 29, 40, 121, 126–9, 131–5, 139, 147. *See also* Kindred

cancer 27, 84, 89, 94, 98
Cann, Rebecca L. 31–4, 40–1, 53
Caribbean 60, 97
Cartwright, Samuel A. 23, 29, 107, 115–17, 147. *See also* Drapetomania
Cavalli-Sforza, Luca 58–60, 62–3
    The History and Geography of Human Genes 59
Celera Genomics 79
Cheddar Man 1, 3–4
Children of Eve (Television documentary) 33
civil rights movement 13, 101, 118, 166 n.91
Clark, Desmond 42
Clarke, David D. 80
class 47–8, 54, 61, 64, 84, 90–1
classification
    of knowledge 151–3
    racial 6, 16, 59, 61–2, 84, 110, 149
climate change 24, 30, 148–9
Clinton, Bill 27, 79, 81
cloning 61, 63–5, 68, 89–90, 96, 128, 170 n.44, 171 n.45
Cohn, Jay 104
Cold Spring Harbor Laboratory 145
Collins, Francis 79–80, 82, 118
colonialism 5–7, 45, 59, 90, 94, 109
colourblindness (political ideology) 13–14, 23, 62, 82, 92, 100, 150
    genetics and 10–18

comic novel 27-8, 84-96
Commission for Racial Equality 2007
  (Britain) 13-14
common ancestor 7, 31, 40, 50
Connor, Steven 24
conservativism 4, 13-14, 35, 43, 48-50, 82, 100, 135, 148
Courlander, Harold 44-5
  The African 44
creation story 34
Crick, Francis 10-11, 90, 145
critical race scholars 6, 8-10, 16, 24
critique 18, 24-5, 93, 118, 149-50
Curtin, Philip 47

Darwin, Charles 18, 23, 27, 33, 62, 68-9, 71, 77, 125, 137
  Expression of the Emotions in Man and Animals, The 68, 71, 77
  Origin of Species 68, 125
Dawkins, Richard 33-4, 55, 74, 136
  River Out of Eden 33-4
Dawson, Ashley 88
decolonizing methodologies 25, 151
Deichmann, Ute 125
Denisovans 33
Dennett, Daniel 41
DeSalle, Rob 146
determinism
  biological 129, 131
  genetic 15-16, 88, 124, 127, 145
Dingwall, Robert 80
disability 131
discrimination 12-14, 54, 62, 66, 68, 72, 82-3, 102, 122-3, 142
disease 16, 45, 121-4, 135, 140
  heart 105, 122, 182 n.101 (*see also* heart failure)
  infectious 121
  mutation 92
  race and 28-9, 107, 115-17
  recessive 58
DNA 29, 33, 57-9, 61, 74, 79, 128, 136, 140. *See also* genes
  ancient 1-3, 156 n.46
  autosomal 60
  double helix 10, 81, 145
  mitochondrial 15, 31-2, 36, 40-1, 43, 50, 53, 58, 60, 73-4
  neanderthal 26, 33
  in palaeoanthropology 26, 39
  popular understandings of 88-9, 123
  sequencing 2, 17, 29, 122
  y-chromosomal 57, 59-60, 73-4
Dolezal, Rachel 101-4
Douglass, Frederick 117
  The Claims of the Negro, Ethnologically Considered 117
Drabble, Margaret 69
Drapetomania 29, 107, 115-17. *See also* Cartwright, Samuel A.
Du Bois, W.E.B. 5, 54, 172 n.79
  Dusk of Dawn: An Essay Toward an Autobiography of a Race Concept 54
Duster, Troy 59, 158 n.72

Edsall, John 11, 157 n.55
education 10-12, 62, 66-70, 75, 90, 94, 153
Eliot, George 69
  Daniel Deronda 75-7
Ellison, Ralph 115
embodiment 29, 42, 55, 122-3, 126, 129, 131-9, 143
emotion 32, 36-7, 42, 54, 62, 68, 70-7, 87, 110, 113, 123, 125
English Defence League 14
Enlightenment, the 7, 67
environment
  biological impact 3, 63, 108, 121-5, 131-2, 135, 139
  cultural 20, 27, 63, 138, 150
  genes and 20, 29, 122-4, 129, 141-2
  literary 23, 142-3
  past 29, 30, 122-3, 130, 134
  racist 5, 25, 30, 121-2, 126-7, 130-2, 140-2, 147
  social 9, 20, 25, 126, 131
epigenetics 3, 21, 29-30, 120-7, 147. *See also* environment
  in contemporary fiction 129-32, 135-41
  race and 22, 25, 126, 127, 139, 142
  racism and 22, 123, 126, 138, 142
  transgenerational inheritance 3, 124-5
Equality Act of 2010 13
Equality and Human Rights Commission 13

Essed, Philomena 65
ethics 59, 74, 87, 98, 101, 172 n.82
ethnic group 54, 58–60, 74–5, 103
ethnicity 12, 15–16, 26, 28, 37, 54, 60, 64–5, 70, 81, 103, 148
  literature and 149–52
ethnology 44–5, 117
eugenics 19, 89, 92, 132
European 5, 33, 40, 44, 52, 59–60, 67, 70, 121, 127, 151
evolutionary history 38–9, 52–3, 55, 58–9
experiment 27–8, 84–6, 89–92, 96–9

Faces of America (TV series) 55
facial expression 23, 27, 45, 62–3, 68, 70–1, 73–7
Fagan, Brian M., *Journey from Eden: The Peopling of Our World, The* 33
family saga 21, 38, 48
Felski, Rita 24
Finding Your Roots (TV series) 55
First Brit: Secrets of the 10,000 Year Old Man, The (documentary) 1–2
Forster, E.M. 28, 84–7, 95–6, 98
  Where Angels Fear to Tread 85
Foster, Eugene A. 57
Foucault, Michel 6
Frankenstein 109
Franklin, Rosalind 145
Fuller, Kathleen 34

Gates, Henry Louis 7, 9, 55, 67, 107, 115, 117, 120
  African American Lives (Television show) 7, 55
  The Signifying Monkey: A Theory of African American Literary Criticism 115
gender 47, 127, 129, 152
genealogy 15, 36, 39, 40, 168 n.121
gene pool 31, 41, 91
genes
  ancestry and 36–7, 43, 74
  as determining 20, 89–90, 129
  development and expression 10, 20, 122, 140, 142
  environment and 20, 23, 29, 122–3, 129
  history and 37, 39, 55, 57, 88
  race and 3–4, 25, 41, 73, 92, 122, 149
  reading and 81–2, 85

genetic ancestry 2, 4–5, 7, 15–16, 23, 26–7, 55, 103. *See also* genetic ancestry testing. *See under* African Americans; genes; genetic science
genetic ancestry testing 4, 7, 26, 55, 57, 60–2, 74
genetic science 5, 7–8, 21, 23–4, 28, 88, 99, 122, 146–50. *See also* genes; determinism
  ancestry and 7, 15, 36, 39, 57–63, 73–5, 148
  as biofiction 5, 10, 23, 26, 147 (*see also* biofiction)
  cultural representation of 23, 26, 95
  in fiction 5, 9, 19, 21, 27, 29, 77, 84, 93, 99, 120, 128
  history of 7–8, 20, 30, 69, 85, 90, 125, 146
  inheritance 29, 129
  language and 14, 79, 81, 106–7, 112
  in literary studies 6–8, 19, 22, 24, 83, 149, 152
  metaphors and 4, 22, 28, 37, 79, 81–2, 125–6
  myths and 89
  narrative and 5, 23, 28, 30, 54, 95, 99–100
  politics and 11, 92, 100, 118, 129, 147–8
  public understanding of 4, 34–5, 58, 88–9, 95, 123, 126–7, 141
  race and 3–5, 7, 9, 11, 14–16, 23–5, 43, 53, 55, 63, 81, 90, 100, 104, 123, 146
  storytelling and 39, 43, 84, 99–100
genomics 3, 18, 79, 81, 85, 92
genotype 58, 62, 88, 103
geography 22, 34, 102, 152
  ancestry 31, 59, 103
  genes 3, 41
  race and 26, 58–60
Gilroy, Paul 7–8, 64, 83
  Against Race 8, 83
Glidden, George 117
Gobineau, Arthur de 6
Goldberg, David Theo 12, 14, 65–6, 83, 92
Gone With the Wind 48
Gould, Stephen Jay 12
Graves, Joseph 145–6
griot 35, 37, 48, 53, 55
Groot, Jerome de 38
Guthman, Julie 134–5, 142

hair 8, 32, 45, 58, 70, 101
Haley, Alex 4–5, 5, 21, 26, 31, 34–5, 35–6, 37–55, 57, 116, 134, 146. *See also* Roots
Autobiography of Malcolm X 45
Hall, Stuart 28, 106, 110–12
Haraway, Donna 10, 19, 74
Hardy, Thomas 69
Head, Dominic 99, 175 n.25
health 2, 6, 103, 107, 124
    of black populations 28, 105, 118, 123
    public 17
    racial disparities in 29–30, 102–4, 118, 120, 122–3, 130
Heard, Edith 126–7
heart failure 28, 101–4, 108. *See also* BiDil
Hemings, Sally 41, 57
history of science 42
Hofmänner, Alexandra 34
holocaust 61
Homo sapiens 31–2, 43
Horton, George Moses 67, 70
Huehls, Mitchum 25
human evolution 31, 33, 36, 39, 43, 55, 58
human genome 7–8, 27, 29, 80–1, 99, 140
Human Genome Diversity Project (HGDP) 3, 15, 21, 26, 58–9, 83, 105, 146, 169 n.27
Human Genome Project (HGP) 3, 6, 21, 27–8, 58, 79, 81–5, 102, 106, 145–6
    anti-racism and 83, 99–100
hybridity 16–18, 84, 87, 175 n.25

immigration 2, 64, 126, 138, 143
indentured labour 45, 48
indigenous populations 58–60
inequality. *See* racial inequality
inherited characteristics 12, 94, 122, 125, 139
interdisciplinarity 23, 30, 150–2
intertextuality 35, 43, 49, 107, 115
IQ 10–12, 42, 145. *See also under* race
Ireland 40
Ishiguro, Kazuo 5, 21, 27, 51, 61, 63, 65, 68–9, 75–6, 128, 147. *See also Never Let Me Go*
    Remains of the Day, The 61
    When We Were Orphans 61

Jackson, Fatimah L. 74
Jasienska, Grazyna 121
Jefferson, Eston Hemings 57
Jefferson, Thomas 41, 57
Jensen, Arthur 10–12
Jim Crow 13
Johnson, Charles 115
Johnson, Linton Kwesi 165 n.59
Johnson, Norman A. 33, 36, 40
    Darwinian Detectives: Revealing the Natural History of Genes and Genomes 33, 36
Jones, Steve 36–7
    The Language of the Genes 36
Journey of Man (Television documentary) 33
Joyce, James 69
Juengst, Eric 61

Kahn, Jonathan 103–4, 118
Kant, Immanuel 6
Kay, Lily E. 81
Keller, Evelyn Fox 20, 141
Kindred. 21, 29, 40, 126. *See also* Butler, Octavia E.
    bodily trauma 128, 130
    intergenerational effects of slavery 127–34, 140
    science and 128–9, 134–5, 141–2
    sexism in 132–3
kinship 5, 43, 54, 59, 62, 69, 73–5
Kipling, Rudyard
    Just So Stories 125
Krieger, Nancy 123
Kunta Kinte 35, 38, 40, 42, 44–50, 116
Kushnuck, Louis 54
Kuzawa, Christopher W. 122

laboratory 34, 86, 97–8, 109, 145
Lamarck, Jean Baptiste 125, 137–8, 140, 147, 184–5 n.27
    Philosophie Zoologique 125
Latour, Bruno 17, 30, 149
Lawrence, Stephen 13, 82
Leakey, Louis 46
Leakey, Richard *Origin of Humankind, The* 33
Leavis, F.R. 85
Leise, Christopher 115, 182 n.105
Levine, Caroline 19, 21, 152

Lewin, Roger 33–4, 163 n.12
  Origin of Modern Humans, The 33
Lewontin, Richard C. 12
Li, Stephanie 115
Literary Darwinism 136
literary form 5, 19, 23, 25–7, 36, 85, 94, 115, 139, 147. *See also* narrative form
  comic 21, 28, 87, 92 (*see also* comic novel)
London 1, 27, 84, 87, 96, 135

Malcolm X 38, 46, 166 n.82
  Autobiography 38, 45
Mansfield, Becky 134–5, 142
Masai 52
materiality 25, 55, 66, 88, 112, 129
Maus, Derek C. 119
Mbembe, Achille 127
McEwan, Ian 136, 139
  Saturday 139
McFadden, Johnjoe 140–1
M'Charek, Amade 19
McKie, Robin 31, 33, 36, 41–2, 53
  African Exodus: The Origins of Modern Humanity 33, 36, 41
melodrama 28, 85–6, 95–9
Meloni, Maurizio 123, 127, 131–2
Memmi, Albert 66
Mendel, Gregor
  Findings in Genetics 46
mental illness 6, 107, 116, 135
microaggressions 92, 123, 132
Midgley, Mary 127
migration 17, 31, 37, 39, 137–8
  migrant 62, 64–6, 137–8
Miletic, Philip 134
missionaries 46–7
Mitochondrial DNA. *See* DNA
mixed race 17, 32
molecular biology 31, 163 n.12
molecular scale 4, 8, 16, 18, 58–9, 123
Moment, Gairdner 54
Morris, Andrea 148
Morton, Samuel George 117
Motherland: A Genetic Journey (BBC2 documentary) 73–4
Muhammad, Elijah 46
Mullan, John 69, 173 n.87
Müller, Ruth 124

multiculturalism 12, 64, 87, 106–11
multi-regional hypothesis 31–2, 41, 52
Murray, Stuart 74

narrative form 4–5, 17, 23, 36, 49, 77, 84, 99. *See also* literary form
Nash, Catherine 15, 170 n.33
National Association for the Advancement of Colored People (NAACP) 101, 104
National Book Award 35
National Human Genome Research Institute (US) 79
Nation of Islam 46
Native Americans 59
Natural History Museum (London) 1
Natural History Museum (Washington) 43
nature 10, 17, 20–1, 41, 52, 85–6, 113, 135, 142, 145
  human 85, 96, 99
Nature 31, 102
Neanderthal 26, 32–3
Nelson, Alondra 15–16, 55, 60
Nerlich, Brigitte 80, 124–5
Never Let Me Go 21, 23. *See also* Ishiguro, Kazuo; cloning
  care 27, 61–6, 69, 71, 74
  cloning and 27, 61–2, 128
  facial expressions, interpretation of 62–3, 68, 70–1, 73, 75–7
  narrative form 62, 68–75
  organ donation 61, 64, 67, 70
  race in 62–8, 73, 150
Newsweek 32
9/11 event 136
NitroMed 104–5
Nordgren, Anders 61
Norrell, Robert J. 40, 44, 49
Nott, Josiah Clark 52, 117
  Types of Mankind 52
nurture 20, 141–2, 145

Obama, Barack 13
Odyssey, The 69
Oikkonen, Venla 32
oncomouse 84
Oppenheimer, Stephen 33, 39, 42, 50–1
  Out of Eden 33, 39, 42, 50–1
oral history 35, 37, 55, 57

Out of Africa theory 31–2, 42–3
Oxford Ancestors 60

palaeoanthropology 26, 31, 36, 39. *See also* DNA
patriarchy 47, 132, 134
Patterson, Christina 94
pharmaceutical 104–8
pharmacogenomics 3, 29, 104, 107, 117, 119, 147, 156 n.46
phenotype 8, 58, 60, 62, 74, 88, 103
Philips, Trevor 14
physiognomy 70
physiology 29, 63, 111–12, 116, 123, 125, 132, 140
Pickersgill, Martyn 124, 127
Pinker, Steven 136
placenta 31, 39, 122
plantation 48–9, 60, 119, 126–8, 130–4
plasticity 29, 121, 127, 135–6
poetry 34, 67, 80, 94
Pollock, Anne 105, 118
polygenism 52, 68
Pope, Alexander 80
popular science writing 4, 22, 33–4, 36, 42, 49, 89, 93, 185 n.29
    Africa and 21, 50, 52
    narrative organization of 37, 39
population genetics 3, 26–7, 39, 58–62
postcolonial studies 17–18, 152
post-genomic biology 19–20, 29, 129, 141–2
post-racial 13, 27, 62, 84, 92, 150
premodern populations 31
Proctor, Robert N. 32
Project Reason 135–6
pseudoscience 7, 45, 47, 129
Puchner, Martin 72
Pulitzer Prize 35

race
    ancestry and 15, 23, 43, 46, 57, 60, 74
    as biofiction 9–10, 18, 21, 25–6, 30, 83, 107, 126–7, 140, 147, 150, 153
    in contemporary fiction 4, 8, 10, 19, 21–3, 26–30, 61–70, 84–92, 99–100, 107–18, 126, 132–40
    debates in science 2, 10–11, 77, 145–6
    DNA analysis 2–3, 8, 26, 53, 55
    fictional or factual status 1, 3–5, 7–9, 18–19, 83, 101, 149
    as genetic difference 2, 14–15, 26–7, 58–9, 62, 105, 108, 134
    genetic status 1–3, 5, 8–9, 11–12, 14, 16, 21, 26, 53, 58, 69, 81, 102–6, 122–3, 147
    identity and 5, 15, 18–19, 40, 54, 62, 74, 106–7, 112, 142
    intelligence and 10–12, 42, 145
    interdisciplinary formation of 5–6, 16, 18, 22–3, 146–7, 152–3
    language and 106, 111–12, 114
    in literary studies 6–9, 15, 22, 24–5, 83, 146, 148, 152
    physical appearance 8, 18, 58, 103, 111
    political erasure 9, 14, 64, 66, 82–3, 153
    politics and 9, 13–15, 25, 83, 118, 148, 150
    public understanding of 60, 99, 102, 108
    and racism 14, 26, 30, 83, 88, 90, 134, 147, 150, 153
    scientific conceptions of 4–6, 17, 61, 92, 146, 149
    self-identification with a 3, 28, 103, 118–20
    social construct 1–3, 8–10, 12, 16, 19, 30, 59–60, 122
Race Relations Act of 1976, 2000 (Britain) 12–13, 82
racial categorization 1, 6–7, 15, 27, 100, 111, 123, 132, 135, 146, 149, 156 n.46
racial group 2, 6, 104, 119, 131, 153
racial inequality 2, 13, 19, 74, 120, 171 n.55
racial medicine 16, 23, 28–9, 101, 103, 107, 111, 117, 119. *See also* BiDil
racial science 5, 7–8, 14, 18, 23, 29, 90, 117, 152. *See also* eugenics
    history of 16–17, 60, 107, 117
racism 1, 14, 26–7, 30, 41, 43, 63, 83, 88, 90, 134, 147, 150, 153
    academic disciplines 5
    biological effects 29, 122, 126–7, 142
    biopower and 6
    environment and 5, 25, 30, 121–2, 126–7, 130–2, 140–2, 147
    epigenetics and 22, 123, 126, 138, 142

as experience 9, 15, 120, 122–3, 132–5, 138–40
in fiction 26, 66, 72, 84, 87–92, 107, 113, 120, 132–5, 138–40
genetics and 2, 7, 28, 30, 50, 53, 58, 146–7
medicine and 23, 108
and race 14, 26, 30, 83, 88, 90, 134, 150, 153
scientific 2, 53, 69, 107, 150
and slavery 43, 45, 117, 129
socio-political 5, 10, 12, 26, 30, 58, 82–3, 100, 153
in UK 12–14, 19
in US 13–14, 19, 146
Ramsby, Howard II 115
Real Eve, The (Television documentary) 33, 50
Reardon, Jenny 9, 58
Reed, Ishmael 115
Reich, David 2–5
Relethford, John H. 33–9
 Reflections of Our Past: How Human History Is Revealed in Our Genes 33, 36, 38
religion 17, 91, 93, 96, 119, 136–7
replacement theory (human origins) 32–3
Roberts, Dorothy 14, 19
Roof, Judith 81, 88–9, 95, 100
Roots. See also Haley, Alex
 African ancestry and 35, 43, 53–4, 165 n.59
 anthropology and 26, 35, 43–53, 146, 150
 awards 34
 enslavement 41–3, 46, 48–9, 54, 116, 134
 genetic ancestry and 4, 37, 40
 historical narrative 41, 47, 55, 166 n.95
 human origins and 37–43, 46
 popular science writing and 4, 21, 26, 36–8, 42–3, 50–2, 146
 representation of Africa in 35, 46, 50, 52, 150
Roots for Real 60, 73
Roots TV series 35–6, 38, 49
Rose, Nikolas 16–18
Rusert, Britt 117

Rushdie, Salman 5, 21, 29, 121, 126, 135–40, 147. *See also Satanic Verses, The*
 Midnight's Children 141

Satanic Verses, The 21, 29, 126–7, 135–43
satire 21, 28, 93, 105, 107, 117
science fiction 21, 61, 93, 95, 117, 128
Second World War 70, 84–5, 98, 157 n.59
Shockley, William 11
Shostack, Sara 23
Sielke, Sabine 148, 152
signification 28–9, 64, 107, 109, 112, 115–16
 floating signifier 28, 106, 110–11
 Signification 107, 115–16
Sims, George 44
single line of descent 40–1
skin 53, 110, 112–13, 125, 130, 142
 colour 1, 3, 8, 28, 64, 92, 103, 106–8, 111, 120
slave narrative 49, 128, 166 n.97
slavery 7, 41–3, 48–9, 54, 57, 114–15, 126, 133, 166 n.95, 189 n.14
 ancestry and 36, 48, 54, 60
 genetics and 41
 intergenerational effects 3, 121, 123, 129–31
 legacies 36, 41, 43, 131, 140
 medicine and 29, 107, 116
 poetry 67
 resistance and 48, 116
slave trade 35, 47, 49, 55
Smith, Zadie 5, 21, 27–8, 84–100. *See also White Teeth*
 Trials of Finch, The 86
Snow, C.P. 85, 148
social science 3, 9, 11, 20, 58, 97, 123, 140
sociobiology 129, 136
sociocritique 16, 18
sociology of science 10, 16–17, 20, 24, 33, 60, 118
Sommer, Marianne 39, 164 n.36
specimen 45, 52, 109, 138
Spector, Tim 122, 125
Spencer, Robert 187 n.91
Squier, Susan Merrill 10, 21
Squires, Claire 87
Steinberg, Deborah Lynn 22, 37, 81–2, 85

Stoddard, Brandon 49
Stoneking, Mark 31, 40
Stringer, Chris 4, 31, 33, 36, 41–2, 53, 164 n.46
  African Exodus: The Origins of Modern Humanity 33, 36, 41
Surai, Bonaventure 47
Sweet, Elizabeth 122
Sykes, Bryan 55
  Seven Daughters of Eve, The 33, 43
systems biology 140

Tattersall, Ian 146
taxonomy 25, 37, 152
Taylor, Helen 38, 48–9
Temu, Arnold 47
Thatcher, Margaret 135
1001 Nights 69
Timmermans, Stefan 23
transracialism 101, 171 n.56
Trilling, Lionel 28, 84–6, 95–6, 98–9
Trump, Donald 14, 148
Tu-Wa-Moja African Study Group 43
23 and Me 60
two cultures 85, 93

UK
  anti-racism 12, 19, 82
  genetic research 1, 13–14, 27
  immigration policies 126
  political culture 2, 11, 13, 148
  racial imaginaries 5, 8–9, 19, 152
  racism 13–14, 19, 126
Uncle Tom's Cabin 49
United Nations Educational, Scientific and Cultural Organisation Statement on Race 12, 157 n.59
United States
  civil rights movement 13, 101, 118, 166 n.91 (*see also* Jim Crow)
  colourblindness in 13, 82 (*see also* colourblindness)
  genetics research 14, 27, 113–14
  health 105, 121
  political culture 2, 11, 13–14, 82, 148

racial imaginaries 5, 13, 18–19
racism 14, 121, 126, 146
slavery and 35, 41 (*see also* slavery)
US Food and Drug Administration (FDA) 28, 101, 104

Venter, Craig 79–81, 136
Vint, Sherryl 131

Wailoo, Keith 35
Wald, Priscilla 50, 53, 155 n.28
Watson, James 90, 145–8
Waugh, Patricia 81–3, 93, 170 n.44
Weinbaum, Alys 63
Wells, Spencer 33, 50, 55
  The Journey of Man: A Genetic Odyssey 33, 50
Werbner, Pnina 17
Whitehead, Ann 65
Whitehead, Colson 5, 21, 28–9, 65, 105–20, 134, 147. See also *Apex Hides the Hurt*
whiteness 6, 64, 108
White Teeth. See also Smith, Zadie
  Forsterian comic mode 26, 85–92 (*see also* Forster, E.M.)
  historical narrative 94
  Human Genome Project and 84
  plot 84–5, 96, 98
  race science 88–90
  racism in 91–2, 98
  science and 93–8
  scientific storytelling and 85, 93, 95, 99
Wilkins, Maurice 145
Williams Johnny E. 92
Wilson, Allan C. 31, 33–4, 40, 58, 163 n.12
Winter, Sarah 69
Wolpoff, Milford 32
Wood, James 86, 96
Worley, Claire 13

Y-chromosome analysis 15, 41, 58–60, 73–4
Young, Robert J.C. 5, 17–18

www.ingramcontent.com/pod-product-compliance
Lightning Source LLC
Chambersburg PA
CBHW052039300426
44117CB00012B/1895